SOLDIERS OF THE

REVOLUTIONARY WAR

SOLDIERS OF THE
REVOLUTIONARY WAR

STUART REID · MARKO ZLATICH

First published in Great Britain in 2002 by Osprey Publishing,
Elms Court, Chapel Way, Botley, Oxford OX2 9LP, United Kingdom.
Email: info@ospreypublishing.com

Previously published as Men-at-Arms 273: *General Washington's
Army (1) 1775-78*, Men-at-Arms 290: *General Washington's Army (2)
1779-83*, Men-at-Arms 285: *King George's Army 1740-93 (1)
Infantry*, Men-at-Arms 289: *King George's Army 1740-93 (2)* and
Men-at Arms 292: *King George's Army 1740-93 (3)*.

ISBN 1 84176 674 7

Series Editor: Martin Windrow
Editor: Sally Rawlings
Index by Alan Rutter

Printed in China through World Print Ltd.

02 03 04 05 06   10 9 8 7 6 5 4 3 2 1

FOR A CATALOG OF ALL BOOKS PUBLISHED BY
OSPREY MILITARY AND AVIATION PLEASE CONTACT:

The Marketing Manager, Osprey Direct USA
c/o MBI Publishing
729 Prospect Avenue, Osceola, WI 54020, USA
Email: **info@ospreydirectusa.com**

The Marketing Manager, Osprey Direct UK
PO Box 140, Wellingborough,
Northants, NN8 2FA, United Kingdom
Email: **info@ospreydirect.co.uk**

www.ospreypublishing.com

FRONT COVER: 'The Battle of Lexington' by W. B. Wollen
(© National Army Museum)

BACK COVER: Light Dragoons (probably Provincials) wearing Tarleton
helmets get in amongst the American battery. (Stuart Reid)

CONTENTS

INTRODUCTION

During the period 1775–78, General Washington commanded three separate armies: the New England Army of 1775; the one-year Army of the United Colonies, renamed Army of the United States in July 1776; and the forces established by the Continental Congress to serve for three years from January 1777, or for the duration. Throughout the American Revolution, the rebel armies consisted of regular troops paid for by the Congress and of militia, volunteers and regulars raised by the states. This study focuses on the systems used by state and Continental authorities to procure clothing materials, the quantities they obtained and the specifications of the uniforms themselves.

The text illustrations include examples of typical arms and accoutrements used by the regular and state forces. A unique feature of this volume is the publication of monochromes of the Smithsonian Institution's collection of military clothing from the period 1775–78. Selected portraits and graphics rendered between 1775 and 1778 illustrate some of the adopted designs. The Plates show many of the distinct uniforms of volunteer companies, Continental regiments of 1776, provincial regulars, light horse, artillery, additional Continental foot regiments, Continental Line at Valley Forge, and independent Continental corps.

The subsequent volume in this series, *General Washington's Army 2: 1779–1783*, will complete this overview of the history of American military uniforms of the Revolutionary War.

George Washington 1776, by Charles Willson Peale (1741–1827). The uniform – blue with buff cape, lapels, cuffs, waistcoat and breeches – was made for him in 1775, probably modelled on the Fairfax (Virginia) Independent Company, which Washington commanded when he was named Commander-in-Chief in July 1775. Buttons and epaulettes are gold. The ribbon is light blue. (Dick S. Ramsay Fund, Brooklyn Museum)

COLONIAL UNIFORMS

Lacking the authority needed to raise regular forces, each of the 13 original colonies of North America, except Quaker Pennsylvania, enacted laws to establish a militia. With the exceptions of New York and South Carolina, no colonial militia law specified uniform clothing; however, each militiaman was supposed to maintain a usable fire-lock, ammunition and a bayonet. Officers were required to maintain a sword.

Owing to limitations in the militia laws, the colonists could only improve their proficiency in the military arts by forming volunteer companies. From 1774, they designated certain militia companies as minutemen – these companies were to be available for service at a minute's notice. Nominally part of the militia, minutemen were equipped and financed by direct local subscription. Independent companies found their own arms and equipment, and each adopted a uniform and established their own training programme.

Although the militia-based organisations enjoyed initial military successes, the committees of safety could not field viable forces without creating new formations that were enlisted for longer terms. In order to achieve this, during 1775 and 1776, the provinces enacted legislation to raise provincial regulars, and appropriated funds to buy material for their clothing. On entering the service of the Continental Congress, many provincials were already in uniform.

Massachusetts

In planning a permanent New England Army, on 23 April 1775, the Massachusetts Provincial Congress resolved that a coat should be given to each soldier as a uniform. A Committee of Supplies was charged with responsibility for collecting and distributing shirts, breeches, stockings and shoes, and following inquiries from General Washington, on 16 August, the council ordered the coats to be shortened so that they could be worn under hunting shirts as a waistcoat without lapels. The number of the regiment was to be displayed on the pewter buttons. By 28 December 1775, around 13,000 uniforms had been made by the people of Massachusetts. At this time Massachusetts had raised 27 regiments.

As a major American port of entry for imported cloth, whose inhabitants were skilled at making clothes, Boston began to receive imported and captured cloth and clothing. Boston also became a centre for the making of clothing for the Continental Army. A Continental Clothing Store was

Grenadier of the Grenadier Company, New York Independent Forces This unique portrait of an enlisted man in a colonial uniform is thought to depict General McKinney.

(Smithsonian photograph, printed by permission of the owners, Mr. and Mrs. Robert C. Pangborn of Bloomfield Hills, Michigan)

opened in Boston in 1777 and then transferred to Springfield in 1778. Massachusetts also boasted a well-established minuteman service and a considerable force of uniformed militia.

Known uniforms were as follows: Salem Rangers – short green coat, gold trim, cap of black beaver with four ostrich feathers, white under dress, black gaiters, ruffles at the wrist; Haverhill Artillery – blue faced buff, buff waistcoats and breeches, yellow buttons, white stockings; Boston Independent Company – black faced red; buttons with the motto '*Inimica Tyrannis*' and the device of a hand holding a drawn sword with the scabbard thrown aside and broken; white waistcoat, breeches and stockings, black half gaiters and feathers, black hats and black cockades; Pittsfield Minute Company – blue coats turned with white; Reading Minute Company – paper caps resembling those worn by British grenadiers; 3rd Bristol County Militia Regiment – officers in blue coats faced red, blue breeches, white stockings, yellow buttons and gold laced hats; Volunteer Company of Matrosses, 1st Hampshire County Militia Regiment – blue faced red, white small clothes, short black gaiters, black fur caps with red cockades; officers had red plumes.

Connecticut

During 1775, the Connecticut General Assembly raised eight provincial regiments. While clothing was not considered a necessity each regiment was allowed a coloured standard: 1st yellow; 2nd green; 3rd scarlet; 4th crimson; 5th white; 6th azure; 7th blue; and 8th orange.

For the campaign of 1776, Connecticut raised eight unnumbered regiments. Each regiment was responsible for obtaining its own uniforms. On 17 July, the Governor and Council of Safety resolved to supply enough home-made cloth of brown or cloth colour for 3,000 coats and waistcoats, 3,000 felt hats, checked flannel or linen for 6,000 shirts, and 6,000 pairs of shoes. On 2 October 1776, the General Assembly agreed to provide clothing for the eight regiments for the next three years. In a letter of 16 December 1776, Daniel Tillinghast, the agent at Providence, instructed Samuel Gray of Windham to make uniforms from cloth that had been bought in Providence from the prize ship *Thomas*. Uniforms were to consist of double breasted 'waistcoats' with lapels of the same cloth stitched down to the body, buttons set without button holes, a small matching cape, short plaited skirts, and sleeves with a small cuff. A jacket was to be worn under this waistcoat. The colours of these garments are described in the section dealing with Connecticut Uniforms on page 34.

Known uniforms were as follows: 1st Company, Governor's Foot Guards of Hartford – scarlet faced black, buff waistcoats and breeches, black fur grenadier caps; 2nd Company of New Haven – for detail see Figure 3 Plate A; Mansfield Militia – grenadiers in blue coats, scarlet waistcoats, white breeches and stockings, scarlet caps striped and tasselled with white, rank and file in white stockings and light blue cockades; Wethersfield Company – uniforms of blue turned-up red.

Rhode Island

On 6 May 1775, three regiments were authorised from among the various county militia companies. These troops marched to Boston carrying provincial blankets and knapsacks, but were otherwise self-clothed and equipped.

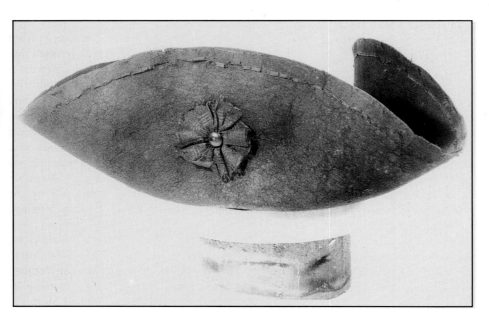

The cocked hat worn by Colonel Jonathan Pettibone of the 18th Regiment, Connecticut Militia, c.1775/6. Made of black wool felt with a small admixture of rabbit fur. It is 20 ¾ inches in diameter, with a 5 inch high crown, and edges bound with ¾ inch wide black silk. (Collections of the Division of Armed Forces History, National Museum of American History, Smithsonian Institution)

During 1776, the 1st and 2nd Regiments became the 9th and 11th Continental Regiments, and two state regiments were also raised for one year. On 23 July 1776, the General Assembly appointed a committee to procure clothing for its Continental troops, but its efforts did not bear fruit until 1777. Independent company distinctions were as follows: Cadet Company of Providence – scarlet coats faced yellow; Independent Troop of Horse, Captain-General's Cavaliers – blue coats faced white, yellow buttons, white jackets and buff breeches; Providence Grenadiers – black leather mitre caps with red backs and a flap on which was painted a gold lion, a gold anchor and edges, and silver scrolls with the words 'God and our rights' and 'Hope'; Newport Light Infantry – distinctive cap with a conical crown made from black leather, the rear turn-up was painted black with gold edging (see illustration below); United Train of Artillery – deserters in 1776 wore brown faced red. A black leather cap with an anchor on the front is associated with this unit.

New Hampshire

On 20 May 1775, the Provincial Congress resolved to raise, but not arm or equip, three regiments to join the New England army. On 21 January 1776, the Committee of Safety issued orders to raise and equip a regiment of rangers under Colonel Timothy Bedel for Continental service in Canada. Among the materials to be bought for this regiment were moose skins for moccasins, 500 pairs of shoes, 720 pairs of snowshoes, 688 blankets, and coarse cloth for Indian leggings, shirting and coats. The three regular Continental regiments raised as New Hampshire's quota were drawn from the militia and from New Hampshire men already serving in the Continental Army in November 1776. Their Continental uniforms are described below.

New York

At the request of the Continental Congress, on 27 June 1775, the New York Provincial Congress authorised four infantry battalions and one artillery company for Canadian service. The following day, Peter T. Curtenius, the state commissary, was ordered to purchase material to make up coats for these troops, and the day after that, the Provincial Congress instructed him that each regiment was to have different cuffs and facings. These four battalions were among the most elaborately uniformed provincial troops at this time, with tape to distinguish drummers' and fifers' coats, laced shoulder straps to distinguish sergeant majors and drum majors, pewter coat buttons with battalion numbers, waistcoat buttons displaying the NY cypher, russia drilling breeches and waistcoats, and narrow brimmed black hats. For the Canadian winter they also had buckskin waistcoats and breeches, woollen leggings, mittens and caps. Regimental uniforms worn until November 1775 were as follows: 1st Regiment – blue faced scarlet; 2nd Regiment – blue faced crimson; 3rd Regiment – variety of colours faced green; 4th Regiment – variety faced blue; New York Artillery Company, commanded by Captain John Lamb – blue coats faced buff, 57 racoon caps were also received in Montreal; Green Mountain Boys – coats of green faced red.

The Provincial Congress decided to import cloth suitable for soldiers' shirts and coarse stockings by employing two or more ships to sail to Europe, obtain the cloth and sail it to St. Eustatius or St. Martin in the West Indies. There it would be off-loaded and picked up by other ships. By 30 April 1776, they had bought 4,393 yards of cloth, $12,869\frac{1}{2}$ yards of linen, 2,861 hats, 473 shirts, 4,711 pairs of shoes and 966 gross of coat buttons.

During 1776 New York raised four additional battalions for its own defence. Having no suitable cloth, for hunting frocks, these battalions wore coats, leather waistcoats and breeches, hats, shirts, woollen hose and shoes. Uniforms worn by Colonel John Lasher's Battalion of Independent Companies of Foot were as follows (all wore white under clothes, half gaiters and black gaiters): Fuziliers – blue faced red, bearskin caps and pouches with a brass plate bearing the word 'Fuziliers' on the cap and

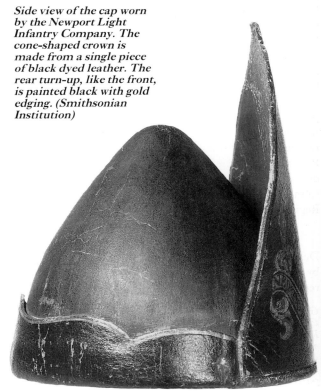

Side view of the cap worn by the Newport Light Infantry Company. The cone-shaped crown is made from a single piece of black dyed leather. The rear turn-up, like the front, is painted black with gold edging. (Smithsonian Institution)

'*Salus populi suprema Lex est*' on the pouch; German Fuziliers – blue faced red, silver lace, bearskin caps with white plates bearing the words 'German Fuziliers' and a tin star above; The Union – blue faced red; Sportsman – green faced crimson, small round hats; The Corsicans – short green coats, small round hats cocked on one side with a red tin heart bearing the words 'God and our Right', and around the crown 'Liberty or Death'; Bold Foresters – short green coats, small round hats turned-up on one side and with a brass plate on the front bearing the word 'Freedom'; Light Infantry – blue faced red; Oswego Rangers – blue coats, and small round hats with a brass plate against the crown bearing the words 'Oswego Rangers'; Rangers – green faced buff, buff waistcoat and breeches, white stockings, and black garters and half gaiters.

Other New York militia uniforms were as follows: Schenectady Minute Companies – one company of blues and one company of greens; Albany County Troop of Horse – blue coats, white buttons and silver laced hats; King's County Troop of Horse – blue coats, red jackets and silver laced hats.

New Jersey

On 3 June 1775, the New Jersey Provincial Congress recommended that each township form and arm a company of 80 men. The Committee of Safety recommended that minutemen companies wear hunting frocks. On 9 October 1775, the Continental Congress asked New Jersey to provide uniforms for two regular regiments for a year. Instead of a bounty, the privates were allowed a felt hat, a pair of yarn stockings and a pair of shoes. For its part, Congress agreed to furnish each man with a hunting shirt and a blanket; however, these were not to be considered as part of the terms of enlistment. Two more foot regiments were added to the state's line in 1776, and an ordinance for raising two companies of state artillery was passed by the Provincial Congress in March 1776. Known uniform details are as follows: Robert Erskine's Independent Company of Foot – green coats; 1st and 2nd New Jersey Regiments (1775–76) – hunting frocks.

Delaware

Delaware placed the militia on a rebel footing in May 1775 by appointing new officers and issuing detailed uniform regulations. A single Continental battalion was authorised by the Delaware Committee of Safety on 9 December. Uniform details were: Dover Light Infantry (1776–77) – green faced red; 2nd Kent County Militia Battalion (1775) – brown faced white; Light Infantry – blue faced white; New Castle County Militia (1775) – for details of this unit see Figure 1, Plate A; Haslett's Continental Battalion (1776) – according to Colonel Haslett's account book and deserter descriptions, blue coats faced red were worn.

Pennsylvania

Rather than accept militia, Quaker Pennsylvania's House of Assembly approved *Articles of Association of Pennsylvania* in August 1775; under these some 46 local battalions of Associators were formed. To ensure Pennsylvania's own defence, on 16 October 1775, the Council of Safety created a company of artillery under Thomas Proctor, and, on 5 March 1776, two state regiments: the Pennsylvania State Regiment of Riflemen and the Pennsylvania State Battalion of Musketry. On 5 October 1776, the two battalions were consolidated into the Pennsylvania State Regiment. Uniform details were as follows: Rifle Regiment – blue faced white, white waist-coats edged with red, buttons engraved with the letters

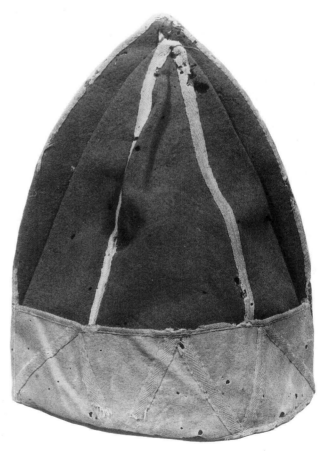

Grenadier mitre cap, 26th Continental Infantry Regiment, 1776. This view shows clearly the straw yellow $3\frac{1}{4}$ inch rear turn-up. The herringbone pattern $\frac{3}{4}$ inch white lace is sewn on in a zig-zag. The back of the front plate and the bag are made of wool in brown – probably the colour of the coat. (Smithsonian Institution)

PRB, black caps marked 'PR', lead coloured fringed hunting shirts; Musketry Battalion – blue faced red, white waistcoats, buckskin breeches, hats bound yellow; State Regiment – blue faced red, white small clothes, buttons with the inscription 'PSR'.

The *Associators'* uniforms were left to their localities, but the state regular forces came under the direct control of the Council of Safety, who appointed Francis Towers as the Commissary of Military Stores. Unless otherwise noted, all regiments wore white belted vests and breeches, white stockings, half boots, black garters and small round hats with fur cockaids. Regimental details were as follows: 1st Regiment – brown faced buff, red waistcoats and brown breeches; 2nd Regiment – brown coats faced red; drummers and fifers scarlet coatee with a brown collar, a blue hat ribbon and a buckstail; 3rd Regiment – drummers and fifers wore white faced brown; one buff taffeta and one Persian blue colour; Light Infantry Company – green with white lapels, jockey caps and feathers; 4th Regiment –

brown faced yellow; 5th Regiment – brown faced red, yellow hunting shirts; Quakers – light blue faced white; Rangers – brown hunting shirts; Light Horse – brown faced white, round hats bound silver, buckstail, yellow standard.

For those battalions in 'Continental Service' the following uniform details are known: 1st – brown faced green, grey waistcoats, buckskin breeches, buttons with the inscription '1P.B' and cocked hats; 2nd Battalion – blue faced red, red waistcoats, leather breeches, and buttons with '2.P.B' on them; 3rd Battalion – brown faced white, buckskin breeches, buttons with the inscription 'No.3', and hats bound white; 4th Battalion – blue faced white, white small clothes, hats bound yellow, red light infantry caps bound black, and white stocks; 5th Battalion – brown faced red, red jackets, buckskin breeches, buttons with the inscription '5.P.B', red, brown and white epaulettes for sergeants; 6th Battalion – blue turned-up red, small round hats.

Maryland

Maryland's Convention organised its forces on 14 August 1775 when it voted for the establishment of 40 companies of minutemen and reorganised the militia. In January 1776, it abolished the minutemen and established a nine-company state regiment, this consisted of two companies of state artillery and seven independent companies – one for each district. The land forces were to have a hunting shirt of colours other than blue. The artillerymen were to receive a new hat, a short coat, waistcoat, breeches and a hunting shirt each year. In the case of the independent companies and the Maryland Battalion the cost of clothing was deducted from pay. The uniform of the 2nd Maryland Artillery Company was blue faced red, yellow button holes and a light jacket; the third's was similar but with white button holes. For details of the 1st Company see Figure 1, Plate E.

Enlisted men of the Maryland Battalion wore hunting shirts, coats, overalls and hats. Officers were clothed in scarlet faced buff. Baltimore Independent Cadets wore coats turned-up with buff, yellow buttons, white stockings and black half boots. In the Independent Companies the hunting shirt was almost universal: in addition the 3rd Company wore black uniforms; the shirts of the 4th Company had red cuffs, and the riflemen of this company were issued capes. In the 5th Company leather caps were worn.

'Rough' sketch dated 9 February 1776 of a knapsack/haversack adopted for use by Maryland, New Jersey, Virginia and Pennsylvania forces. (Smithsonian photograph, MdHR 4561, Maryland Hall of Records)

Virginia

Following the expiry of the Militia Law in March 1775, the Convention of Delegates resolved to replace the militia with two regiments of regulars, two frontier independent companies and a battalion of minutemen. These units were recruited from the militia in each of the sixteen provincial districts. Minutemen and regulars who signed up without their own clothing would be furnished, at public expense,

Rifleman, Captain Church's Company, 4th Pennsylvania Battalion, Summer 1776. He wears a short blue double-breasted regimental coat faced white, white waistcoat, drilling breeches and a red cap bound black. (Peter F. Copeland)

with a hunting shirt and a pair of leggings. The number of regular regiments was increased to nine on 1 December 1775, and the Convention of Delegates added hat binding, facing cloth and leggings to the clothing allowance. At this time, a Public Store in Williamsburg was established, which, under William Aylett, Commissary of Supplies was to provide arms, accoutrements and clothing. Throughout the war, the Virginia Public Store clothed the state's land and naval forces, and its Continental regiments, from the profits of tobacco export.

The clothing of the constituent units of the Minute Battalion and the independent companies varied quite markedly. Uniform details were as follows: Fairfax County Independent Company (1774–76) – blue turned-up with buff, plain yellow metal buttons, buff waistcoat and breeches, white stockings. In addition George Washington procured, for this unit, a colour bearing the motto '*Aut Liber aut Nullus*', officers' gorgets and halberds, and shoulder knots for sergeants and corporals; Prince William County Independent Company of Cadets – the unit's colour, officers' sashes and gorgets, and gold shoulder knots for sergeants and corporals were supplied by General Washington; Independent Company of Alexandria (1775) – for this unit Washington provided a pattern of hunting shirt, cap and gaiters; Culpeper County Minute Battalion (1775–76) – the colour for this battalion displayed a coiled rattlesnake in its centre, below it the words 'Don't tread on me', at the sides 'Liberty or Death', and at the top 'The Culpeper Minute Men'. The men wore brown linen hunting shirts dyed green with the inscription in large white letters on the breast, 'Liberty or Death', buckstail for cockades, blue stroud leggings with scarlet garters and

13

horn buttons, leather shoulder belts for tomahawks, and scalping knives; Prince William County Minute Battalion (1775) – blue hunting shirts and red leggings.

Of Virginia's regiments in Continental service the following uniform details are known: 1st – dyed hunting shirts faced scarlet, blue overalls, round hats, black camp colours, racoon rifle pouches and blue kersey watchcoats; 2nd – purple hunting shirts, blue kersey watchcoats and white camp colours; 3rd – dyed hunting shirts and blue leggings; 4th – red faced green, and yellow buttons; 5th – hunting shirts; 6th – short brown oznabrig hunting shirts, colour and cuffs faced with red, drummer's and fifer's shirts were white with brown cuffs (for further detail see Figure 3, Plate C); 7th – black hunting shirts, blue waistcoats, and leather breeches; 8th – brown hunting

shirts and trousers, blue coats, yellow buttons, and buckskin breeches; Light Horse – blue close bodied coats with red cape and cuffs, leather breeches, a pair of pistols and holsters, a tomahawk, a spear and a saddle; Artillery Company – coats of blue faced white.

North Carolina

North Carolina raised two battalions of regulars in 1775, and placed them on the Continental establishment in order to secure support for uniforms from the Continental Congress. On 24 December 1775, the Council of State resolved that in districts where Continental troops were stationed, paymasters would buy cloth to be made into coats, waistcoats and breeches for the two battalions. In addition to the regulars, each of the six regional military districts was required to raise a ten-company battalion of minutemen whose bounty consisted of a uniform that comprised a hunting shirt, leggings or spatterdashes, and black garters.

To provide for its nine Continental regiments, North Carolina's delegates to the Continental Congress informed the Council of Safety on 2 August 1776 that they had appointed James Mease one of the Continental commissaries. Mease was employed to make up cloth short coats, breeches, stockings, shoes and shirts. A later requisition included such items as hats, cartouche boxes, canteens and regimental colours. On 18 October, Mease consigned to the Council of Safety at Halifax: 560 coats mixed faced red, 592 coats drab faced blue, 16 drummers coats in blue faced drab, 608 coats brown faced white, 16 drummers coats white faced brown, 411 coats drab faced red, 476 coats brown faced red, 506 pairs of drilling breeches, and 500 oznabrig shirts. No record has been found of the distribution of this shipment.

South Carolina

South Carolina's militia of 14,000 officers and men was organised into 12 regiments of foot and one of horse. In addition the First Provincial Congress formed volunteer companies and troops of horse. On 4 June 1775, the Provincial Congress authorised the raising of two regiments of foot and one of rangers as regulars on South Carolina's establishment.

Captain Jacob Shubrick, 2nd South Carolina Regiment of the Continental Line, by Henry Benbridge. Probably painted after Shubrick's death at Fort Moultrie in June 1778. He wears a grenadier officer's uniform consisting of a black mitre cap, garters, scabbard, spatterdashes and stock; silver crescent, epaulettes, buttons and sword hilt; blue coat; scarlet lapels, cape, cuffs and lining; white waistcoat, breeches, stockings, and frills. (The Society of the Cincinnati Museum, Anderson House, Washington DC)

The known uniform details of South Carolina's militia are as follows: 1st Regiment (June 1775) – officers' regimentals were blue faced buff, cap and feather, however from 1776 regimentals were to be blue faced red; 2nd Regiment (June 1775) – officers' regimentals blue faced scarlet, cap and feather, and crescent in front bearing the motto 'Liberty', two regimental standards, one red and one blue (see illustration on page 38 for detail of the blue standard); 3rd Regiment (Rangers) (December 1775) – equipped as riflemen, uniforms were of blue faced white, fronted caps inscribed with the motto 'Liberty or Death' were also worn; Edisto Island Volunteers (1775) – blue coat with white cuffs and lapels, white waistcoat and breeches and fan-tail hat; Captain Charles Drayton's Volunteers (1775) – officers in scarlet frock coats, faced with white and silver metal; St Helena Volunteers (1775) – blue coatees faced red, standing collar, white small clothes, black kneebands and gaiters, beaver cap with silver crescent and inscribed with the motto 'Liberty or Death', white plume on the right and black ostrich plume on the left; Regiment of Horse, Provincial Militia (1761–75) – blue coats with yellow buttons and crimson lining, cuffs, lapels and waistcoat; blue breeches, gold laced hat, officers' waistcoats laced, blue saddle cloth and blue fringed holster; Artillery Company of Charleston (1757–76) – blue coatee, crimson lapels and cuffs, gilt buttons, blue waistcoats and breeches; Light Infantry Company of Charleston (1773–75) – scarlet short coats faced black were worn with gold lace for officers and plain lace for soldiers, white waistcoats and breeches, black caps with black feathers and a silver crescent inscribed with the motto '*Pro patria*' completed the uniform.

Georgia

The poorest and least populated of all the provinces, Georgia had to rely on help from the Continental Congress to begin raising a regular regiment. A volunteer company of light infantry and one of grenadiers existed in Savannah, but, like the regulars, no information on uniforms is available.

CONTINENTAL UNIFORMS

On 18 July 1775, the Continental Congress resolved to inform each province that all men entering a military association should come with a good firelock, bayonet, cutting sword or tomahawk, cartridge box with 24 rounds, a powder horn with 2 lbs powder and 2 lbs lead in a bag, and a knapsack.

The procurement of military clothing was assigned to the Continental Quartermaster General at Cambridge, Major Thomas Mifflin, appointed 16 June 1775. Mifflin's appeals of 6 and 11 September to Congress for funds to buy coarse woollens compelled the delegates to debate the neglected issue of clothing the two armies Congress had raised – the Cambridge Army, commanded by Washington, and the Northern Army, campaigning against Canada. On 23 September 1775, Congress voted to form a committee to buy £5,000 worth of woollens, to be placed in the hands of the Quartermaster General. For his trouble, Mifflin received a commission of five per cent of the prime cost and charges attributable to this activity. To supply its Northern Army, on 2 November 1775, Congress ordered Francis Lewis and John Alsop of New York to purchase 3,000 felt hats, 3,000 caps, 3,000 pairs of buckskin breeches, 3,000 waistcoats, 3,000 pairs of shoes, and 300 watchcoats of fearnought or duffel.

Provision of uniforms

As domestic supplies of cloth rapidly dwindled and prices soared, the Continental Congress committee recommended, on 23 December 1775, the importation of 60,000 striped blankets, 120,000 yards of blue and brown broad cloth, 10,000 yards of different coloured broad cloths for facing, and 3,000 yards of duffel. As a result of this report, on 3 January 1776, Congress authorised the Secret Committee to negotiate contracts with merchants, such as Nicholas and John Brown of Rhode Island, to take commercial voyages with the object of importing the above cloth. Among the early results of this effort was the aptly named brig *Happy Return*, which brought over 2,000 yards each of brown and blue cloth into Providence.

Supplementing this commercial activity, the Committee of Secret Correspondence ordered Silas Deane of Connecticut, then representing the 13 colonies in France, to apply for clothing and arms to be paid for by remittances as soon as navigation opened.

It was not until 19 June 1776 that Congress recommended that the rebelling colonies should provide each soldier enlisted from their colonies with a suit of clothes for

the 1777 campaign. This was to include buckskin waistcoat and breeches, a blanket, a hat or leather cap, two pairs of hose, two shirts and two pairs of shoes. Congress would pay for them and would be reimbursed from soldiers' pay. Most of the states had already taken action to clothe their troops, but where necessary they appointed commissaries to represent the Continental effort. Many agents, such as Samuel Allyne Otis of Boston, Daniel Tillinghast of Rhode Island, James Mease of Philadelphia and William Aylett, simply served both masters.

Following the creation of a war department in the form of the Continental Board of War and Ordnance, on 9 October 1796 Congress resolved to appoint a Commissary of Clothing for each of the regional armies. George Measam, a native of Canada, was appointed to the Northern Army, and James Mease, the Continental agent in Philadelphia, was appointed by General Washington on 10 February 1777 to the broader position of Clothier General.

In the meantime, General Washington was putting his army into some measure of order. Washington's General Orders of 14 and 24 July specified the following rank insignia for officers and non-commissioned officers: commanders-in-chief – a light blue ribbon across the breast between the coat and waistcoat; major generals – a purple ribbon; brigadier generals – a pink ribbon; aides-de-camp – a green ribbon; field officers – a red or pink cockade; captains – yellow or buff; subalterns – green; sergeants – an epaulette or strip of red cloth sewn on the right shoulder; and for corporals one of green. For all men on duty without uniform, Washington recommended, but did not order, a practical and inexpensive uniform of a hunting shirt and long breeches made gaiter fashion. He went on to try to convince the governors of Rhode Island

Right: Georgia four spanish milled dollars certificate, c.1776. The figure in the bottom right hand corner wears a Scottish bonnet with a feather in the front, single breasted jacket, fringed kilt, overalls and moccasins. (Private Collection)

GEORGIA.　　　No. *646*

THIS CERTIFICATE intitles the Bearer to FOUR SPANISH MILLED DOLLARS, or the Value thereof, according to Refolution of CONGRESS.　　§1§ FOUR §1§

DOLLARS.

Left: Georgia three dollar certificate, dated 10 September 1777. The figure wears a Kilmarnock bonnet, single breasted jacket, wide kilt, leggings and moccasins. (Smithsonian photograph)

and Connecticut and the Continental Congress to adopt the hunting shirt as the standard American uniform.

Washington's dream of a hunting shirt clad army was shattered by the lack of tow cloth in both Connecticut and Rhode Island. At a meeting of delegates from the Continental Congress held at Cambridge on 20 October, it was agreed that clothing provided by the Continent was to be paid for from the soldiers' wages – 10 shillings per month. Cloth for this purpose was to be dyed brown, and regimental distinctions were made in the facings. On 17 November 1775, Washington ordered the officers commanding the 26 Continental Regiments of Foot to meet at the office of the Quartermaster General at Cambridge to agree uniforms for their regiments.

To make these uniforms, the Quartermaster General could draw on captured British uniforms amounting to 338 scarlet faced pale buff coats of the 22nd Regiment of Foot, 336 scarlet faced buff coats of the 40th Foot, two bales containing 420 yards of blue broad cloth, and four casks and nine bales of cloth and clothing sent by Francis Lewis to John Alsop in Cambridge. These were to be made up into 2,000 blue, brown and green coats and waistcoats, faced in red, blue, pink, green, yellow, white, buff, brown and crimson. The $\frac{6}{4}$ wide cloth would provide $2\frac{1}{2}$ yards to make up a short coat and a belted waistcoat, like those of the Philadelphia *Associators*. Some 2,000 felt hats with white binding were also to be forwarded.

The regimentals drawn by the colonels of the 26 Continental regiments became available for delivery at cost on 5 January 1776. On 20 February, Washington ordered that each regiment was to be furnished with colours that would match the regimental uniform. The suit of colours

of each regiment consisted of two standards and four colours for each grand division. The first standard was to be the Union, and the second was to be in the colour of the facings and marked with the number of the regiment and a motto.

Uniforms and colours of the Continental Regiments of Foot

1st Regiment

Officers wore green coats and breeches. The regimental standard featured a tiger enclosed by netting, defended by a hunter in white and armed with a spear, on a crimson field with the motto 'Dominari Nollo'. For details of the uniforms of enlisted men see Figure 2, Plate B.

7th Regiment

Sailor's dress. This regiment's standard had a white field with a black thorn bush and a flesh coloured hand extended to pluck the bush. The standard bore the motto 'He that touches me shall prick his fingers'.

11th Regiment

Men wore brown hunting shirts and coats faced with white. Officers' uniforms had silver lace.

12th Regiment

Blue coats faced buff.

13th Regiment

Regimental standard was light buff, with a pine tree and a field of Indian corn. The standard depicted two officers in regimental uniform, one wounded in the breast with blood streaming from the wound pointing to several children under the tree, with the motto 'For posterity I bleed'.

15th Regiment
At Trenton, on 25 December 1776, Fife Major Isaac Greenwood lost his pack containing a suit of blue turned-up with white, and silver laced; Captain Ebenezer Sullivan, when taken prisoner on 20 May 1776, lost his blue coat faced white with two gold epaulettes, white jacket and breeches, gold laced hat, and blue surtout coat with green velvet collar.

16th Regiment
Deserter reports indicate uniforms of green and a standard of red on a white field.

17th Regiment
Regimental coats had black lapels, these were made for Lieutenant Jabez Fitch on 14 February 1776.

18th Regiment
A deserter had a cloth coloured coat faced buff. The uniform of the regiment was a narrow brimmed felt hat bound white. The regimental standard was buff.

22nd Regiment
Lieutenant Roger Hooker's inventory of personal possessions included a scarlet faced buff coat with a gold

epaulette, a blue coat faced with red, a red duffel watchcoat, a red and a white pair of breeches, two white, one blue and one red vest, two pairs of black silk knee garters, two beaver hats, one which was trimmed with gold, four white shirts, one white goat skin haversack, a cartouche box and a bayonet belt.

24th Regiment
A deserter report describes a man in a Continental coat and jacket (July). The regimental standard was buff with a red field, white thorn bush with a flesh coloured hand extended to pluck it, and the motto: 'He that touches me shall prick his fingers'.

25th Regiment
One blue and buff coat issued at Albany on 20 September 1776; the regiment was credited with 601 uniform coats and 270 waistcoats.

26th Regiment
Uniforms consisted of a brown coat, blue jacket and white breeches, for further details see Figure 1, Plate B. For detail of regimental mitre caps see the pictures on pages 7 and 44. The unit's standard was straw coloured.

Regiment of Artillery (Knox's)
According to the papers of Henry Knox and the orderly book of Captain Ezra Badlam, the regiment had blue coats, red two inch wide lapels, cape and cuffs, white lining, gold buttons, white waistcoats, buff leather breeches, blue stockings, black half-gaiters, and black hats with black cockade and gilt buttons; drummers' and fifers' coats were scarlet faced blue.

Major Jeremiah Dugan's Canadian Rangers
Officers received blue and red cloth, coarse linen, buttons and thread to make a coat, waistcoat and breeches, and a pair of moccasins. Enlisted men received blanket coats, spotted swanskin waistcoats, cloth breeches, russia sheeting shirts, ratteen leggings, mittens, shoes and milled caps.

Grenadier mitre cap, 26th Continental Infantry Regiment, 1776. Full front view. This example is believed to have been worn by Corporal Ansel Pope, Captain Thomas Mighill's Company. The front of the cap is 12 inches high, 10½ inches wide at the base and covered with red wool. Embroidered in white thread on the front is the monogram 'GW' and a sunburst. The cap itself is edged in white herringbone tape. The 4 inch high flap is in the facing colour of straw yellow, with gold edging. (Collections of the Division of Armed Forces History, National Museum of American History, Smithsonian Institution)

Uniforms and specifications 1777–78

When Congress established a new Continental Army of 88 battalions of Line infantry, five regiments of artillery, one of artillery artificers, 16 additional regiments not assigned to any state, five regiments raised in 1776 for the war (1st and 2nd Canadians, German Battalion, Warner's Green Mountain Boys, the Maryland and Virginia Rifle Regiments), four regiments of light dragoons and a squadron of Provost Guards, the clothing of these troops became the conflicting objective of Congress, the individual states and Washington's subordinate commanders. In this process, Washington's role was that of a referee.

Continental clothing depots were established either in camp with the armies or in convenient locations. Before the fall of Philadelphia, Congress instructed Mease to buy up all available supplies of cloth, caps and hats in Philadelphia. After the capture of Philadelphia, York and Lancaster served as the locations for Continental clothing stores in Pennsylvania.

To serve the Northern Army, clothing stores were established first in Albany and then, in 1777, in Fishkill and Peekskill, New York. Assisting Mease were clerks, storekeepers and a deputy in each state. Clothing was issued direct to non-commissioned officers, and appropriate amounts were deducted from soldiers' pay.

Mease's direct responsibilities included the line, cavalry, artillery and additional regiments within his reach,

Etching, 'The Death of Warren' frontispiece from Brackenridge, The Battle of Bunkers-Hill (Philadelphia, 1776). This contemporaneous illustration is not based on any known British or European work; therefore, it may be considered a faithful depiction of the military dress worn by defenders of the famous hill. Note the dragoon sleeve and the narrow cape and lapels on the coat of the kneeling figure. Three background figures have short hunting shirts with fringed capes, flopped hats turned-up, and leggings or overalls worn into the shoes. (Library of Congress)

Massachusetts Provincial Congress coat, reconstructed by Peter F. Copeland. Made by various Massachusetts townships in response to the call of the Provincial Congress for uniforms for the troops raised by the colony. It had no lapels and was faced with the material of the coat, The number of the regiment was displayed on the pewter buttons. Made of homespun cloth, these coats were used extensively by New England forces during 1776.

altered by removing the white lapels from the 47th's coats and using them as cuffs and capes on those of the other two. Hoping to issue these to Colonel William Grayson's Additional Regiment of Foot from Virginia, Mease found that Grayson had already settled on 400 blue faced red coats. The Commander-in-Chief's Guard was to have facings of buff, but with this colour in short supply, Mease substituted yellow.

In the Northern Department, on 5 September, George Measam, from Albany, informed General Gates of the arrival from Boston of a 'fine' parcel of 581 blue and red uniforms, and from James Mease in Philadelphia of 386 brown faced red coats, 118 brown faced white, 150 brown faced green, 136 blue faced red, 60 drab faced red, 96 drab faced green and 20 drummers' and fifers' coats of green faced blue. On 5 October, Measam received from Massachusetts 600 coats blue faced white, 104 brown faced white, 470 brown linen shirts, as well as various other items of clothing. While the above totals 1,847 coats, an account for the Northern Army in the US National Archives enumerates 3,497 coats issued during 1777.

Notwithstanding this effort, complaints of lack of clothing kept coming to General Washington, who blamed much of the shortfall on individual officers, accusing them of neglecting their men, inflating their requirements, and engaging in other time-honoured practices.

Mease, in a letter dated 4 December 1777 to Washington, asked to be relieved of his duties owing to ill-health, but promised to fulfil his responsibilities until a successor was named.

Accounting to the Board of War Committee on Clothing, Mease reported on all issues, including those to the Northern Army, but excluding South Carolina and Georgia which did not file clothing returns. On 1 January 1778 issues stood at: 22,586 coats, 21,880 waistcoats, 22,237 pairs of breeches, 53,002 shirts, 53,658 pairs of shoes, 44,818 pairs of stockings, 10,451 hats, 11,308 blankets, 6,087 hunting shirts, 14,936 pairs of overalls, 1,276 pairs of mitts, 514 pairs of boots, 1,162 milled caps and 337 gaiters and garters. To measure the adequacy of this distribution against requirements, exclusive of the artillery, the strength of Washington's army in December 1777 was 10,276 rank and file present and fit for duty out of a total 25,985.

During 1777, Washington issued no order specifying a uniform colour or pattern for the Continental Army, but on 28 December 1777, he accepted a uniform pattern recommended by the Marquis de Lafayette for the 1778 issues. Washington described it as a 'waistcoat, in the French fashion', with large lapels turned back in fair weather and buttoned over the breast in cold. It had a high standing $1\frac{1}{2}$ inch collar and three inch cuffs of a different

but not the Continental service departments such as the Quartermaster General, the Hospital, and the Commissary General of Military Stores, all of which took care of their own personnel.

Mease first made use of captured British clothing. Writing to Washington on 12 May 1777, he proposed issuing to Colonel John Moylan's 4th Continental Light Dragoons some 250 scarlet faced blue coats of the 8th and 21st Foot. For the outcome of this expedient move, see Figure 1, Plate D. The remaining 450 coats of these two regiments were shortened and their body linings removed. Coats belonging to the 47th, 53rd and 62nd Foot were

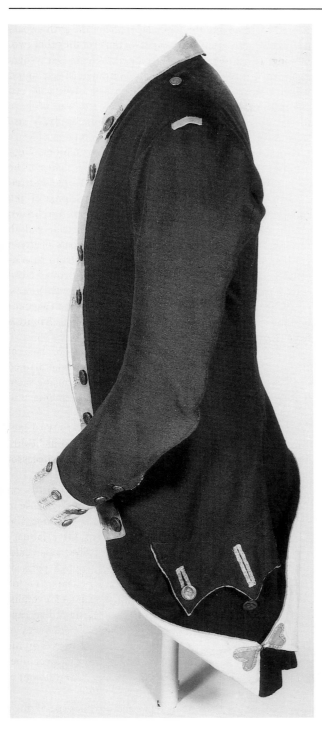

colour; these varied to distinguish regiments. Lafayette's round hat had a three inch brim turned up on one side and adorned with a small feather, an under jacket without a pocket or belt, and either overalls or breeches and stockings. Rather than wear stockings, he recommended the soldiers grease the inside of their shoes and cover the shoes with half gaiters.

Imported Uniforms 1777–78

The Continental Congress first ordered imported ready-made uniforms when on 17 February 1777 the Secret Committee instructed the Continental Commissioners at Paris to obtain 40,000 uniforms in green, blue and brown, with facings. The coats and waistcoats were to be short skirted and made to suit men of stouter stature than those of France. Orders were for batches of 10,000 or less. The uniforms were either brown or blue and had red facings and white metal buttons. They were to include white cloth waistcoats and breeches. A contract of 6 August 1777 for 5,000 coats specifies red linings as well as facings and collars. The other contracts call for white linings.

Uniforms that did reach the Continental Clothier were highly praised by George Measam: they were good quality

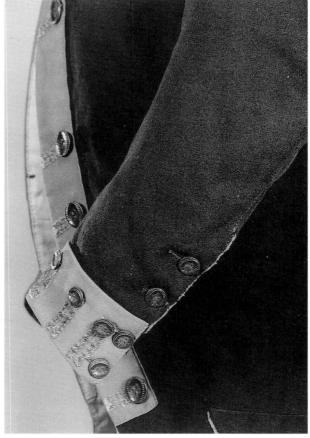

Regimental coat of Colonel Peter Gansevoort, 3rd New York Regiment of the Continental Line, 1777–79. The skirts are hooked back revealing red hearts with silver lace and the $\frac{1}{2}$ inch wide red welt edging on the pocket. Shoulder strap retainers were red, 2 inches long and $\frac{1}{2}$ inch wide. Note the narrow red welt marks on the cuffs. (Smithsonian Institution)

cloth, lined with white serges, and had white waistcoats and breeches. The breeches were made for knee-buckles, which were not supplied, the coats were well cut, being large and warm with the lapels made to button over the breast and belly, with plain white buttons and slash sleeves made to button underneath. The coats and waistcoats were lined with white serge and the breeches with strong brown linen. Stockings were lead coloured.

No uniforms for non-commissioned officers or drummers and fifers were received in these consignments. As of 23 July 1778 Mease reported the arrival of the following imported clothing: 22,596 coats, 23,074 waistcoats, 23,074 pairs of breeches, 1276 suits in the brig *Three Brothers*, 12,098 shoes, 16,130 stockings and 4,986 blankets. This clothing was to be distributed to the Continental Infantry which in December 1778 returned 17,343 rank and file fit for duty.

Allocation of these uniforms was determined by a lottery held in two drawings by Washington's aides-de-camp. On 28 October 1778, they drew lots to determine which colour – brown or blue – went to which state line.

The results of the first draw were: blue for North Carolina, Maryland, New Jersey and New York; and brown for Virginia, Delaware, Pennsylvania, Massachusetts, New Hampshire and Hazen's Regiment. States that drew brown coats participated in a second lottery for access to any remaining undistributed blue coats. A record of 4,232 brown and blue coats, and the same number of white waistcoats and pairs of breeches, distributed to Gate's Division between 4 and 11 November 1778, confirms the lottery's allocations.

In April 1778, the Continental Board of War prepared an estimate for 100,000 uniforms to be imported for the campaign of 1779. The suits were to be sized as the French uniforms, except that the skirts of the coat were not to reach below half-way down the thigh. When made up, the clothing was to have extra cloth at the seams, to enable it to be altered if too small, and sleeves wide enough to give the soldier the free use of his arms. The coat was to button as far as the waistband, and the buttons were to be of block tin or brass, solid cast, with a strong eye or shank. Each button bore the inscription 'USA' in Roman letters. The linings,

Cartouche of 'A Map of that part of Pensylvania [sic] now the Principle seat of War in America wherein may be seen the Situation of Philadelphia, Red Bank, Mud Island, & Germantown...'. Etching 1777. The officer represents the American forces and shows a pattern uniform that resembles that used pre-1775. (Library of Congress)

except for those of the Artillery, were to be the same colour as the facings, and the sergeants' clothes were to be of a better quality.

Infantry uniforms were to be blue faced white, blue faced scarlet, white faced blue, blue faced yellow and green faced white. The drummers' and fifers' uniforms were reversed, and 1,200 of the soldiers' coats were to be furnished with knots for corporals. For light dragoons, complete suits, including cloaks, were to be of green faced white, blue faced white, white faced blue and blue faced yellow, with trumpeters' coat colours reversed. Corporals' knots were to be fixed to 120 privates' coats in each group. Plain caps with green, black, red and white horsehair crests were ordered in proportion to the suits. Material for officers' uniforms, following the same colour schemes as those of the infantry, light dragoons and artillery were also estimated. Officers' buttons were to be white and yellow with the letters 'USA' stamped on them. The officers were to have white worsted hose, fine linen for shirts and cambric stocks. For enlisted men, the estimate specified hats laced with white bindings and feathers of the Kevehuller cock, black stocks, brass shirt-sleeve buttons and stock buckles.

Continental Artillery

Descriptions of deserters, tailoring orders of Brigadier General Henry Knox and comments on orders for clothing for the Artillery by Messrs Otis and Andrews reveal the following uniform details: black coats lapelled with red, plain yellow buttons, white waistcoats, breeches and stockings, black garters, cocked hats, hair cockades and white tassels. The above details are supported by clothing records of the 2nd and 3rd regiments.

The first consolidated delivery of clothing to all four regiments was in October 1778. Officers received regimental coats and brown breeches. For non-commissioned officers and drummers, Knox requested two-inch wide white leather sword belts to wear over the shoulder. Hats for the whole brigade were to be cocked without being cut, and ornamented with a piece of bearskin. Drummers' and fifers' hats were to be cut round and turned-up on one side. An invoice in the National Archives, prepared by the Board of War on 30 April 1778 for clothing to be imported from France, details the Artillery clothing for the campaign of 1779 as: suits of black faced with scarlet, with yellow trimmings and lined in white. Coats for corporals, gunners and bombardiers were to have knots, while those of the drums and fifes were to be scarlet faced with black.

In April and May 1778, Harrison's 1st Continental Artillery Regiment received from the Virginia Public Store: 221 blue coats with red lapels, 74 striped waistcoats and pairs of breeches and 30 red jackets and pairs of

Colonel Henry Jackson of Jackson's Additional Continental Regiment of Foot, after an original in the Essex Institute of Salem, Massachusetts, by an unknown artist. Painted while Jackson's regiment was stationed at Dorchester Heights in 1777, he wears blue faced buff, buff waistcoat and breeches, black cocked hat and white ruffles. (Peter F. Copeland)

breeches. Two Maryland companies, that joined the 1st Regiment in July, were also uniformed in blue faced scarlet. And in October 1778, the regiment received 142 yards of black cloth from the Virginia clothier at camp.

The 4th Continental Artillery Regiment was a Pennsylvania state regiment until transferred to the Continental Army by an act of the General Assembly of 18 June 1777. For details of its uniforms, see the Pennsylvania section below.

Benjamin Flower's Regiment of Artillery and Artificers does not appear to have been uniformed during this period.

Continental Light Dragoons

On 7 March 1778, Major General Horatio Gates, President of the Board of War, informed the governors of the states that the minimum needed to equip a horseman for the field was: a straight bladed sword, three feet long, open guarded and with a leather scabbard; a pair of pistols and holsters; a sword belt; a carbine belt with a running swivel; a cartridge box to buckle round the waist and 12 tin pipes for the cartridges; a helmet of jacked leather, guarded by

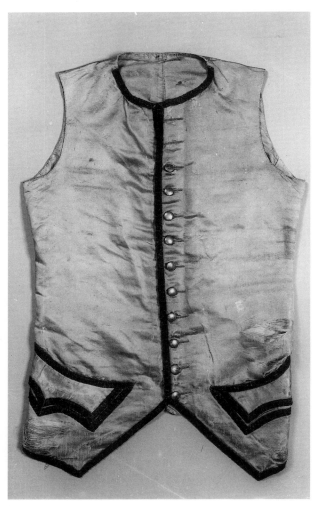

Waistcoat of Major General Adam Stephen. White silk front and back, silver lace and buttons. Stephen, a veteran of the French and Indian War, commanded the 4th Virginia Regiment of the Continental Line until promoted to brigadier general on 4 September 1776. He was promoted once more, this time to major general, on 19 February 1777, Stephen was 'dismissed [from] the service' for drunkenness at Germantown. (Collections of the Division of Armed Forces History, National Museum of American History, Smithsonian Institution)

several rows of small chains with iron or steel hoops, or a hat with a metal scull piece inside the crown; a saddle, saddle cloth, breast plate, crupper, saddle straps and pad; saddle bags; a double-reined bridle with curb and snaffle bit, and a halter; a cloak sufficient to cover all the arms and accoutrements; and a pair of boots and spurs.

1st Light Dragoons

On 13 April 1777, Colonel Theodrick Bland issued a complete regimental order that included: brown coats with a green interrupted lapel, a standing collar and angular cuff, gold buttons cast with a horse and the number '1', and button holes; green vests without skirts; buff breeches; (for trumpeters see Figure 3 Plate D); for farriers and saddlers plain brown coats with green lapels, white sword belts and slings, leather caps with perpendicular fronts, green turbans with yellow tassels, and plain leather holster caps marked with the number '1'. Cloth for the regimentals, which was used until 1780, was obtained from the Virginia Public Store and the helmets and boots came from Baltimore.

2nd Light Dragoons

Other than their own clothes and horse equipment supplied by Connecticut, and a few hunting shirts provided by the Continental Clothier General, the 2nd had no uniform in 1777. When in 1778 Lieutenant Colonel Blackden went to New England to contract for boots, breeches and coats, all the regiment could boast of was 149 heavy horsemen's swords with steel scabbards taken from General Burgoyne. A fragment bill signed by Samuel Blackden in the National Archives is for brass for helmets.

3rd Light Dragoons

Some of the Virginia-recruited troops of this regiment joined wearing Virginia Light Horse uniforms. By mid-September 1777, the Clothier General had issued 246 coats, 81 vests, 47 pairs of breeches and eight pairs of boots to the regiment. However, a pattern uniform seems only to have been adopted in April 1778 when Colonel George Baylor purchased from the Virginia Public Store: 178 yards of white cloth, $77\frac{1}{4}$ yards of blue and other cloths, and 48 black feathers for the officers. On 27 September 1778, Captain Robert Smith was sent to Otis and Andrews in Boston to obtain regimental uniforms. Otis and Andrews had no difficulty making cloaks for the regiment, but a shortage of white cloth meant that the uniforms were not delivered until 1779.

4th Light Dragoons

The use of captured British clothing by this regiment is discussed earlier in this chapter. For further detail see Figure 1, Plate D.

North Carolina Light Horse

Raised in North Carolina for Continental service, this troop was uniformed by the Clothier General with 70 coats, 70 waistcoats, 70 pairs of breeches, 70 hunting shirts, 70 pairs of shoes and 59 pairs of boots. While serving at Fort Pitt in 1778, the troop also received blue and red cloth from the store keeper of the Western Department.

Continental Legionary Corps

Armand's Corps

On 17 May 1778, the Continental Board of War authorised Colonel Armand, Marquis de la Rouerie – commander of the independent corps of Major Ottendorf, to form a corps of Free and Independent Chasseurs. After examining the needs of his new corps, Armand wrote to Lieutenant Colonel Alexander Hamilton on 5 November 1778 requesting 100 knapsacks, 141 pairs of woollen breeches, 141 worsted caps, 112 pairs of long gaiters, 24 cloaks and 24 linen wraps from the store at Fishkill.

Lee's Legion

Formed as a detachment from the 1st Continental Light Dragoons, Lee's Legion did not possess a distinct uniform until July 1778 when Major Henry Lee purchased 305 yards of buff cloth, 130 yards of green cloth and 156 pairs of yarn hose from the Virginia Public Store.

Pulaski's Legion

A clear picture of the uniforms worn by men of Pulaski's Legion in 1778 can be constructed from a general return of clothing and accoutrements preserved in the New York Historical Society, (see Figure 3, Plate H). During 1778, the Legion received 619 coats, 262 leather jackets, 353 pairs of leather breeches, 222 linen jackets, 85 hunting shirts, 533 caps, 374 pairs of boots, 156 boot buckles, 154 great coats, 350 pairs of gaiters, 250 gaiter tops, 348 leather cockades, 400 stars, 400 feathers, and 234 fur skins. Some 1,835 yards of blue, red, grey, white and other cloth were used to make uniforms for riflemen, dragoons and infantry. Musicians had red coats and trumpeters' coats were bound with silver.

Additional Continental Regiments of Foot

Sixteen regiments were raised regionally but not adopted by any state, so their clothing had to come from the common pool of Continental stores or commanders had to find alternative sources.

Armaments of the American Rebels. Pen sketch with hand colouring, $11\frac{1}{2}$ by $16\frac{1}{4}$ inches. The artist Charles Blaskowitz was the map maker for Major General Howe. Figure 'A' represents a floating battery or gondola built at Cambridge 'by the Rebels' in October 1775. Note the tree displayed on the colour. 'C', 'D' and 'E' are pole arms '. . . in Use in the Rebel Army'. (Library of Congress)

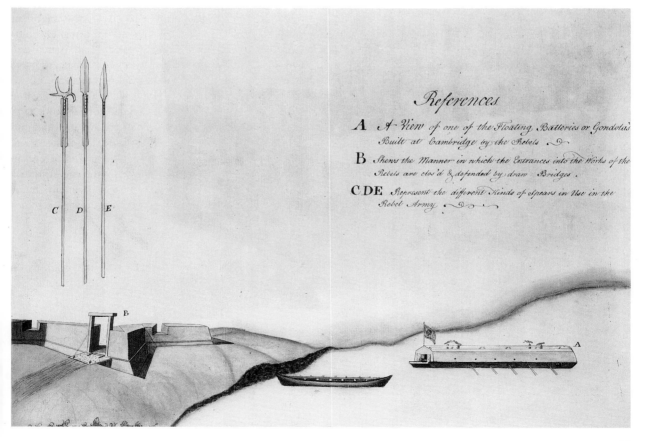

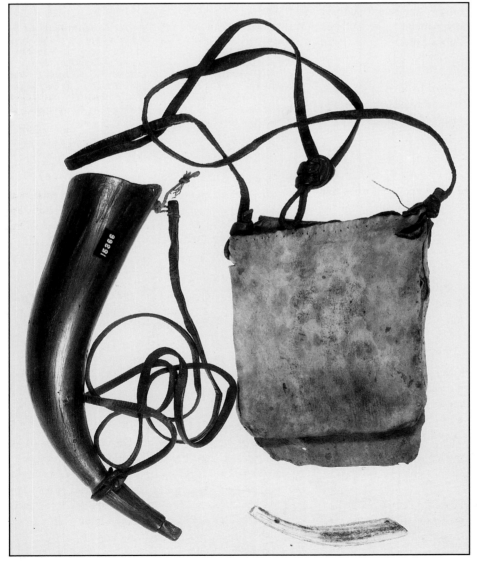

Committee of Safety musket. (Collections of the Division of Armed Forces History, National Museum of American History, Smithsonian Institution)

Powder horn, bullet pouch and powder measurer carried by Captain William Walton, 1st North Carolina Regiment of the Continental Line. (Collections of the Division of Armed Forces History, National Museum of American History, Smithsonian Institution)

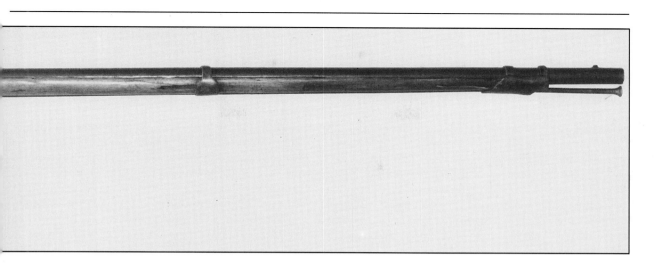

David Forman's
Deserter descriptions and an eye-witness account of the Battle of Germantown describe red coats faced buff, a white jacket, buff breeches and pewter buttons marked '31'.

Nathaniel Gist's
Deserter descriptions specify brown turned-up green, white shirts and brown yarn stockings.

William Grayson's
Blue turned-up with red, red shalloon lined shoulder straps and button holes; on 10 June 1778, the regiment received coats for 180 privates, 29 sergeants and eight drummers from Virginia sources.

Thomas Hartley's
1777: blue coats with white collars, white jackets and buckskin breeches; 1778: blue faced yellow and caps. For further detail see Figure 1, Plate F.

David Henley's
During 1777, 165 soldiers each signed receipt rolls for a hat, coat, waistcoat, shirt, pair of breeches, stock, two pairs of stockings and two pairs of shoes. Deserter descriptions indicate blue regimentals. On 13 October 1778, General Sullivan ordered Henley's, Lee's and Jackson's regiments to be clothed in blue and buff.

Henry Jackson's
This unit's uniform of blue and buff, lined white, white waistcoat and breeches and large hats with white binding was obtained in Boston by Colonel Jackson. For further detail see Figure 2, Plate F.

William R. Lee's
From deserter descriptions it seems that this unit's 1777 uniform included a blue regimental coat faced white.

Oliver Spencer's
By 23 September 1777, the Clothier General had issued the regiment 300 coats, 300 vests, 300 pairs of breeches, 100 pairs of shoes, 110 pairs of hose, 80 shirts, 70 hats or caps, 100 hunting shirts and 165 pairs of overalls.

Seth Warner's
At Albany the regiment received 186 coats, 205 waistcoats, 1,223 pairs of breeches, 65 woollen overalls, 624 shirts, 171 pairs of stockings, 61 hats or caps, 101 hunting shirts, 110 pairs of trousers and 150 blankets.

Samuel Blatchley Webb's
On 18 January 1777, Washington ordered Webb to appropriate captured scarlet clothing sufficient for one regiment. For detail see Figure 3, Plate F.

The uniforms of the regiments of William Malcolm, John Patton, Moses Rawling, Henry Sherburne, Oliver Spencer, Charles Mynn Thruston and Seth Warner are unknown for this period.

Commander-in-Chief's Guard
On 1 January 1778, the Clothier General issued: 90 coats, jackets, pairs of breeches and hats; 94 shirts; 91 pairs of shoes; 111 pairs of stockings; 9 blankets; 1 pair of boots; 180 gaiters or garters; and 90 cockades. Washington expressed a preference for blue and buff, and a miniature portrait of the Guard Commander, Major Caleb Gibbs, shows this combination; in June 1778, 150 suits were reserved for the Guard.

German Battalion

The company book of Captain Philip Graybill's Maryland company in the Maryland Historical Society shows linen hunting shirts for each man. In 1778 a Jacob Smith was wanted for impersonating an officer of the battalion. He was seen wearing a blue coat turned-up with red, a buff jacket and breeches, and blue stockings.

1st Canadian Regiment

In 1777, the regiment received, from the Albany Public Store, 119 pairs of breeches, 62 swanskin jackets, 62 check shirts and 3 blue coats; the Massachusetts Historical Society has clothing returns from 1778 that show caps, shoes, mittens, jackets with sleeves, overalls and coats for some companies.

2nd Canadian Regiment

The men of this regiment wore brown coats with white cuffs and buttons. Waistcoats and breeches were white, black caps were also worn. For further detail see Figure 1, Plate H.

Marechausee Corps

On 14 November 1777, Captain Bartholomew von Heer proposed a Provost corps of 63 men with regimentals of green, or blue coats with black facings; when Congress established this corps on 27 May 1778, Washington wrote to Nathanael Greene, then Continental Quartermaster General, stating that they were to be armed and accoutred as light dragoons.

Invalid Corps

On 23 September 1777, they received from the Clothier General 86 coats, 99 vests, 30 pairs of breeches, 141 pairs of shoes, 107 pairs of hose, 144 shirts, 49 hats or caps and 98 pairs of overalls; in April 1778, Colonel Lewis Nicola, Commandant of the Regiment of Invalids, informed General Washington to be on the lookout for an Invalid wearing a British uniform of a red coat faced buff or white with buttons bearing the number 26. A deserter from the Boston detachment was advertised on 18 January 1779 as wearing a regimental coat of brown faced with red.

Light Corps

On 4 November 1778, Major Thomas Posey's Corps received 80 brown faced red suits, white waistcoats and breeches and grey hose from the Clothier General.

General Staff and Aides-de-Camp

No uniform regulation or details of dress of army staff were published during this period, but personal tailoring bills, correspondence with family members and portraits of general officers and their aides-de-camp indicate that blue faced buff, yellow buttons, gilt epaulettes and buff waistcoats and breeches were the prevalent fashion.

General Washington's uniform of 1776–77 is illustrated in a portrait by Charles Willson Peale. It shows Washington in what was to become his identifying

Hanger and scabbard carried by Brigadier General Richard Montgomery, killed in the assault on Quebec, 31 December 1775. *(Collections of the Division of Armed Forces History, National Museum of American History, Smithsonian Institution)*

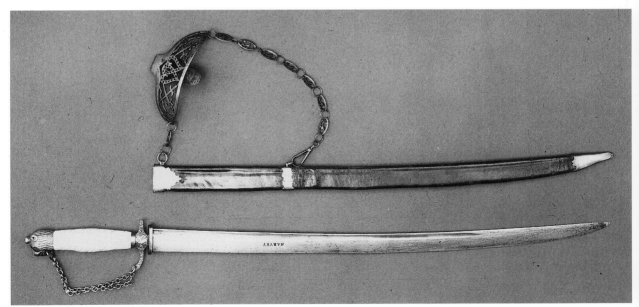

uniform, possibly made for him by Richard Peacock in January 1776. Washington's accounts in the Washington Papers at the Library of Congress indicate that a coat was made for him on 28 April 1777. In March 1778, George Gibson, a quartermaster at Lancaster, sent him two pieces of blue and buff cloth of 20 yards each. At General Washington's order, in November 1778, Otis and Andrews made a blue drab surtout coat with blue covered buttons.

From their personal papers, it is evident that Horatio Gates and Nathanael Greene, as general officers, also adopted the blue and buff uniform with buff waistcoat and breeches.

Continental Service Departments

Engineers
On 16 July 1776 at Ticonderoga, Colonel Jeduthin Baldwin reported the loss of a blue coat and 'jackoat' full trimmed with narrow gold lace, a hat, a pair of silver shoes and knee buckles.

Quartermaster General's Department
In January 1778, enlistment advertisements from the Quartermaster General's Department for waggoners and drivers stipulate that those signing on for three years or the duration would receive annually a suit of clothing, a great coat and a pair of boots. Clothing forwarded in December 1778 by Colonel Jacob Weiss to Colonel Udney Hay, Deputy Quartermaster General, for Quartermaster Artificers consisted of fully lined brown cloth coats, leather breeches, yarn stockings, shoes, white linen shirts and striped Indian blankets.

Corps of Waggoners
Colonel Henry Luterloch recommended to Washington in December 1777, that the Waggoners should wear a plate or badge on their breasts in order to identify the department they worked in.

STATE UNIFORMS 1777–78

While each state had the responsibility for clothing their own regular corps and, in some cases militia, due to failures in Continental Clothing departments, they also undertook to supply their quota of Continental troops.

Sword and scabbard carried by Brigadier General Daniel Roberdeau, Pennsylvania Associators. (Collections of the Division of Armed Forces History, Museum of American History, Smithsonian Institution)

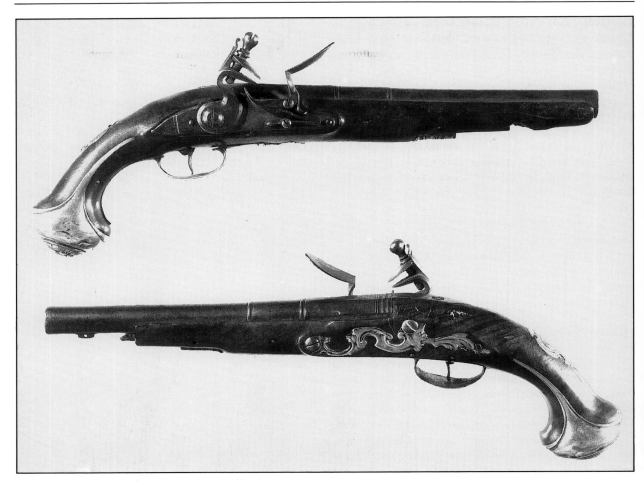

Pair of flintlock pistols
owned by Major General
Charles Lee. (Collections
of the Division of Armed

Forces History, Museum of
American History,
Smithsonian Institution)

Connecticut

On 7 February 1777, Governor Trumbull wrote to
General Washington that British clothing of scarlet and
buff and scarlet and blue being held in Dartmouth could be
of great use to the Connecticut Line. Acting on
Washington's approval, on 15 February 1777, the Council
of Safety voted that Colonel Jedediah Huntington's 1st
Regiment should have the red coats.

For the period 1777–78, the Connecticut Line
exemplified the effort required to dress the troops of a
given state. On 28 February, Andrew Huntington, a
deputy purchaser of clothing, advertised for home-made
blue, brown or red cloth for coats, white flannel for
waistcoats and breeches, and white yarn for stockings. On
12 September 1777, the Governor and Council of Safety
resolved that each town in the state was to donate a shirt, a
hunting frock, a pair of woollen overalls, one or two pairs of

stockings and a pair of shoes for each soldier in the army
belonging to that town.

For the next campaign, the Governor and Council of
Safety resolved, on 10 December 1777, to apply to Samuel
A. Otis and Benjamin Andrews, the Continental purchasing commissaries at Boston, for delivery of cloth with
trimmings sufficient for 4,000 men. The resultant regimental uniforms of 1778 were as follows: 1st Regiment –
red faced white, white waistcoat and breeches, small round
hats, drummers and fifers wore grey-brown faced light
brown, and white small clothes, officers had silver
epaulettes and hat cords; 2nd Regiment – dark brown
faced white, brown vests and breeches, and hats turned-up
on one side, drummers and fifers wore green faced brown;
3rd Regiment – light brown faced red, red or green lining,
green waistcoat and breeches and yellow buttons; 4th
Regiment – brown faced red, light brown small clothes and
yellow binding on hats; 5th Regiment – blue turned-up
with scarlet, green vests and breeches, drummers and fifers
wore yellow faced brown; 6th Regiment – blue faced white,
lined white, white small clothes, and leather caps; 7th

Regiment – miniature of Lt. Augustine Taylor, by John Ramage, unlocated: scarlet coat, white facings and waistcoat, and rose red sash; 8th Regiment – in 1777 uniforms were blue faced scarlet, in 1778 they were scarlet and white.

Rhode Island

On 21 January 1777, the Rhode Island Council of War resolved that Daniel Tillinghast should collect cloth and trimmings for 1,000 coats and pairs of breeches. Tillinghast contracted with various local tailors to make up the cloth, and in April, John Reynolds was empowered to go beyond the state in search of additional cloth.

When, in late August 1777, these efforts to purchase and make clothing did not meet expectations, the 1st Rhode Island Continental Regiment mutinied in late August 1777. Some relief for the two Continental battalions came on 14 January 1778, with the dispatch of eight cases and one cask of clothing to the Rhode Island Brigade at Valley Forge.

When raised in December 1776, the men who enlisted for the State Brigade of two foot and one artillery regiments did not receive clothing, but those who needed uniforms could buy them from the regimental quartermaster. Later, on 19 December 1777, on authorising the re-enlisting of the State Brigade, the General Assembly

Cap worn by the Newport Light Infantry Company, Newport, Rhode Island, 1774–1776. Nothing is known of the uniform of the Company; however, the cap has a $10\frac{3}{16}$ inch high front plate still bearing the royal cypher in silver. On a light blue oval, the female figure America, robed in white and red, stands over broken chains and holds a staff topped by a liberty cap. The belt and scroll with the name of the company are painted gold. (Collections of the Division of Armed Forces History, National Museum of American History, Smithsonian Institution)

stipulated that in addition to a bounty payment, each man would receive a hat, a uniform coat, two waistcoats, two pairs of breeches, three shirts, three pairs of stockings, two pairs of shoes, a hunting shirt and a pair of overalls.

Known uniform details are as follows: 2nd Rhode Island Regiment – deserters from the regiment in 1777 wore brown regimental coats faced with red, brown breeches and black sleeved jackets; 1st Rhode Island State Regiment – a deserter advertised on 13 December 1777 wore a blue coat faced with yellow; 2nd Rhode Island State Regiment – for detail see Figure 2, Plate H; Rhode Island State Artillery Regiment – blue faced red, leather breeches, white waistcoats; drummers in blue coats trimmed with blue and white saddle lace.

Massachusetts

On 10 January 1777, the Massachusetts Council resolved to issue a warrant on the Treasury for four thousand pounds to form a Committee for Clothing. On 17 January,

the Massachusetts Board of War resolved to import from the French merchants Messrs Pliarne, Penet and Company cloth of chocolate, pompadour, claret, berry and blue, with yellow, green, red, buff and white for facings, and if these were not available, white cloth with blue facings. By 31 January, the Northern Army was richer by 870 suits of clothing, 95 coats, 171 jackets, 134 overalls, 358 shirts and 457 pairs of hose. An additional 2,300 suits were dispatched by the Continental Agents for the Northern Army to Bennington on 14 February 1777. During that month, the Massachusetts Board of War ordered from Messrs Jacques Gruel and Company 40,000 four-point blankets, 70,000 yards of wool for clothing 20,000 men, 132,000 yards of coarse linen for soldiers' shirts, 20,000 coarse soldiers' hats, 3,000 pieces of ravens duck for tents, 40,000 pairs of shoes fit for soldiers, 40,000 white stockings and 60,000 yards of brown russia drilling for waistcoats and breeches.

Between February and August, the state issued around 2,000 hunting shirts, and the same number of coats, waistcoats and jackets to its infantry and artillery regiments. For the purpose of accountability, on 31 July 1777, the Massachusetts Board of War defined a suit of clothes as a hat, coat, jacket, breeches, shirt, a pair of stockings and a pair of shoes.

The Massachusetts Line was not arranged until 1779, therefore no regimental breakdown by number is practical for 1777–78. Known uniform details are as follows: Bailey's – at Dorchester on 28 September 1778, an officer requested a blue coat lined white, white or buff facings, plain white buttons and white waistcoat and breeches. On 10 November 1778, 358 suits of imported brown faced red coats and white waistcoats and breeches were received; Greaton's – uniforms were brown faced white in 1777; Rufus Putnam's – from November 1778 uniforms of blue turned-up white, with white lining were to be worn; Thomas Nixon's – on 21 February 1778, the Public Store, Albany, received 340 coats, 18 drummers' and fifers' coats, 340 pairs of breeches, 309 waistcoats, ten green and blue jackets, 50 shirts; and 100 pairs of hose; Ichabod Alden's – received at Albany on 31 January 1778 were 200 coats, 201 waistcoats, 200 pairs of breeches, 199 shirts, 203 pairs of shoes, 99 pairs of hose, on 15 February, 35 caps, on 25 October 1777, 186 milled caps, and on 4 November 1778, 300 imported brown faced red uniforms and white waistcoats and breeches; Michael Jackson's – on 25

Deputy Quartermaster General Morgan Lewis, Northern Department, unattributed. Appointed 12 September 1776, Lewis served throughout the war. He is shown here in a blue coat without collar, scarlet lapels, white waistcoat and shirt ruffles. (The Society of the Cincinnati Museum, Anderson House, Washington DC)

1: Private, Lower Regt. of New Castle, Delaware Militia, 1775-76
2: Grenadier, Captain John Lasher's New York City Grenadier Co., 1775-76
3: Captain Benedict Arnold, Governor's 2nd Co. of Guards, 1775
4: Colonel John Cadwalader, 3rd Bn. Philadelphia Associators, 1775-76

A

1: Grenadier, 26th Continental Regt. of Foot, 1776
2: Rifleman, 1st Continental Regt. of Foot, 1776
3: Chaplain William Emerson, 2nd Continental Regt. of Foot, 1776

B

1: Corporal, 3rd New Jersey Bn., 1776
2: Captain, Light Infantry Co., 2nd S.C. Regt., 1776-78
3: Corporal, 6th Virginia Regt., 1776-77

1: Trooper, 4th Continental Light Dragoons, 1777-78
2: Capt. Samual Chandler, 11th Connecticut Militia Regt., Light Horse Co., 1776-77
3: Trumpeter, 1st Continental Light Dragoons

D

1: Matross, 1st Co. of Maryland Artillery, 1776
2: Captain, Georgia Artillery, 1778
3: Gunner, 4th S.C. Regt., Artillery, 1775-78

E

1: Private, Thomas Hartley's Additional Continental Regt. of Foot, 1777
2: Private, Henry Jackson's Additional Continental Regt. of Foot, 1777
3: Ensign, Samuel Blatchley Webb's Additional Continental Regt. of Foot, 1777

1: Private, 4th New York Regt. of the Continental Line, 1778
2: Fifer, 1st New Hampshire Regt. of the Continental Line, 1778
3: Private, 10th North Carolina Regt. of the Continental Line, 1778

G

1: Private, Light Infantry Co., 2nd Canadian Regt., 1777-78
2: Private, 2nd Rhode Island State Regt., 1777-78
3: Dragoon, Pulaski's Legion, 1778

November 1777, James Keith received 18 pairs of blue breeches. The following year he received 277 imported brown faced red uniforms, white waistcoats and breeches; James Wesson's – Captain Nahoum Ward died on 6 March 1778 owing for a red coat faced white, on 10 November 1778, 332 suits of imported brown faced red uniforms and white waistcoats and breeches were received; Thomas Marshall's – on 9 November 1778, they received 255 imported blue faced red uniforms and white waistcoats and breeches; Ebenezer Francis's, later Benjamin Tupper's – on 9 November 1778, the unit received 334 imported blue faced red uniforms and white waistcoats and breeches; Gamaliel Bradford's – deserter reports of 1777 indicate a scarlet coat faced black, leather breeches and a beaver hat; in November 1778, the unit received 278 imported suits of blue faced red, and white waistcoats and breeches; Massachusetts State Train of Artillery – blue faced red, blue waistcoats and breeches. Officers' coats were trimmed with gold lace edged lapels and button holes; white watch coats.

New Hampshire

On 21 January 1778, a New Hampshire Board of War was established to supply the Continental regiments with clothing and other necessities. During March 1778, the Board of War sent to Exeter green serge to be made into coats, waistcoats and breeches. On 30 May, 25 June and 29 July, 805 hats, 501 pairs of leather breeches, 229 blankets, 1925 shirts, 56 pairs of hose, 493 pairs of overalls, 148 waistcoats, 105 rifle frocks, 885 pairs of shoes, and various amounts of cloth were despatched. The results of the Board of War effort are illustrated in Figure 2, Plate G. In addition to clothing, the state made a green and a blue silk colour for the 1st and 2nd regiments during 1778. The 1st Regiment lost its white suit of colours in 1777.

On 16 November 1778, the New Hampshire Regiments received their most complete supply of uniforms consisting of 1,105 imported coats of brown faced red, 1,105 imported waistcoats, pairs of breeches, shirts and pairs of lead coloured hose.

Pennsylvania

Having successfully uniformed its battalions for 1776, Pennsylvania turned to the Continental Clothier General for uniforms. As of 23 September 1777, James Mease reported to General Washington that the 12 Pennsylvania Line regiments plus Colonel Walter Stewart's State Regiment had received: 3,915 coats, 4,927 vests, 3,552 pairs of breeches, 9,153 pairs of shoes, 7,600 pairs of hose, 9,588 shirts, 2,328 hats or caps, 674 hunting shirts and 2,045 pairs of overalls. Yet shortages persisted. When, on 16 November, Mease was visited at Lancaster by the

Colonel John Cox, Assistant Quartermaster General, after a miniature by Charles Willson Peale, taken at Valley Forge on 2 March 1778. He wears a blue coat, off-white facings, gilt epaulettes and buttons. (Peter F. Copeland)

commanders of the 5th, 8th, and 10th regiments, he was unable to comply with their requisitions. As a result, the officers bought enough cloth to make 550 coats: 100 brown faced white, 100 blue faced white, 300 blue faced red, and 50 brown faced green.

A 3rd Pennsylvania Regiment receipt book credits the regiment with 254 coats – 200 blue and red, 27 blue and white, 23 red, two white and blue and two sergeants' red regimental. It also lists quantities of blue cloth breeches and waistcoats. By 21 November 1778, Brigadier-general Anthony Wayne's division received new clothing, bound its hats with white and used buckstail for cockades.

The officers of the Pennsylvania Line were among the first to be taken care of by their home state. After December 1777, officers who could claim arrears in clothing could draw, at state expense, superfine broad cloth of brown, blue, claret or other colours, a pair of cotton stockings, a pair of worsted stockings, one pair of fine shoes, a shirt, a stock, two dozen small gilt buttons, shalloon, mohair and linen.

Blue silk standard with the gold embroidered unit designation of the 2nd South Carolina Regiment of the Continental Line. It was presented to the regiment on 1 July 1776 at Charleston, SC. Captured on 9 October 1779 during the Siege of Savannah, it is now in the United States. (Smithsonian Institution)

In May 1777, the State Clothier provided Thomas Proctor's Artillery Regiment with 200 drilling jackets, 200 pairs of shoes, 200 shirts, 200 pairs of hose, 100 pairs of shoes and 100 pairs of buckskin breeches. On 14 July, the State Treasurer paid a bill from Philip Heyd, a Philadelphia tailor, for 13 red regimental coats for the band at 25 shillings per coat. Proctor also contracted with the Pennsylvania Commissary, James Mease, for 100 regimental coats.

New Jersey

Like Pennsylvania, New Jersey turned to the Continental Clothier General for uniforms. On 9 May 1777, James Mease informed Colonel Dayton, on the road from Boston, that he had addressed to the 3rd Regiment 325 blue coats faced red and 12 red coats faced blue for the drums and fifes. Mease had already sent 104 blue coats which were different from the old regimental uniform illustrated in Figure 1 Plate C. These coats were found by George Measam in the Fishkill, New York, clothing store in June 1778.

On 22 May 1778, the New Jersey Council of Safety appointed Major Enos Kelsey commissioner for purchasing clothing for the state's Continental troops. His main responsibility was to buy flax to make into linen. Lieutenant Colonel Israel Shreve of the 2nd New Jersey bought cloth for all New Jersey Continental Line officers and blue breeches for his own regiment. The Israel Shreve Papers at Rutgers University Library contain a receipt dated March 1778 signed by Lt. Derick Lane, for broad cloth in blue, claret and black, red shalloon, brown durant and scarlet. The quantities translate into a blue coat faced in scarlet and lined with red shalloon. The claret coloured cloth might have been used for the waistcoat and breeches, and the rest to make an overcoat. Getting the New Jersey Line into a single uniform took until 1779. The New Jersey State troops – two regional artillery companies – only received hats from the commissioners. The militia light horse officers may have had blue regimental coats turned-up with red and blue saddle clothes edged with white, like the suit advertised by John I. Schenk in the *Pennsylvania Gazette* of 17 March 1778.

New York

With the help of the Continental Clothier at Albany and the efforts of Peter Courtenius, New York clothed its five regiments during 1777. According to a return dated 15 November 1777, John Henry, Commissary of Clothing, accounted to the New York Line for the following: white or check linen and flannel shirts, 4,017 shoes, 4,662 stockings, 3,466 overalls and trousers, 2,425 hats and bonnets, 1,692 upper and under vests, 1,109 pairs of leather and cloth breeches, and 2,675 frocks. George Measam's provision of regimental coats to the New York regiments proved ample until 21 August 1778, when New York's Governor, George Clinton, ordered Henry to issue substantial quantities of every article of clothing for the five regiments.

1st Regiment

In 1777 at Albany the regiment was supplied: 131 drab coats, 30 short blue coats, four brown coats, six grey ratteen short coats, 160 short ratteen coats, 77 swanskin jackets, two crimson and 97 pairs of everlasting breeches, and 18 hats; in August 1778, Governor Clinton ordered a suit of clothes for each officer and enlisted man, the officers' regimentals being blue turned-up with red.

2nd Regiment

In 1777 at Albany the regiment was supplied: five hats, 242 coats, 158 waistcoats, six pairs of breeches, 95 shirts, 274 pairs of hose, 46 pairs of shoes, 242 caps, 248 mittens and 105 blankets; on 10 March 1777, Colonel Philip Van Cortlandt wrote that he hoped the New York Convention would provide his regiment with colours corresponding to his uniform of scarlet with white lappets; in 1778, regimental deserters wore brown-sleeved jackets, black breeches, white woollen stockings and round hats.

3rd Regiment

In 1777 at Albany the regiment was supplied: 467 coats, 34 pairs of breeches, 256 shirts, 420 stocks, 436 pairs of hose, 582 shoes, 400 caps, 400 mittens, 133 blankets, and 568½ yards of cloth, including 60 blue coats with red facings and white lining, and hats; on 16 March 1778, at Albany a further 225 pairs of shoes, 36 pairs of hose, 297 rifle shirts, 27 dozen buttons and 40 pairs of breeches were supplied. Colonel Gansevoort's regimental coat is illustrated in the pictures on pages 17 and 39.

4th Regiment

Between 19 June 1777 and 30 May 1778, Captain Nathan Strong's company received 24 coats, 28 hats, 26 pairs of breeches, 30 stockings, 48 frocks, 48 overalls, and 51 pairs of shoes; in August 1778, a deserter wore a brown homespun coat and jacket with linen overalls. For further detail see Figure 1, Plate G.

Front and rear views of the regimental coat of Colonel Peter Gansevoort, 3rd New York Regiment of the Continental Line, 1777–79. Blue wool with red cape, lapels, cuffs, and front edge of skirts and pockets, white lining and turnbacks. Non-military silver buttons, with raised milled oval on ivory or bone back and quatrefoil button shank indicator. (Gansevoort-Lansing Collection, Smithsonian Institution)

Delaware

With only one Continental battalion, Delaware relied upon the uniforms left over from 1776, to which yellow hat lace was added as a regimental distinction. At the end of 1777, Lieutenant Colonel Charles Pope was sent to Delaware by General Washington to re-clothe the regiment for the coming year. A clothing factory at Newark, established by State Clothier Thomas Rodney, made shirts from linen and 250 pairs of breeches from brown drilling. In June 1778, 19 seamstresses made 427 shirts for the regiment, and on 17 December 1778, the Delaware Assembly voted to instruct the State Clothier General to provide each officer with a coat, a waistcoat and a pair of breeches, or, in lieu, the sum of £80 for past services.

Virginia

In 1777 Virginia's Continental regiments converted from hunting shirts to regimental coats. To induce the Virginia Line to reinforce Washington, the Continental Congress promised to supply sufficient scarlet cloth to face their clothes. Detachments of Virginia troops joined the Army partially uniformed by their home state and hoping to have their uniform completed on arrival in camp, with round hats with two inch brims, prescribed the previous winter in Williamsburg.

In January 1778, Virginia's 15 regiments, consisting of 4,465 rank and file present or fit for duty, were credited with 6,211 coats issued by the Clothier General. State cloth imported from France on the Virginia state sloop *Congress* was deposited at Lancaster on 2 December 1777 and handed to Virginia agents to be made into clothing. With the cloth in hand, Brigadier General George Weedon excused from duty the tailors in his 2nd Virginia Brigade to make up the clothing. On 29 December 1777, Weedon recommended to Washington that the uniform should be a short coat, cuffed and caped in different colours, a short waistcoat without shirts, a small round hat, black leather or hair stocks, and overalls in both summer and winter. Mease had such a uniform – drab coloured country-made cloth with scarlet cuffs and collar – made at Lancaster in March for the 9th Virginia.

Other uniforms of the Virginia Continental regiments were: 1st, blue faced scarlet; 2nd, blue faced blue and white button holes; 3rd, pale blue coats faced blue, and green waistcoats; 4th, blue coats, white breeches and waistcoats; 5th, purple linen coats; 6th, blue coats and brown small clothes; 7th, brown faced scarlet; 8th, blue coats and buff small clothes; 12th blue turned-up white; 13th, blue cuffed yellow and blue breeches; 14th, white hunting shirts; 15th, brown faced buff.

Device of the regimental standard of the 2nd South Carolina Regiment of the Continental Line. A tree trunk is topped by a red liberty cap, one blue and one faded red standard, a buff coloured drum, the motto in gold 'Vita potior libertas' and the year '1775'. The wreath on one side has acorns and on the other small white flowers. (Smithsonian Institution)

At the end of 1778, the Virginia Public Store in Philadelphia sold the officers enough cloth for a blue or brown faced scarlet uniform. Virginia's state regulars were uniformed as follows: 1st State Regiment – blue coats, striped jackets, drilling breeches, caps with bands and buckles, and white shalloon camp colours; 2nd State Regiment – blue or brown coats turned-up and lined red, caps as 1st Regiment; State Artillery Regiment – blue coats, red lapels and cuffs, red lining and small clothes, cocked hats and yellow buttons; State Garrison Regiment – as State Artillery Regiment but white buttons; French Company – blue coats, scarlet lapels, buff breeches and waistcoats; State Laboratory – blue suits and check shirts; Volunteer Cavalry – blue coats edged white, white waistcoats, leather breeches, and hats with black feathers.

Maryland

Due to the lack of clothing for the seven regiments of Maryland troops, Washington despatched Lieutenant Colonel Adams to buy clothing in Maryland with $2,000 to be drawn from the Continental Paymaster. Acting on this request, Governor Johnson appointed clothing agents across the state to buy up cloth, clothing and blankets. By the end of 1777, Maryland's Continental troops were issued with 137 regimental suits, 692 coats, 723 vests, 279 pairs of breeches, 539 hats, 79 hunting shirts, 696 overalls and 1,974 shirts.

The capture in Wilmington, Delaware, of a brig laden with the baggage of three British regiments, and the later despatch of James Calhoun, of Baltimore, as state clothier at camp, covered the Maryland Line for 1778. By this time, the uniform had been established as blue coats faced red with white waistcoats and breeches. The troops at Wilmington also converted captured British goods into scarlet waistcoats and breeches. The 4th Regiment wore brown coats procured in Baltimore by Colonel Samuel Smith, and reserved the blue faced red coats for drums and fifes.

North Carolina

In August 1777, a 10th Regiment and an artillery company were added to the state's Continental quota. For the original nine regiments, the only additions in 1777 to the uniforms that were received at the end of 1776 were 679 coats and a proportion of other articles, delivered by the Clothier General.

Governor Richard Caswell, following the rules laid out by the Continental Clothier General, sent to James Mease over 4,000 yards of blue, brown, green and white woollen cloth, 300 blankets, 1,500 yards of osnaburg and shoes and stockings that had been destined for the North Carolina regiments during 1778. At Kingston in February, officers received blue cloth, red facings and gilt buttons. The rank

Colonel George Baylor, 3rd Regiment of Continental Light Dragoons, miniature taken by Charles Willson Peale at Valley Forge in the Spring of 1778. White uniform, stock and ruffles, dark blue lapels and cape edged in silver, silver buttons, epaulettes, and belt buckle; black sword belt. (The Society of the Cincinnati Museum, Anderson House, Washington DC)

and file received brown cloth, red facings and white buttons. The 10th North Carolina (see Figure 3, Plate G) was clothed from the Virginia Public Store. Recruits enlisted in April 1778 for nine months to fill the state's Continental regiments were to have a bounty suit provided by their home militia, this consisted of a hunting shirt, a sleeved waistcoat, one pair of breeches, shoes, stockings, two shirts, and a hat.

South Carolina

During 1777–78, South Carolina continued to clothe its regiments without Continental supplies. It even sent its own representative, Commodore Alexander Gillon, to France to negotiate imports of fabrics. On 30 January 1778, the firm of Lozy and D'Lombard received at

*Colonel Thomas Crafts,
Massachusetts State Train
of Artillery, after an
unattributed miniature.
Blue faced scarlet uniform*
*worn by the regiment until
1779. Lace, epaulettes and
buttons are gold; white
waistcoat and stock.
(Peter F. Copeland)*

Charleston and sold to South Carolina: 4,217 yards of blue
and 643 yards of buff wool, and 10,339 yards of white cadix
and tricot cloth.

Changes in uniform principally affected the 3rd
Regiment. This began life as a mounted riflemen unit and
was transformed into an infantry unit with Charleville
muskets, blue coats faced scarlet, white buttons, black
cocked hats laced black, white small clothes and French
full-length white leggings. See Figure 3, Plate E, for the
uniform of the 4th Regiment.

Georgia

Georgia's four Continental regiments had locally made
uniforms that consisted of short waistcoats over jackets,
kilts worn over overalls and Kilmarnock caps. General
orders of 21 May 1778 prescribe the camp colours each
battalion was allowed: 1st, blue field with yellow inser-
tions; 2nd, white and blue; 3rd, green and white; and 4th,
red and blue. Portraits of Joseph Habersham of the 1st
Georgia Battalion and Major Joseph Woodruff of the
Georgia Artillery show officers in proper regimental coats.
Habersham is in a blue coat faced, cuffed and caped in
yellow, a yellow waistcoat, a white egret plume in his hat,
and a gilt gorget with a coiled rattlesnake engraved on it.
See Figure 2, Plate E, for the artillery uniform.

CONCLUSION

From April 1775 to the end of 1778, the uniforms of
General Washington's armies changed considerably. At
the beginning of the rebellion, only the independent
companies and some minute militia companies reported in
uniform. However most rebelling provinces quickly init-
iated efforts to clothe their troops. While many uniforms
were made available, little standardisation could be
achieved due to the lack of a general clothing warrant, and
conflicts between Congress and the states over local
purchases and the importation of materials.

Although hunting shirts were initially ordered as
uniform by New Jersey, Maryland, Virginia and North
Carolina, and favoured by Washington and the Continental Congress, by the end of 1777, the preferred uniform
was the regimental coat. However, no standardisation of
colour was achieved. Among the 22,586 coats known to
have been issued during 1777, blue, black, grey, drab,
green, red, brown and white are all recorded, and even
with the arrival from France in late 1778 of over 20,000
brown and blue coats, complete uniformity was still
elusive.

Select Bibliography

Published Works

Walter Clark (edit), *The State Records of North Carolina*
(Raleigh 1886–), vols. 11–13.

Donald H. Cresswell (comp.), *The American Revolution in
Drawings and Prints, a checklist of 1765–1790 graphics in
the Library of Congress* (Washington DC, 1975)

Georgia Historical Society, *Collections* (Savannah 1902),
vol. 5.

Philip M. Hamer (edit), *The Papers of Henry Laurens*
(Columbia, SC 1968–), vols. 12, 13.

Hugh Hastings (edit), *Public Papers of George Clinton,
First Governor of New York 1777–1795* (Albany 1900),
vols. II and III.

Charles H. Lesser (edit), *The Sinews of Independence
Monthly Strength Reports of the Continental Army*
(Chicago 1976).

Captain Fitzhugh McMaster, *Soldiers and Uniforms:
South Carolina Military Affairs 1670–1775* (Columbia,
SC 1971).

William James Morgan (edit), *Naval Documents of the
American Revolution* (Washington DC), 9 vols.

E. B. O'Callaghan (edit), *Documents Relative to the
Colonial History of the State of New York* (Albany 1857),
vol. 8.

Edward W. Richardson, *Standards and Colours of the
American Revolution* (1982).

Erna Risch, *Supplying Washington's Army* (Washington DC 1981).

William L. Saunders (edit), *Colonial Records of North Carolina* (Raleigh, NC 1890), vol. 10.

Charles Coleman Sellers, *Portraits and Miniatures by Charles Willson Peale* (Philadelphia 1952) and *Charles Willson Peale With Patron and Populace* (Philadelphia 1969).

Richard K. Showman (edit), *The Papers of General Nathanael Greene* (Chapel Hill, NC 1976), vols. 1, 2.

Robert G. Stewart, *Henry Benbridge (1743–1812) American Portrait Painter* (Washington 1971).

John B. B. Trussell Jr., *The Pennsylvania Line Regimental Organization and Operations, 1776–1783* (Harrisburg 1977).

William B. Wilcox (edit), *The Papers of Benjamin Franklin* (New Haven 1983), vols. 23 and 24.

Robert K. Wright Jr., *The Continental Army* (Washington, DC 1983).

The Company of Military Collectors and Historians series: *Military Uniforms in America* (cited as MUIA) and *Military Collector and Historian, passim*.

Manuscripts

US National Archives: Record Group 360, M247, *Papers of the Continental Congress,*(1774–1789) *passim.*; Record Group 93, M859, *Miscellaneous numbered records (The Manuscript File) in the War Department collection of Revolutionary War Records passim.*; M853, *Numbered record books concerning military operations and service, pay and settlement of accounts and supplies in the War Department collection of Revolutionary War Records passim.*; Virginia State Library, Archives Division, Williamsburg Public Store, *Daybooks* and *Journals* (1776–1778); US Library of Congress, *George Washington Papers*, series 4, rolls 33–55, series 5, rolls 115–117; *Peter Force Historical Manuscripts*, series 9, boxes 9–34; New York Historical Society, *The Horatio Gates Papers* (1726–1828), rolls 3–8, 20; *Day Book of John Tayler, Storekeeper, Albany* (January 1776–April 1777); *Duer papers, vol. 1*; New York Public Library, *Gansevoort-Lansing Papers*, box 21; New York State Archives, *New York State Accounts Audited*, vol. A; *Philip Van Rensselaer Papers of the Historic Cherry Hill Papers*, Acct. No. SC14764; New Jersey State Archives, Department of Defence Records and numbered records 6930–10699; Rutgers University Libraries, *Papers of Israel Shreve, Papers of Gershom Mott*; Connecticut State Library and Archives, series 1–3, military records 1775–1778, *Jonathan Trumbull Collection*; Yale University Library, *Deacon Nathan Beers Collection*; Maryland Hall of Records, *Maryland State Papers (Series D, Revolutionary War Papers)*; Massachusetts Archives, *Board of War*

Major Nicholas Rogers, aide-de-camp, after a portrait by Charles Willson Peale, taken in October 1778. Rogers wears a blue coat with buff lapels and pointed cuffs, gold buttons and epaulettes, and green silk ribbon. Note the unusual lapels, these should be compared to the portrait of Colonel George Baylor which appears on page 41 and the lapelettes mentioned in the order for the uniforms of the 1st Continental Light Dragoons, see page 20. Note also the double-breasted waistcoat. (Peter F. Copeland)

Papers, Revolution Council Papers, Revolutionary War Rolls (all *passim.*); Massachusetts Historical Society, *Papers of William Heath*, rolls 6–11, *Miscellaneous Bound Volume 15, 1776–1778*; New Hampshire Archives, Record Group 7, *Military Records – Colonial Period*, boxes 2–11; American Philosophical Society Library, *Papers of Benjamin Franklin*, vols. 42, 61; Historical Society of Pennsylvania, *Papers of Anthony Wayne*, vols. 1, 2; *William Irvine Papers*, vol. 1; *Cadwalader Collection, General John Cadwalader Section*; Pennsylvania Historic and Museum Commission, RG 27 records of Pennsylvania's Revolutionary governments 1775–1790, *Board of War Minutes 1777*, RG 28 records of the Treasury Department, *State Store Journal 1776–1777*; Brown University, Anne S. K. Brown Military Collection, *Miscellaneous Papers of Henry*

Jackson; Rhode Island State Archives, vols. 7–16, 18, *Letters to the Governor*, vols 3, 8, 10–12; University of Virginia Microfilm, *Lee Family Papers 1742–1785*, rolls 3–5.

THE PLATES

A1: Private, Lower Regiment of New Castle, Delaware Militia, 1775–1776
The field officers of the militia agreed that the upper, middle and lower regiments should be uniformed in short light blue coats, lined white, with slash pockets and false slash sleeves, plain small white buttons and button holes on each side of the breast, short white belted waistcoats, white breeches, black garters, white stockings and half spatter-dashes; small round hats, without button or loop, bound black with a ribbon around the crown the colour of the facings. The upper regiment wore cuffs and capes of white, the middle wore buff, and the lower wore green. (*Delaware Archives.*)

A2: Grenadier, Captain John Lasher's New York City Grenadier Company, 1775–76
See the portrait on page 4 for further detail. The motto on the cap is adapted from the text found on the German Fusiliers' pouches. (*MUIA Plate No. 562.*)

A3: Captain Benedict Arnold, Governor's Second Company of Guards, Connecticut, 1775
On 28 December 1774, 65 New Haven gentlemen agreed to form themselves into a volunteer company. On 2 February 1775 they voted that the dress of the company be 'a scarlet coat of common length, the lapels, cuffs and collar of buff, and trimmed with plain silver wash buttons, white linen vest, breeches and stockings, black half-leggings, a small fashionable and narrow [hat]'. After petitioning the General Assembly to be named 'Governor's Second Company of Guards', they were mustered into the 2nd Regiment of Militia of the Colony, and Benedict Arnold was named Captain. (*History of the City of New Haven*, New York 1885, pp. 649–650.)

A4: Colonel John Cadwalader, 3rd Battalion Philadelphia Associators, 1775–76
Colonel Cadwalader's uniforms were made on 20 May and 7 September 1775 and included a $\frac{1}{4}$ of a yard of white cloth for cuffs and lapels, 38 coat and 36 vest buttons, white dimity for vest and breeches, black silk garters, white taffeta facings, a blue striped saddle cloth, black bearskin holsters, a round hat, rose and band, two silver epaulettes with bullion fringe, and an eagle head silver mounted hanger with black ebony handle and chains. (General John Cadwalader Section, Cadwalader Collection, Historical Society of Pennsylvania.)

B1: Grenadier, 26th Continental Regiment of Foot, 1776
Regimental commander Colonel Loami Baldwin listed a London brown coat of uniform with epaulettes, light blue jacket and white breeches in his invoice of clothing dated 10 June 1776. Members of the regiment claimed for losses of grenadier caps and coats. (Revolutionary War Rolls, Vol. 58, Massachusetts Archives; David Library of the American Revolution.)

B2: Rifleman, 1st Continental Regiment of Foot, 1776
Colonel Edward Hand ordered 2,000 yards of linen for frocks and trousers for 624 men. This was to be dyed green and trimmed in red. (*Papers of Edward Hand*, Vol. 1, f.5 and box, Historical Society of Pennsylvania.)

Grenadier mitre cap, 26th Continental Infantry Regiment, 1776. Reconstruction based on D. W. Holst's analysis of thread holes showing the probable arrangement of the damaged portion of the front flap revealing a pattern of Roman numerals 'XXVI'. (Smithsonian photograph)

B3: Chaplain William Emerson, 2nd Continental Regiment of Foot, 1776

On his way to join his regiment as chaplain, the Rev. William Emerson asked his wife to turn and face his blue coat with black. This coat, along with a black cloak, black jacket and breeches, beaver hat, and sword, was included in the inventory of his estate. (*Diaries and Letters of William Emerson 1743–1776* (n.p., 1972), pp. 105, 127.)

C1: Corporal, 3rd New Jersey Battalion, 1776

In April 1776, three deserters from Captain John Moss's Company were advertised in the *Pennsylvania Packet* wearing new hats bound with white, new regimental coats of drab faced with blue, buckskin breeches, new shirts and shoes. A portrait of Major Joseph Bloomfield by Charles Willson Peale shows pointed cuffs, slash sleeves with four small buttons and silver shoulder knots.

C2: Captain, Light Infantry Company, 2nd South Carolina Regiment, 1776–78

According to regimental orders of 20 June 1775, every officer was to provide himself with a blue coatee, faced, cuffed and lined scarlet, white buttons, white waistcoat and breeches, a black cap and black feather. The lapels were narrow and the $\frac{5}{8}$ inch white metal buttons were stamped with a '2'. This figure is based on Henry Benbridge's posthumous portrait of Captain Charles Motte, who fell in the Siege of Savannah in 1779. (*MUIA Plate No. 450.*)

C3: Corporal, 6th Virginia Regiment, 1776–77

On 2 August 1776, Colonel Mordecai Buckner ordered the regiment to adopt the following uniform: short, hanging just below the waistbannd of the breeches, brown oznabrig hunting shirts faced on collar and cuffs with red, drummers' and fifers' shirts were white with brown cuffs; corporals to have red twist shoulder knots. From the Virginia Public Store, the regiment received blue duffel cloth for leggings and striped cloth for breeches and waistcoats. Hats had a two inch wide brim with black ribbon binding and were cocked up on the left side. (*Orderly Book, 6th Virginia Regiment, 1776–1778*, Americana Collection, National Society Daughters of the American Revolution.)

D1: Trooper, 4th Continental Light Dragoons, 1777–78

General Washington allowed the Clothier General to issue 240 red faced blue coats of the 8th and 21st Foot to the 4th Light Dragoons. Orange coloured hunting shirts concealed the red coats; black leather breeches and British-style leather helmets. (*George Washington Papers*, Series 4; *Revolutionary War Rolls*, jacket 14, roll 115.)

Captain Daniel Parker, 3rd Continental Artillery Regiment, unattributed. Parker resigned his commission on 3 October 1778, but his coat appears to be blue rather than black. Lapels and cape are red, as is the backing to the epaulette which is of gold lace to match the buttons. A gold welt edges the white waistcoat; white cravat and ruffles. (Photo by James Kochan, Morristown National Historical Park)

D2: Captain Samuel Chandler, 11th Connecticut Militia Regiment, Light Horse Company, 1776/7

He wears a blue frock coat with gold epaulettes, a white waistcoat trimmed with gold lace, white breeches and a gold laced hat. Based on Captain Chandler's portrait by Joseph Chandler, National Gallery, Washington DC.

D3: Trumpeter, 1st Continental Light Dragoons

This figure wears a green faced brown tunic with a brown fringe hanging from the shoulders, white belts, brown trumpet banners, black caps with green turbans and yellow tassels.

E1: Matross, 1st Company of Maryland Artillery, 1776

Deserters from Captain Nathaniel Smith's Company of Artillery wore new felt hats with white loops, white pewter buttons marked 'MM1' vertically, blue regimental coats turned-up with light grey, grey waistcoats, leather breeches and blue yarn stockings. (*Maryland Journal and Baltimore Advertiser*, 1 May and 14 August 1776; *Maryland State Papers*.)

E2: Captain, Georgia Artillery, 1778
The uniform of black coat, scarlet lapels and cape, gilt buttons and epaulette conforms to that of the Continental Artillery. The white waistcoat with heavy gold lace and buttons and the red egret feather are shown in a portrait of Major Joseph Woodruff of the Georgia Artillery.

E3: Gunner, 4th South Carolina Regiment, Artillery, 1775–78
Men of this regiment wore blue coats with small standing collars and red tabs and lapels, dragoon sleeves and angular cuffs; blue breeches and waistcoats were worn in winter, white in summer. Hair was cut for wearing with caps. (*MUIA Plate No. 485*, and Henry Benbridge's painting, *Death of Colonel Owen Roberts*.)

F1: Private, Thomas Hartley's Additional Continental Regiment of Foot, 1778
Hartley informed General Washington he had ordered uniforms of blue faced white cut in the style of 'His Excellency's' uniform; caps were also ordered. (George Washington Papers, roll 40.)

F2: Private, Henry Jackson's Additional Continental Regiment of Foot, 1777
Colonel Jackson obtained in Boston British accoutrements and arms and a uniform of blue and buff, lined white, white waistcoat and breeches and large hats with white binding. (Colonel Henry Jackson to Messrs Otis and Andrews, Camp Pautuxet, 14 October, 1778, Anne S. K. Brown Military Collection, Providence, Rhode Island.)

F3: Ensign, Samuel Blatchley Webb's Additional Continental Regiment of Foot, 1777
In 1777 the regiment obtained captured British uniforms which were faced with white then changed to yellow in 1778, with white waistcoats and breeches. (Samuel Blatchley Webb Papers, series 2, box 12, folder 8, Yale University.)

G1: Private, 4th New York Regiment of the Continental Line, 1778
As his officers had already obtained this uniform, in September 1778 Colonel Henry B. Livingston requested suits of white regimentals turned-up and lined with scarlet, caps with black hair, black knee garters, black or scarlet stocks, and brass knee and shoe buckles. (Dreer Collection, series 51:1, p.72, Historical Society of Pennsylvania.)

G2: Fifer, 1st New Hampshire Regiment of the Continental Line, 1778
On 30 May 1778, New Hampshire's Commissary of Military Stores shipped to Valley Forge: 12 yellow regimental coats, 12 pairs of green breeches and 12 jackets for the drummers and fifers of the 1st and 3rd regiments. (Commissary Papers, box 3, RG 12, New Hampshire Records and Archives.)

G3: Private, 10th North Carolina Regiment of the Continental Line, 1778
This soldier, like many of his comrades, has no footware and his feet have become covered with mud. His uniform has also seen better days, the blue faced green coat has

Reconstruction of the imported coat of 1778. Over 20,000 coats made in France were received by the Continental Army during 1778. (Peter F. Copeland)

Fragment of New Standard Number 1 for the Army of the United States. This standard corresponds to the first of 13 'New' standards with division colours recorded as being held in the Continental Store in mid-1778. The full return is in the US National Archives. It has a green ground, mixed from a pale blue warp and a pale yellow weft. It is 70 inches on the hoist, and around 78 inches on the fly. There are 13 stars in the circular form of the Union. (Collections of the Division of Armed Forces History, National Museum of American History, Smithsonian Institution.)

become faded and worn, as has his hat. His ragged appearance is typical of many Continental units during the harsh winter at Valley Forge.

H1: Private, Light Infantry Company, 2nd Canadian Regiment, 1777–78

This private wears a brown coat with white cuffs and buttons, and a white waistcoat. Hanging from the crossbelt of his cartridge pouch is a picker and brush for cleaning the flintlock he carries over his shoulder.

H2: Private, 2nd Rhode Island State Regiment, 1777–78

Deserters from the regiment wore blue sailors' jackets, small round hats and striped flannel overalls. (*Providence Gazette,* 3 January, 1778.)

H3: Dragoon, Pulaski's Legion, 1778

The appearance of Pulaski's legion owed much to the unit's Polish origins and the efforts of General Count Pulaski. The dragoon illustrated here wears a short blue coat with bound frogged button holes in the Polish manner. His cap is decorated with grey fur. He leans on his lance and carries his musket slung over his shoulder.

INTRODUCTION

General Washington's armies of 1775–78 were clothed in a variety of uniforms (see MAA 273, *General Washington's Army 1: 1775–1778*). With the receipt in late 1778 of over 25,000 uniforms imported from France this miscellaneous clothing began to disappear; thereafter much of the Continental Army was uniformly clothed in blue or brown coats faced with red. Similar difficulties with procuring uniforms confronted the state and local armed forces not under Washington's direct command. During the phase of the war covered by this volume the hitherto pre-eminent role of Congress in procuring clothing for the Continental Army shifted to the individual states. As a consequence of their uneven performance the Board of War and subsequently the Commander-in-Chief were compelled to guide the states and local commanders by issuing written orders prescribing Continental uniforms. How this came about, and the specifics of some of these uniforms, form the subject of the present volume.

CONTINENTAL UNIFORMS 1779–1782

Epaulette of Lt.Col. Burgess Ball, 1st Virginia Regiment: two rows of gold lace ¾ inch wide, laid on cream coloured wool, 6 inches long, strap 1½ increasing to 2 inches wide, crescent 4 inches wide; bullions – outer 2¼ and 2½ inches long, ¼ inch diameter, inner ¹⁄₁₆ inch diameter. (Division of Armed Forces History, National Museum of American History, Smithsonian Institution)

Even with most (though not all) of the Continental regiments north of South Carolina wearing the imported clothing, complete uniformity for all troops remained an elusive goal. Not only were these uniforms issued to the infantry only, but they lacked hats, shoes and other accessories. In its resolution of 23 March 1779 regulating the Clothing Department, the Continental Congress deplored that the '. . . discretionary changes of the uniforms of regiments have proved inconvenient and expensive: the Commander in Chief is therefore hereby authorized and directed . . . to fix and prescribe the uniform, as well with regard to the colour and facings, as the cut or fashions of the clothes to be worn by the troops of the respective States and regiments . . .'. At the same time the Board of War proposed a single ground colour for all uniforms, with differences only in the facings to distinguish between the Continental regiments of geographically contiguous groups of states.

Board of War Estimate for Campaign of 1780

A single uniform was the basis of the Board of War Estimate of Stores to be Imported for the Campaign of 1780, submitted to the Continental Congress on 11 June 1779. This estimate, for 104,040 suits of uniform, specified dark blue uniform coats for all combat arms, with buff, white, red, and blue facings for infantry; red facings with yellow button holes for artillery, and white facings for light dragoons. Specifications included:

Coats: full cut, skirts to mid-thigh, to button over the stomach and the capes to close over the neck in winter, reinforced elbows, extra cloth for alterations, to come in three different sizes; trumpeters, drummers and fifers reversed the facing colours, except those of blue facings to be laced white; light dragoons shorter than infantry; waggoners grey or brown. *Buttons*: white of block tin, yellow of brass, USA in Roman letters on each, hat and cap stamped with state abbreviation or USA cypher. *Hats*: four inches deep crown; cocked; infantry bound white, artillery yellow; waggoners round and flat. *Stable jackets*: green. *Leather caps*: light dragoons, crested with green horse hair, light infantry, drummers and fifers. *Waistcoats*: white wool, waggoners grey or brown. *Breeches*: white wool with fall front and reinforced seat, waggoners grey or brown, dragoons leather. *Overalls*: white wool for winter and linen for summer. *Shirts*: body 1 to 1¹/₁₆ yards long, sleeves ⁹/₁₆ yard long to ¹⁰/₁₆ long, two buttons on collar, one on underpart of each sleeve. *Stocks*: black velveret line with linen, ends of black fustian, buckles white metal. *Regimental colours*: silk cloth of crimson, blue, white and buff with gold fringe, gold and blue cords and tassels.

General Order 2 October 1779

At a time when the Continental Army was suffering from want of clothing the office of Clothier General was vacated by its first incumbent, James Mease. The Resolution of 23 March 1779 specified how the Clothier General, each Sub- or State Clothier and the Regimental Clothiers were to discharge the distribution function of their respective responsibilities; but neglected to deal with procurement. General Washington tried to fill the void with instructions to George Measam, Agent Clothier at Springfield, Massachusetts, to forward to Headquarters at Fishkill, NY, all shirts, overalls, hunting shirts, shoes and stockings that were available at Boston and other Eastern ports.

After a number of worthy civilians and officers turned down the honour of being named Clothier General, Colonel James Wilkinson accepted on 25 July 1779. Wilkinson took over a Department run by Measam and others which, by 16 August 1779, had assembled in Philadelphia 10,000 coats, 8,000 waistcoats, 7,000 breeches and overalls, and had 30,000 shirts being made; at Springfield about 6,000 suits, 4,100 blankets, 7,000 linen overalls plus 20,000 more already sent on, and about 4,000 hats.

Notwithstanding this supply, the Continental Board of War assigned Wilkinson to request the individual states to take on the clothing of their own Continental Lines. To this end Wilkinson sent a circular letter to each state governor informing them to purchase shirts, shoes, hats and blankets as the most urgently required items. States inclined to purchase woollen clothing need not procure breeches, but were instead to obtain overalls lined to

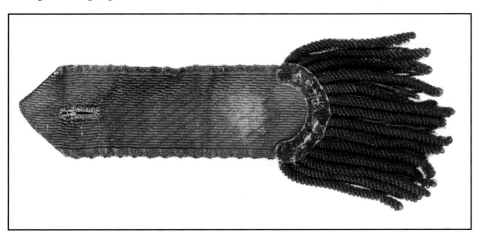

Epaulette of Major Jacob Morris, silver gilt strap, crescent and bullion. (Morris Collection, Smithsonian Institution)

the knee with linen; and were to ensure that their purchases conformed to the uniform agreed on for the whole army, which was to have a blue ground with facings of different colours for each group of states:

White
    New Hampshire
    Massachusetts   *Vests and overalls of the*
    Connecticut   *whole to be white*
    Rhode Island
Buff
    New York
    New Jersey
Scarlet*
    Pennsylvania
    Maryland
    Delaware
    Virginia
Blue, button holes trimmed with white tape or worsted lace:
    North Carolina
    South Carolina
    Georgia

General Washington passed this decision on to the Continental Army in the form of his General Order of 2 October 1779, which added:

Scarlet facing and lining; yellow buttons, button hole and hat binding, and coat edged with narrow lace or tape:
    Artillery and Artillery Artificers
White, white buttons and lining:
    Light Dragoons

(*Pennsylvania, Delaware, Maryland and Virginia were to assume red, rather than scarlet facings. With the exception of the replacement Continental battal-ions maintained from 1781–83 by North and South Carolina, this order applied until 1783.)

At the time this order was being issued, the Deputy Clothier General in Philadelphia was shipping to Newburgh, NY, the following uniforms:

Coats		Vests		Breeches	
Blue and red	1,787	white	450	white	450
Brown and red	1,743	brown	180	brown	157
Brown and buff	526	blue	1,650	blue	235
Green and red	225	green	420	leather	564
Light coloured and red	99	red	405	red	135
Black and red	700				
Light blue and red	200				

Overseas procurement

During 1779 Continental agents in France and Spain continued their attempts to acquire military clothing and stores. In August 1779 the Continental Frigate *Deane* and the supply ship *Duchesse de Grammont* between them carried 16,709 each of soldiers' coats, waistcoats and breeches. On 28 December 1779 Jonathan Williams wrote to Dr. Benjamin Franklin, Continental Commissioner in Paris, that he was able to obtain cloth of royal blue and red-brown suitable for coats and white tricot for waistcoats and breeches. By February 1780 Williams was busy fulfilling an order for 10,000 suits of clothing based on a Congressional specification of blue coats faced white and

Pair of holsters owned by Maj.Gen. Charles Lee who presented them to Maj. Jacob Morris after the battle of Monmouth. Made of dark leather, overall length is 30 inches, each holster is 13½ inches long.

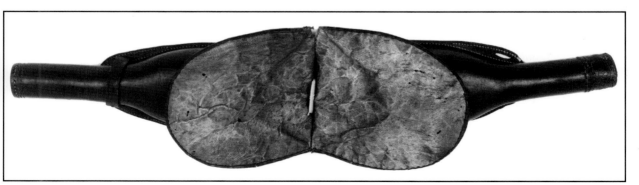

cocked hats with white lace; unfortunately, lack of shipping space seriously delayed this consignment.

Better fortune attended the Continental cause when, on 9 August 1780, a combined French and Spanish fleet captured a large stock of British clothing, which was obtained in Cadiz, Spain, by Richard Harrison, the Congressional representative to the Court of His Most Catholic Majesty. Shipped on 12 March 1781 in 123 bales, 56 casks and a trunk, it comprised: 3,683 coats, 2,714 breeches, 737 waistcoats, 3,781 shirts, 3,752 stocks, 7,495 pairs of hose, 3,312 plain and laced privates' and 217 sergeants' hats, 6 silver laced sergeants' caps, and 2,271 pairs of shoes. The arrival in September of this clothing, along with the cloth contained in the cargoes of the store ships *Cibell*, *Olimpe*, and *Duque de Trouin*, made up for the capture in April 1781 of the Continental frigate *Confederacy*, and in June of the *Marquis de Lafayette*, with 20,000 suits of uniform.

While the store ships carried blue, white and buff cloth for coats and facings, ticken for overalls, ready-made shirts, hats, hose and shoes, sergeants' and cavalry swords, calfskin haversacks, and other accoutrements, the British uniforms were immediately sent to the care of Major General William Heath at Continental Headquarters, Newburgh, where, on General Washington's orders, the red coats were dyed brown. The lines of New Hampshire, New York, and New Jersey and the 10th Massachusetts Continental Regiment received the brown coats in early 1782, thus changing the ground, but not the facing colour.

During 1782 Thomas Barclay, the Congressional agent for procuring clothing abroad, shipped 92 bales and 1 trunk containing blue, white and scarlet cloth, along with hats, buttons and officers' quality cloth. With the war winding down and American credit abroad suffering an ever greater deflation, only three Continental cargoes were received in 1783: on 14 May, 26 September and 9 December. Consisting mainly of arms and accoutrements, these shipments also included 530 horseman's caps, 2,000 worsted epaulettes, 767 silver epaulettes, 3,594 linen haversacks and 1,394 swords and scabbards.

Uniform of Lt.Col. Tench Tilghman, aide-de-camp to General Washington. Dark blue coat; buff cape, lapels, cuffs and breeches; gilt epaulettes and buttons. The waistcoat is not original. (Maryland Historical Society, Baltimore)

Generals, staff and officers' uniforms

At Short Hills, New Jersey, on 18 June 1780, General Washington issued a General Order prescribing, for the first time, the uniforms of general officers and staff and a new system for distinguishing rank:

Major Generals Blue coats, buff facings and linings, yellow buttons, white or buff small clothes, two epaulettes with two stars on each, a black and white feather.

Brigadier Generals Same uniform as Major Generals, one star on each epaulette, white feather.

Colonels, Lieutenant Colonels, Majors Uniform of their regiments and two epaulettes.

Captains Same, epaulette on right shoulder.

Subalterns Same, epaulette on left shoulder.

Aides-de-camp Uniform of ranks and corps or of their general officers. ADCs to Commander-in-Chief, white and green feather; to Majors and Brigadier Generals, green feather.

Inspectors Blue feather.

Corps of Engineers Blue faced with buff, red linings, buff small clothes.

Other officers Plain uniforms and swords.

All officers, GO of 19 July 1780: Cockades emblematic of the expected union with France, black ground with white relief.

John Moylan, Assistant Clothier General, reported the total clothing issued through February 1780 to the Continental Army under General Washington's direct command: 14,911 coats, 14,619 vests, 11,220 breeches and overalls, 11,558 pair woollen hose, 30,317 pair shoes, 11,920 shirts, 10,590 hats, 4,935 blankets, 70 pair boots, 43 cloaks and watch coats, 438 pair leather breeches, 2,715 woollen caps, 3,138 pair mitts, 20 hunting frocks, 216 canvas and linen overalls, 60 shoe buckles, 3,206 pair woollen socks, and 2,583 stocks.

Following the reduction of the Continental Line infantry to 49 regiments or battalions, General Washington, in General Orders of 15 November 1780, allowed, within the limits of the established uniform, the newly arranged officers to agree upon a fashion for their regimentals.

Estimates for 1781

Among the military stores needed for the campaign of 1781 were: 29,447 coats of the same quality and

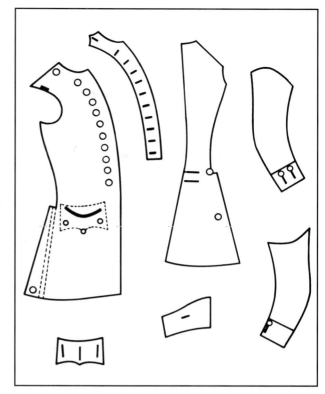

Uniform coat of Lt.Col. Tench Tilghman, pattern drawing by Donald W. Holst.

colours as those estimated in 1780; white stable jackets with sleeves and collars; and 600 yards of blue silk, yard wide, for regimental colours.

On 6 May John Moylan was appointed Clothier General by Congress. According to a French officer who witnessed the American army passing in review at Dobbs Ferry, NY, on 9 July 1781, some regiments wore white cotton clothing consisting of coat, jacket, vest, trousers buttoned from the bottom to the calves, and black caps with white plumes. Another French observer was struck by the ragged and barefoot condition of the Americans, except for the artillery, the only troops in uniform.

At Yorktown, September–October 1781, General Washington's army consisted of relatively well-uniformed Continental units: the Light Infantry Division, two battalions each from Pennsylvania, Maryland, New York and New Jersey, Hazen's 2nd Canadian Regiment, the Rhode Island Regiment, Gaskin's Virginia Continentals, 2nd and 3rd Continental Artillery Regiments, 4th Continental Light Dragoons, and Armand's Legion.

Changes of 1782

With part of the Main Army in brown uniforms, General Washington strove to improve the uniformity of his troops. On 14 May 1782 he ordered the non-commissioned officers to obtain worsted shoulder knots: sergeants, one on each shoulder, and corporals, one on the right, or a piece of white cloth substituted. Chevrons, in a herring-bone form, extending from seam to seam three inches from and parallel with the shoulder seam, on the left arm of rank and file for each three years of faithful service, were ordered on 7 July 1782; on 11 August they were ordered to be of the colour of the facings. On 2 December Major General Benjamin Lincoln, Secretary at War, informed General Washington that the lack of financial resources militated against further substantial purchases of cloth for 1783; therefore, it was the decision of the Continental War Office that all coats of all arms would be faced with red, with white lining and buttons.

Washington's General Order of 6 December

Washington, Lafayette and Tilghman at Yorktown, *by Charles Willson Peale, 1784. All foreground figures in blue coats, with buff lapels, capes, cuffs, waistcoats and breeches. Note difference between lapels. (Maryland Commission on Artistic Property of the Maryland State Archives, Special Collection 1545–1120)*

1782 accordingly specified this uniform for cavalry and infantry, while the Corps of Artillery and the Sappers and Miners retained their current uniforms. This order was expanded upon by Washington on 15 December, to advise the officers that the regimental coats need not all be made in the 'samed mode' but that each line or corps could agree among themselves on any distinctions they wished to adopt as to the fashion of the lapels, cuffs, buttons, and the like.

The Southern Army 1782–83

During 1782 the Southern Army under Major General Nathanael Greene, still actively campaigning in South Carolina and Georgia, received the following clothing from the Clothier General:

April 30 sergeants' hats, silver laced; soldiers' hats, small fan-tailed worsted tassels; caps for pioneers; sergeants' shirts ruffled at bosom and wrists.

6 May Enough linen to make coatees.

15 November Continental and captured Hessian clothing, consisting of 889 overalls and 860 pair breeches as follows:

Coats	Facings	Lining
Continental clothing:		
37 cavalry—		
blue	white	short skirts
341 infantry—		
blue	white	
305 ditto	red	
Captured Hessian clothing:		
3 sergeants'—		
blue	black	red
8 sergeants'—		
blue	yellow	red
3 sergeants'—		
blue	red	red
22 sergeants'—		
blue	yellow	yellow
9 drummers'—		
yellow		white
21 privates'—		
blue	white	red
19 privates'—		
blue	red	red
109 privates'—		
blue	yellow	red

Detail of Washington, Lafayette and Tilghman at Yorktown. *The foreground figure is an American officer in blue coat with scarlet cape, cuffs, lapels and lining. The flag has red and white stripes and a* blue canton with eagle seal, gilt finial and cords. (Maryland Commission on Artistic Property of the Maryland State Archives, Special Collection 1545– 1120, Smithsonian Photograph)

Changes of 1783

Notwithstanding the change in facings, the non-arrival of sufficient amounts of scarlet cloth necessitated the issue of further orders to maintain a degree of uniformity among those (mostly Northern) regiments directly under General Washington. On 14 February 1783 Washington had to explain that the coats issued the previous year would have to be turned and worn again, but that their length must be shortened, and that scarlet only sufficient for the capes, cuffs, and perhaps half-facings would be furnished. Scarlet cloth remained so scarce that when a small supply did arrive in camp, General Washington held a lottery among the regiments.

The intentions of the Continental Congress with regard to the Army's uniforms are best illustrated by

the estimate prepared on 5 June 1783 by Samuel Caldwell, a former assistant Continental Clothier. This pattern constitutes the first and most detailed specification of Army uniform surviving in the papers of the Continental Congress:

Coat: of an average size, 1⅝ yards blue ⁶⁄₄ cloth for outside, ⅕ yard scarlet cloth for facing, 1½ yards oznabrigs for pockets, staying and sleeve linings, 1½ yards white shalloon for skirt lining and facing the forepart, 32 large buttons, 2 small buttons, 4 hooks and eyes. *Vest*: skirts ⅝ yard white ¾ cloth, ⅜ yard oznabrigs for pockets and staying, 1¼ yards flannel for lining, 11 small buttons. *Breeches*: ¾ yard white ⁶⁄₄ cloth, 1⅝ yards dowlas or best oznabrigs for lining and pockets, 2 large buttons, 12 small buttons. *Woollen overalls*: 1⅜ yards blue ⁶⁄₄ duffil, ⅝ yard oznabrigs for pockets and stays, 2 large and 5 small buttons. *Linen overalls*: 2¼ yards ravens duck, ¼ yard oznabrigs for pockets. *Hunting shirt*: 2 yards brown Russia sheeting, thread and fringe. *Body shirt*: 3⅜ yards white Irish linen. *Shoes*: one pair. *Stockings*: one pair, of white yarn. *Hat*: felt, finished with metal button, white looping. *Stock*: black leather lined with white jean.

Continental Corps

Uniforms of these units of foot not belonging to a particular state Continental Line, as well as of the light horse and artillery, which differed from, or were not mentioned in, the General Orders of 2 October 1779 and 6 December 1782, are described in this section:

Artillery

The Brigade of Artillery received its new uniforms on 6 January 1780, consisting of 887 coats, 1,320 vests, 1,209 breeches and overalls, 2,837 pair woollen hose, 1,611 pair shoes, 831 shirts, 96 blankets, 60

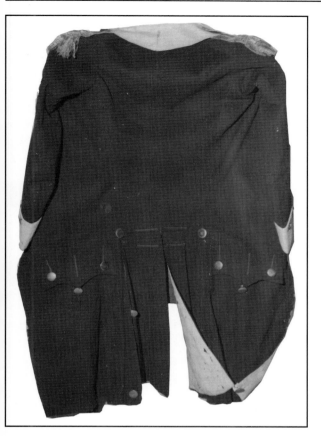

Uniform coat of Lt.Col. Tench Tilghman; side view with skirts unhooked (far left), side view with skirts hooked (left) and back view (above). (Photos by Robert L. Klinger, courtesy of Ms. Christina Klinger)

shoe buckles and 341 stocks. Thereafter, due to dispersal of the Continental Artillery to various theatres of operations and garrisons, distributions of clothing were made regimentally.

Regimental distinctions:

1st Authorized uniform, but lacking lace or edging, fifers with red lapels, black and white feathers for officers; see also portrait of Captain Frazier.

2nd Regimental order of 22 October 1780 specifying the officers' uniform includes: *Coat* Lapels, cuffs and cape 2½ inches wide, cape and lapels button on shoulder, all button holes vellum bound, bound shoulder strap opposite epaulette, 10 buttons paired on each lapel; *cuffs* round, 4 small paired buttons, slit, hooks and eyes; *skirts* to the knee joint, waist of medium length, 4 buttons on each fold, 4 button holes below back seam, small heart bound at turn-up; *pockets* scalloped, 4 paired buttons. *Hats:* gold but-

ton, loop and cocking cords; for sergeant's uniform, see Plate D2.

3rd In May 1781 a deserter was described as wearing a short blue coat, red cuffs and cape, pewter buttons and red watchcoat; for regimental band uniform, see Plate D1.

4th In 1779–80, General Sullivan's campaign, a small blue regimental standard; for officers' uniform see Plate D3. In January 1782 a deserter was described in a light blue coat faced red, round hat with broad gold lace band, and striped ticken trousers.

Colonel Jeduthan Baldwin's Regiment of Artificers Officers' regimentals blue and red, yellow buttons. In September 1780 a deserter was described in short white sleeved jacket and overalls, large round hat and silver shoe buckles.

Colonel Benjamin Flower's Regiment of Artillery and Artificers In 1779, coats dark faced red, red jackets, white ticken breeches; in March and June 1780 deserters were described in blue regimental coats faced red; portrait of Benjamin Flower by James Peale (private collection, Baltimore, MD) shows blue regimental coat, red narrow cape, lapels, angular cuffs, waistcoat and breeches, gold-bound button holes, inch-wide lace on waistcoat edge and pockets, gold epaulettes and bound shoulder wings, black feather and gold hat loop and band.

Independent Corps

Commander-in-Chief's Guard June 1782 inspection return, clothing in use: 64 coats, 66 vests, 66 breeches, 66 linen overalls, 132 shirts, 66 stocks, 132 stockings, 66 shoes, 61 buckles, 66 hats and 66 blankets.

German Battalion Brown coats and green waistcoats and breeches provided by Maryland.

Continental Rifle Corps 24 September 1779, effects of deceased Captain Livingham include one regimental coat of black turned up with red, and red plush breeches.

Corps of Invalids For Philadelphia Detachment, see Plate B1. Boston Detachment, August 1781, wore British uniforms of the 5th Foot, scarlet faced with green.

1st Canadian Regiment In January 1781 received 114 each of coats, vests, woollen overalls, shirts and hose, 123 shoes, 100 hats, 100 blankets, and 114 pair woollen socks.

Standard of Pulaski's Legion – crimson silk with gilt embellishments. (Maryland Historical Society)

2nd Canadian Regiment In April 1779 two drummers deserted in white coats faced pale blue, white jackets and dark coloured breeches. In March 1780, received 454 coats, 460 vests, 460 breeches or overalls, 460 pair woollen hose, 700 pair shoes, 560 shirts, 460 hats, 75 blankets and 200 stocks. On 22 July 1780 Major Torrey advertised the loss of a superfine blue coat with scarlet facings not quite made up, 2 pair olive coloured jean overalls, white shalloon enough for lining 2 coats, and a fine linen hunting shirt. In February 1783 Captain Carlile advertised a lost light-coloured watch coat with red cape.

Additional continental regiments of foot

The following table includes only those additional regiments which had new uniforms between 1779 and 1781, when they were merged into the Continental Line.

Regiment	Coat	Facing	Other items
Thomas Hartley's	blue	yellow	—
Henry Jackson's	blue	buff	blue overalls
Moses Rawling's	brown		brown jacket
Henry Sherburn's	See Plate F3		—
Samuel B. Webb's	scarlet	yellow	—

Legions

Armand's See Plate F1.

Henry Lee's See Plate F2. In 1782 Lee presented each officer with 1½ yards of blue cloth, 36 coat buttons, and one gold epaulette.

Pulaski's See illustrations for Legion standard. In February 1779 a deserter was described in brown short coat, large beaver hat, leather breeches, shoes and stockings.

Light Dragoons

Regiment	Coat	Facing	Stable Jackets	Caps	Other
1st					
1779	red-brown	pale-green			
1780–81	See Plate A4				
1782–83	blue	white			
2nd					
Guidon, see illustration p 13.					
Standard, blue 25½ × 38½ inches, union of 7 red alternating with 6 light blue stripes, gold scrolls, rest same as Guidon					
Sword, see illustration p 14.					
1780–81	green	white	blue	brass	green cloaks
1782–83	blue	scarlet	See Plate A2 and portrait of Lt.Col. Benjamin Tallmadge		
3rd					
Officer, see Plate A3					
Trumpeter	blue	white			
Troopers	same as officer		white and blue	light blue turbans	blue cloaks
4th					
1779–80	green	red		bearskin	green cloaks red cape
1781–82	blue	white	brown		
1783	blue	scarlet			
Trumpeter, see Plate A1					

Light infantry

In the reorganization of 1779 each of the infantry regiments was to designate one or more companies as eligible for drafting into a temporary detachment of light infantry. On 15 June 1779 a total of 16 companies were organized into four battalions of four companies each. Since they were considered as drafts, General Washington refused the request of the Light Corps Commander, Brigadier General Anthony Wayne, for a separate uniform for his troops; Wayne nonetheless authorized the use of caps ornamented with hair as a Corps distinction. When re-formed in July 1780 the Continental Lines could field a Light Corps of 12 battalions of 48 companies and 2,400 rank and file. This Corps was placed under the command of the Marquis de Lafayette, who immediately prescribed a uniform of linen hunting shirts and overalls and small round hats cocked up on one side.

Colours presented to the corps by the Marquis were made in France, of white silk with *fleurs de lys* and a striped canton. As a further mark of his esteem the Marquis presented each officer with a gilt smallsword, epaulette, cockade, red and black feathers, blue cloth and trimmings for a regimental coat, and leather caps with white horsehair crests. The privates had two black feathers, one tipped with red; corporals, drummers and fifers received a piece of silver lace for a 'right line' on the front of their caps. For the sergeants, see Plate G2.

In September 1782 the Corps of Light Infantry was in brown with green cuffs and lapels, and white overalls tucked into black gaiters. In 1783 General Washington ordered the Light Corps to retain uniforms of blue faced white.

Service departments

Hospital Department October 1780, hospital stewards received clothing left behind by deceased patients. Officers of the department were allowed by the Continental Congress to draw clothing in the same manner as line officers. See also the portrait of Doctor Barnabas Binney.
Corps of Sappers and Miners Blue faced with buff lined red, buff smallclothes; for officer, see Plate B2.
Quartermaster General's: Company of Ferrymen Brown coats, white vests and breeches. *Corps of Waggoners* 1779, deserter described in cloth coloured coat, red cuffs and cape, white jacket, brown breeches; 1780, issues of blue greatcoats, brown coats, jackets and breeches; see also Plate B3.
Commissary General of Military Stores Deputy-Commissary John Collins, who broke gaol on 1 May 1781, wore a suit of 'good brown clothes, French lapelled'.

Flags and colours

13 May 1779 Brigadier General Henry Knox proposed two standards for each regiment: a Continental Colour, and a Regimental or State Colour of the colour of the uniform with the number of each regiment.

Guidon, 2nd Continental Regiment of Light Dragoons – silk, 24 inches hoist, 28 inches fly, 9¾ inch square union, seven silver ¾-inch-wide stripes alternating with six pink stripes, pink field, blue ball, gilt arrows and bolts, silver wings, black letters, on green scrolls, 14-inch-long scroll. (Smithsonian Institution)

14 September 1779 General Washington agreed with the proposal of the Continental Board of War for a standard with a union and with emblems in the middle, with the addition of the number of the regiment and the name of the state to which it belongs inserted within the curve of a serpent.
28 February 1780 Plan approved for two colours, one the standard of the United States, the other the regimental standard of the colour of the facings.
November 1780 Military stores on hand at Philadelphia included 11 new standards, 42 new division colours, 40 sets of tassels.

Military stores

Camp kettles 26 June 1782: 9¼ inches wide and hold 9½ quarts each, with covers that could be used as frying pans.
Drums 16 September 1780: each included 25 brass nails, 75 iron tacks, 1 gill varnish, ½ ounce Spanish brown paint, 2 drum heads, 1 snare, 1 chord, 10 drum ears, 3 coards of fir wood.
Haversacks 1781: 15 inches high, 6 inches in the bottom, 7 inches in the flat, 16 inches broad, belt 27 inches long and 3 wide.
Knapsacks 1782: 180 pounds Spanish brown paint, one yard of linen each.

Lt.Col. Benjamin A. Tallmadge, 2nd Continental Light Dragoons, by John Ramage, c. 1785. Dark blue coat, scarlet cape and lapels; silver epaulettes, buttons, and lace; white waistcoat, stock and frills. This uniform represents the fulfilment of the 1783 regulations for cavalry. (Litchfield Historical Society)

Sword associated with Lt.Col. Benjamin A. Tallmadge, 2nd Continental Light Dragoons. 'POTTER' stamped on riccaso of blade, black leather wrappings, overall length 43¼ inches. (Smithsonian Institution)

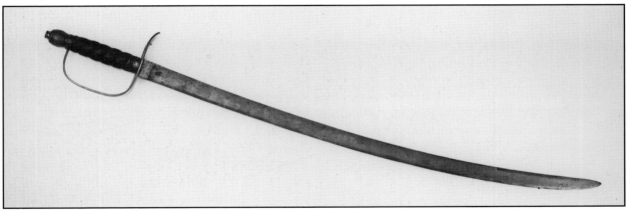

Tents Allocated for each Line regiment, 27 May 1779: field officers, one markee and one horseman's; company officers, one horseman's each; adjutant, quartermaster, surgeon and mate, one walled tent; sergeant-major and quartermaster sergeant, drum and fife major, company non-commissioned officers, one common shared; every six privates, including drums and fifes, one common shared.

STATE UNIFORMS

Massachusetts

In spite of the Royal Navy's blockade of its coasts, Massachusetts sent its Brigantine *Nants*, Captain Williams, on 13 January 1779 to Messrs. Joseph Gardoqui and Sons of Spain with an order for 5,000 blankets, 50 pieces of blue cloth with appropriate amounts of white shalloons and trimmings, 30 pieces of buff or white cloth, 1,000 pair thread hose for officers, and 2,000 pair white hose for soldiers. By combining the proceeds of such imports with donations collected in the countryside, Messrs. Wales and Davis, the state commissaries to the Massachusetts Line, amassed by 2 June 1779: 11,718 shirts, 14,401 pairs of shoes, 14,570 pairs of stockings and 1,956 blankets. Supplementing these supplies, in September 1779 the Massachusetts Board of War ordered from Boston hatters 700 strong and well-made felt hats properly cocked and trimmed. By 27 November 1779 the Line had received 2,802 coats, 2802 vests, 1,868 breeches or overalls, 1,245 hose, 1,245 shirts, 300 shoes, 2,000 hats and 792 blankets.

During 1780 the Massachusetts Line drew 670 coats, 669 vests, 341 hose, 888 shirts, 3,167 shoes, 1,262 hats, 2 blankets, and 3,380 linen overalls.

On 5 January 1781 a committee of officers appointed to fix the Massachusetts officers' uniform reported the colour of the coats, waistcoats, linings and buttons to be agreeable to the General Orders of 2 October 1779:

Coat Length to upper part of knee pan, cut high in the neck, with ⅝ above the waist and ⅜ for skirts, 4 hooks and eyes on the breast, to button or hook as low as the 4th button, no edging, vellum lace or other

Officer in uniform of 3rd Continental Light Dragoons, unattributed. White coat, waistcoat, shirt and frills; light blue lapels and collar; silver epaulettes, buttons and button holes; black stock. (Private collection, Smithsonian Photograph)

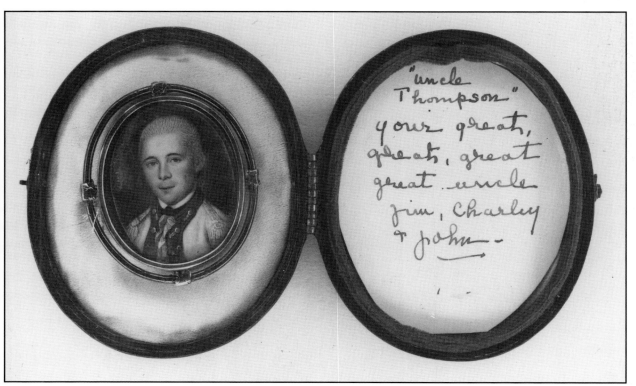

ornamentation. *Collar or cape* Peaked behind and in proportion to lapels. *Lapels* Three inches at top tapering to $2^3/_{10}$ as low as the waist, wing to button within an inch of the shoulder seam to small button on the cape, 10 large buttons and open worked button holes each. *Epaulettes* Directly on top of the shoulder joint on the same button with the lapels. *Cuffs* Round and close, 3 inches deep, 4 large buttons and close worked button holes. *Pocket flaps* Scalloped, set on a curved line from bottom of the lapel to the bottom on the hip, 4 button holes, 2 inner close worked, 2 outer open. *Skirts* Hook up with a blue heart at each corner, bottom cut square, fold on each with one button on hip, one at bottom and 2 in centre, at equal distance with those of lapels. *Waistcoat* Single breasted, 12 buttons on the breast, pocket flaps 4 close worked buttons and 4 buttons below flaps. *Breeches* Half fall, 4 buttons on each knee.

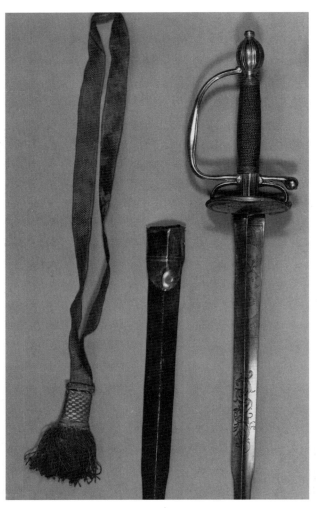

French épée d'officier, sword knot and scabbard, presented by Lafayette to Lt. James Giles, 2nd Continental Artillery, serving with the Light

Hats Military cock, small silver regimental button and loop. *Buttons* Number of the regiment in centre with such devices as directed by field officers. *Stocks* Black.

Ezra Lunt, State Clothier to the Commonwealth, reported delivering on 16 January 1781: 14,255 pair hose, 14,223 pair shoes, 11,224 shirts, 3,740 blankets, 2,659 felt hats, 360 epaulettes, 3,508 coats, 2,660 frocks, 3,446 overalls, 2,018 vests and 2,000 breeches. In order to finance this great effort the state engaged in some creative fund-raising by announcing in the 2 July 1781 issue of the *Boston Gazette* a state lottery for the 'SOLE Purpose of Cloathing the ARMY', issuing 120,000 tickets at 3 Spanish milled dollars each.

The results of the lottery and imports from Holland allowed Wales and Davis to forward on 21 December 1781: 1,540 pair shoes, 1,310 blankets, 1,335 shirts, 1,489 pair hose and 900 hats, with the expectation that 2,000 suits of uniform clothing would soon follow. When the uniform clothing arrived at Newburgh on 27 January 1782 it was sufficient to clothe all Massachusetts Line regiments except the 10th, which had to settle for brown-dyed captured British uniforms. As a final distinction for its troops, the Commonwealth in April 1782 delivered 2,000 pairs of buff-coloured breeches. No doubt, as the best uniformed component of the Northern Continental Army, it was the royal blue coats with white lapels and cuffs of the Massachusetts Line that impressed the reviewing French officers at Ver Plank's Point on 22 September 1782.

Regimental distinctions:

2nd 21 January 1779: 4 yards of grey cloth and 3½ yards milled flannel for a greatcoat for Captain Judah Alden. 5 October 1779: Lieutenant Colonel Ezra Badlam requested the Massachusetts Board of War for scarlet broadcloth for a close bodied coat and the uniform 'of our Regiment is Blue Turnd up with white'. 22 August 1780: brigade order, to bind hats with old tent cloth.

3rd 14 October 1779: report of a stolen blue lapelled coat edged red and lined blue, Continental buttons

Division, 9 September 1780. (Morristown National Historical Park, Morristown, NJ. Photo by James M. Kochan)

set in wood, resembling silver, a silver epaulet, lined red. March 1783: inspection return includes 2 colours, 9 swords, but no espontoons.

4th 20 January 1779: Colonel William Shephard drew 4 yards brown cloth for an outer coat. 5 March 1779: deserter described in blue faced white, white jacket, brown overalls and cocked hat bound white. 10 June 1779: a drummer, and the drum- and fife-majors, deserted in white faced blue, white breeches and white stockings. 19 May 1780: two deserters described in regimental coats faced green. August 1781: caps. May and July 1782: light infantry uniform included white wings and cords on the arms and pockets, half boots, cap with cockade on one side and red tipped plume on the other and white turban around the crown; drummers, fifers and sergeants wear a black plume in addition to the white regimental feather, see Plate H1 for private's uniform.

5th 11 January 1779; 12 yards gray cloth for officers' greatcoats. 22 July 1779: deserter described in blue coat faced white, lined red, and small brimmed hat.

6th 5 January 1780: Colonel Thomas Nixon bought a scarlet coat. 13 January 1782: drew 402 yards blue cloth for 257 coats at 1⁹/₁₆ yards cloth per coat, 71 yards white cloth for facings at ³/₁₆ yard per coat, 449¾ yards serge for lining, 289 yards linen for pockets and trimmings at 1½ per coat. 29 March 1782: 31½ yards white cloth for 21 Music coats at 1½ yards per coat, 3⁵/₁₆ yards blue cloth for facings, 88½ yards serge for linings, pockets, etc.

7th 16 January 1779: two officers drew 5¼ yards claret cloth for greatcoats. 19 April 1781; regimental order that skirts of coats to come within two inches of the knee pan. 24 March 1783: deserter described with both a new greencoat faced red, and a blue coat with green cuffs and collar, white tape button holes, leather breeches.

8th 22 August 1780: brigade order to bind hats with old tent cloth. 21 September 1780: hats to be cut into caps; uniform of the rank and file to be altered to that of the Massachusetts Line. March 1782: inspection return, in hand: 1 colour, 21 espontoons, 11 swords, 387 muskets, 386 bayonets, 393 cartridge boxes, 9 drums, 9 fifes, 403 coats, 419 vests, 398 breeches, 290 woollen overalls, 346 linen ditto, 389 hats, 555 stockings, 337 shoes, 99 buckles, 4 socks, 6 watch coats,

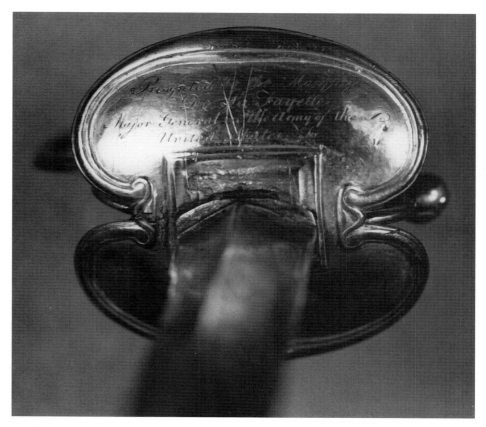

Detail of épée d'officier. (Morristown National Historical Park, Morristown, NJ. Photo by James M. Kochan)

Barnabas Binney, Surgeon, Continental Hospital Department, c. 1779–83 – an unattributed portrait. Blue coat, lapels and cape; white waistcoat, stock and frills; silver buttons. The General Order of 18 June

1780 recommended that officers without military rank wear plain coats, cocked hats and swords. (The Society of the Cincinnati Museum, Anderson House, Washington, D.C.)

245 blankets, 1 marquee tent, 1 horseman's tent, 64 common tents, 433 knapsacks, 464 canteens, 24 axes, 9 spades, 3 picks and 58 camp kettles.

9th 22 August 1780: brigade order to bind hats with old tent cloth. 21 June 1781: regimental order to cut hats into caps.

10th 3 January 1782: clothed with brown-dyed British coats. 27 May 1782: deserter described in dark brown coat, British worsted laced facings, old white waistcoat, white breeches and stockings and round hat with worsted binding. 14 June 1782: inspection report, in use 362 coats, 395 vests, 377 woollen overalls, 408 linen ditto, 310 hats, 68 caps, 537 shirts, 194 stocks, 413 hose, 323 shoes, 153 buckles, 231 blankets, 1 marquee, 13 horsemen's and 77 common tents, 420 knapsacks, and 431 canteens. 25 March

1783: Inspector of the Northern Army recommends to General Washington that since the men of the regiment were distributed into other regiments it was time to exchange their brown coats for blue ones.

11th See portrait of Captain Stephen Abbott.

Massachusetts State Train of Artillery July 1779: deserter described in new regimentals, blue faced blue, trimmed with white edging. 11 December 1779: Colonel Paul Revere received 12 sergeants', 6 drummers' and 147 privates' coats. October 1780: a Pine Tree flag made for Castle Island in Boston Harbour.

Militia of Essex and Suffolk Counties See portrait of Jacob Herrick.

Company of Indians, Machias Blue coats, white shirts, hats.

New Hampshire

In March 1779 the New Hampshire Board of War sent to its Continental troops 909 black stocks, 2,846 pairs of shoes, 1,086 leather knee garters, 20 pairs of boots, and 243½ yards of linen. As of 10 March 1780 Joseph Leigh, State Clothier, had issued to the three New Hampshire Continental regiments: 636 coats, 596 vests, 333 breeches, 22 linen overalls, 151 woollen overalls, 170 shirts, 673 stockings, 1,679 shoes, 1,128 hats, and 8 hunting shirts. Due to a severe shortage of cloth in New Hampshire these articles were supplied by the Continental Clothier. Nevertheless, Colonel Henry Dearborn reported to the State Board of War on 30 June 1780 that one fifth of the troops were totally destitute of a shirt, except for old jackets without sleeves with old stockings drawn over the arms. So bad had the situation become for the New Hampshire troops that in December 1781 they were the first line to be designated by Major General William Heath to receive the captured British uniforms.

Completely outfitted in these uniforms, hats, waistcoats and breeches, the two remaining regiments decided at some time before September 1782 to embellish their coats with stars resembling French decorations. In January 1783 General Washington ordered the Continental Clothier at Newburgh, New York, to immediately issue new uniforms to the two regiments.

Regimental distinctions:

1st 20 July 1779: bill for 2½ yards of green taffeta for regimental colours. 1781: blue coat binding.

2nd March 1781, specifications for officers' uniform: *Coat* To extend to the middle of the knee joint, middling waist, edged or bound with ³/₁₀ inch wide white lace, all buttons set in pairs, 2 inches between each, 2¾ between pairs, white lining. *Collar or cape* 2½ inches front, 2 on top of shoulder, 3½ at point behind, edges bound. *Lapels* Short, bound edges 2½ inches wide at top, 2¼ middle, 2⅛ bottom, 'frog' or wing 2½ inches at joint with top of lapel, 1¾ middle, 2 top attached to epaulette button, one pair buttons set below facings on each side in line with vest, false button holes. *Pocket flaps* Surrounded by lace, 9 inches wide, 4 inches deep at the end and centre points. *Cuffs* Round, 2½ inches deep, 4 large buttons, 2 small buttons on the underside of the cuff slit. *Skirts* Folds bound, two buttons on upper part of each fold with false button holes, the upper one ranging with upper part of pocket flap, one button on middle and one on lower end of each fold, small narrow lace bound blue diamonds on corners of the folds. *Waistcoat or jacket* Pocket flaps like those of the coat with laced button holes and lace on the opposite breast. 1782: see Plate G1 for a private's uniform.
3rd 1781: brown coat binding.
New Hampshire Battalion March 1783: inspection return lists 167 rank and file, in use 1 colour, 210 muskets, 210 bayonets, 210 cartridge boxes, 1 drum, 3 fifes, 224 coats, 223 vests, 224 breeches, 84 hose, 176 shoes, 289 shirts, 148 hats, 114 blankets, 3 watch coats, 78 knapsacks, 6 canteens, 12 axes, 1 pick, and 9 portmanteaus.

Connecticut

The Connecticut Continentals began 1779 with a reputation for having more clothing than any other line. Accordingly, when the previous year's supply proved inadequate by mid-year, no further issues were made by Continental Clothiers without specific orders from the Commander-in-Chief. To come to the aid of its troops, Connecticut accelerated the gathering of donated clothing from its constituent counties and attempted to provide new recruits with complete uniforms before they joined their regiments. In order to justify their requirements, the Connecticut Division was ordered on 11 April 1779 to carefully distinguish in their returns as 'jackets' those garments which were with folds such as were worn by the British Light Infantry. Brigadier General Huntington's Brigade of the 1st, 2nd, 5th and 7th Regiments received a 'goodly supply' of French clothing in June; Brigadier General Samuel Holden Parson's Brigade of the 3rd, 4th, and 6th Regiments had to wait until November. At Stoney Point, New York, on 24 November 1779 the seven regiments

Portion of marquee dining tent used by General Washington. (Smithsonian Institution)

Silhouette of Col. Michael Jackson, 8th Massachusetts Continental Regiment, after an original in the Jackson Homestead, Newton, MA. The cockade is tinted red, white and blue. (Peter F. Copeland)

received 1,401 French and 654 Philadelphia-made coats, 1,314 French and 741 Philadelphia-made vests, 692 French breeches, 678 woollen overalls and 700 blankets, for 2,854 rank and file. From the state came 1,555 shirts, 1,749 shoes and 128 pair linen overalls.

Division orders of 25 August 1780 recommended that hats be cut into the form of light infantry caps, with black hair.

Regimental colours of the Connecticut Line were each of a different ground colour with the number of the regiment in large characters, the device on one side the Connecticut Arms and on the other the motto and device of the 30 Dollar Bill.

By December 1780 Elijah Hubbard, the State Clothier, could report to Governor Trumbull that the officers of the Connecticut Line were clothed, but would need new uniforms for the campaign of 1781. A complete supply was required for the five regiments in the newly consolidated Line. In order to finance the procurement of clothing or, in lieu thereof, to induce the citizenry to donate the necessary articles, in May 1781 the General Assembly passed a law requiring a poll tax to be paid either in specie or silver or in actual cloth: whitened yard wide tow cloth suitable for shirts, white ¾ yard wide woollen plain cloth for vests and overalls, plain blue wool for coats, and white woollen stockings. When offered captured British coats in December 1781 the Connecticut officers declined to receive them, opting to retain their blue regimentals. At a meeting of the officers in the three Connecticut regiments remaining in December 1782, a uniform for the Line was finally agreed upon:

Coat Reaching to the knee band, skirts hooked up, 4 buttons on folds. *Facings* 10 buttons; soldiers' to lap sufficiently to cover edge of cape; officers' lap 4 inches on cape. *Cuffs* Round, 4 buttons on each, soldiers' slit on underside 3 inches and hooked. *Pocket flaps* 4 buttons. *Hats* Bound white, cocked.

Regimental distinctions:

1st February 1779: deserters described in scarlet faced with white, white jacket and breeches, round hats, fifers in snuff faced with light brown, round hat bound white. March 1781: drummers and fifers in white faced with blue. April 1781: drums to be painted with the number of the regiment and the Connecticut Arms. June 1781: leather caps with forepieces for entire regiment, with distinctions for sergeants, drummers and fifers and officers. June 1782: inspection return lists in use 353 coats, 352 vests, 153 woollen breeches, 355 linen overalls, 415 shirts, 331 hose, 360 hats, 23 espontoons, 12 swords, 370 muskets, 371 bayonets, 372 cartridge boxes, 10 drums and 9 fifes.

3rd 1779: Samuel Richards, Regimental Clothier, received from both the state and Continental clothiers 1,018 linen overalls, 1,108 shirts, 1,354 pair shoes, 445 frocks, 463 black stocks as a gratuity from the state, 349 coats, 345 vests, 351 pair woollen overalls, and 136 hats. 1782–83: see Plate H4 for a sergeant's uniform. 12 February 1782: Nathan Beers drew from Continental Clothier cloth for 20 'Musicks coats 30⅞ yards white cloth, 3⅞ yards blue for facings, 36¾ yards serge for lining'.

4th 1782–83: complete with leather caps and short regimental coats.

5th 2 March 1782: butternut coloured watchcoat lost by Captain Bates. 1782: lapels to be 2½ inches wide.

6th 20 July 1780: a receipt submitted by Wensley Hobby of Middletown, Connecticut, for painting and gilding 27 officers' and painting 401 privates' leather caps; see also illustrations of uniform.

7th 22 September 1779: Regimental order to supply rank and file with sailors' jackets and overalls.

8th March, April 1779: deserters described in new red regimental coats faced white, brown vests and leather breeches, old cartridge boxes.

Connecticut State Regiment of Guards 1782–83: 710 pair shoes, 355 pair woollen overalls, 355 shirts, and white and blue cloth for coats, vests and other garments for officers and men.

11th Regiment of Militia July 1780: deserter described in blue coat faced white, white buttons, belted striped jacket, white shirt and overalls.

24th Regiment of Militia July 1782: inventory of Ensign John Jameson's estate listed a blue coat and jacket, pair of boots and silver stock buckle.

State Garrison Artillery Regiment 1779–80: Captain Adam Shapley's Company lost deserters in brown jackets and straight bodied coats, round hats, buff under jackets and overalls, a grey overcoat.

Yale Students' Company See portrait of George Welles.

Rhode Island

In order to reinforce the two Rhode Island battalions, the June 1780 session of the General Assembly voted to allow each new enlistee one pair of overalls, one linen frock or hunting shirt and one pair of stockings. The men raised under this act were to be considered a separate battalion, while the two existing Continental battalions were to be merged under the command of Lieutenant Colonel Christopher Greene. Once the regiments comprising the line had been discharged in 1780, the state was in a position to furnish its now consolidated single Continental battalion with clothing of every description.

Regimental distinctions:

1st May 1779: received regimental coats, waistcoats and breeches. 12 April 1780: deserter described in red faced white. 1780: clothing received from the state amounted to 1,269 shoes, 315 coats, 287 vests, 407 woollen overalls, 299 hats, 803 shirts, 65 stockings, 6 hunting shirts, and 524 linen overalls.

2nd 4 January 1779: new bound hats. February 1779: blue and scarlet cloth sufficient for a suit of uniform issued to each officer. September 1779: two men deserted in rifle frocks, small felt hats and overalls,

Gen. Stephen Abbott, as a captain in the 11th Massachusetts Continental Regiment, after a copy of an original lately in the collections of the Essex Institute, Salem, MA. Note the angular cuffs and double-breasted waistcoat. (Peter F. Copeland)

one in a white coat, jacket and overalls. October 1779: received distribution of coats, waistcoats and breeches. November 1779: corporal deserted in blue coat faced white and lined yellow, private in blue coat faced red, lined white. February 1780: inspection return – 'This Regiment is Well Disciplined & well Clad, their Arms are in very good order', with 226 coats, 225 waistcoats, 6 pair breeches, 225 pair woollen overalls, 213 shirts, 193 stocks, 270 pair shoes, 235 hats, and 25 epaulettes good.

Capt. Jacob Herrick, Commissioned Adjutant, Middlesex Regiment, Massachusetts Militia, 1780, after a pastel in the collections of the Essex Institute. Light blue coat, buff cape and lapels; silver buttons and epaulette; white stock and ruffles. (Peter F. Copeland)

Rhode Island Regiment See Plate H2 and H3.

State Regiment of Artillery 2 June 1779: memorandum signed by Colonel Robert Elliott, to the Council of War, of clothing wanting for the 27 officers for the 1779 campaign, specified blue broadcloth for coats, buff for waistcoats and breeches, scarlet for coat facings, and beaver hats; rank and file, round hats bound yellow, blue regimental coats faced red, green or white waistcoats and breeches.

Bristol County Militia August 1780: deserter described in a dark jacket lined in yellow, beaver hat, striped flannel trousers, striped shirt, and a black and white striped blanket marked in two places JP.

Providence County Militia September 1781: deserter described in a blue sailor's jacket, red and white overalls and grey felt hat.

New York

An order of late 1779 or early 1780 specifies the uniform of the troops raised by New York as conforming to Continental specifications, but adds that sergeants' coats had to be made of better cloth and with worsted epaulettes; for uniforms of drums and fifes, see Plate G3. On 26 December 1779 James Black, New York Clothier, issued to the line of 988 rank and file a total of 693 coats, 690 waistcoats, 520 breeches, 61 linen overalls, 317 shirts, 529 hats, 7 bundles of worsted epaulettes, and 260 blankets. At state expense, the non-commissioned officers and privates were to receive 1,800 regimental coats, 1,800 woollen vests, 1,800 woollen overalls, 3,600 pair shoes, 1,800 blankets and 1,800 hats, while the officers were to be granted 200 dollars to defray the cost of making up a suit of regimental clothing.

In July 1780 the troops received coats of blue faced with white, which could be changed to buff by applying clay to the facings. Brigade orders of 6 September 1780 specified that the New York brigade's hats should be cut down to caps and covered with white hair. On 21 December 1780 the regiments were sent some 40 hogsheads of clothing amounting to 944 coats, 1,349 vests, 1,577 woollen breeches or overalls, 2,095 shirts, 3,519 shoes, 657 hats, 57 light infantry caps, and 28 watch coats.

According to General Washington's Order of 31 December 1781, the New York and New Jersey lines were to receive complete issues of the brown-dyed captured British uniforms.

Regimental distinctions:

New York Brigade standard, 1779–80 Blue canton with white stars, white field with 8 horizontal red stripes.

1st June 1782: inspection reports regiment in exceeding good order, clothing extremely well attended to, in use 522 coats, 513 vests, 515 breeches, 494 woollen overalls, 510 linen ditto, 929 shirts, 443 shoes, 505 hats, 355 blankets, 942 hose, and 219 socks.

2nd ca. 1780–81: Uniform order – the colour to be agreeable to the General [order of 2 October 1779]:

Coat To the upper part of the knee pan, ⅝ to the waist, ⅜ below. *Collar* Three inches broad at the button hole, point behind. *Lapels* Three inches at the

1: Trumpeter, 4th Regiment Continental Light Dragoons, 1779-81
2: Trooper, 2nd Regiment Continental Light Dragoons, 1782
3: Officer, 3rd Regiment Continental Light Dragoons, 1781
4: Trooper, 1st Regiment Continental Light Dragoons, 1781-83

WB/ 95

A

1: Sergeant, Philadelphia Department, Continental Corps of Invalids, 1781
2: Officer, Corps of Sappers and Miners, 1782-83
3: Waggoner, Quartermaster General's Department, 1779

B

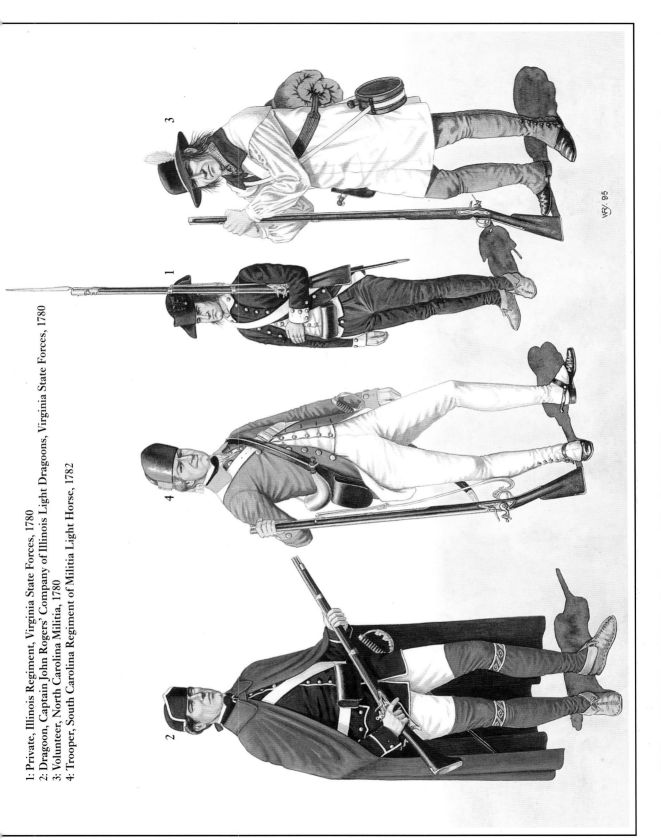

1: Private, Illinois Regiment, Virginia State Forces, 1780
2: Dragoon, Captain John Rogers' Company of Illinois Light Dragoons, Virginia State Forces, 1780
3: Volunteer, North Carolina Militia, 1780
4: Trooper, South Carolina Regiment of Militia Light Horse, 1782

C

1: Bandsman, 3rd Continental Artillery Regiment, 1782-83
2: Sergeant, 2nd Continental Artillery Regiment, 1780-82
3: Officer, 4th Continental Artillery Regiment, 1779

D

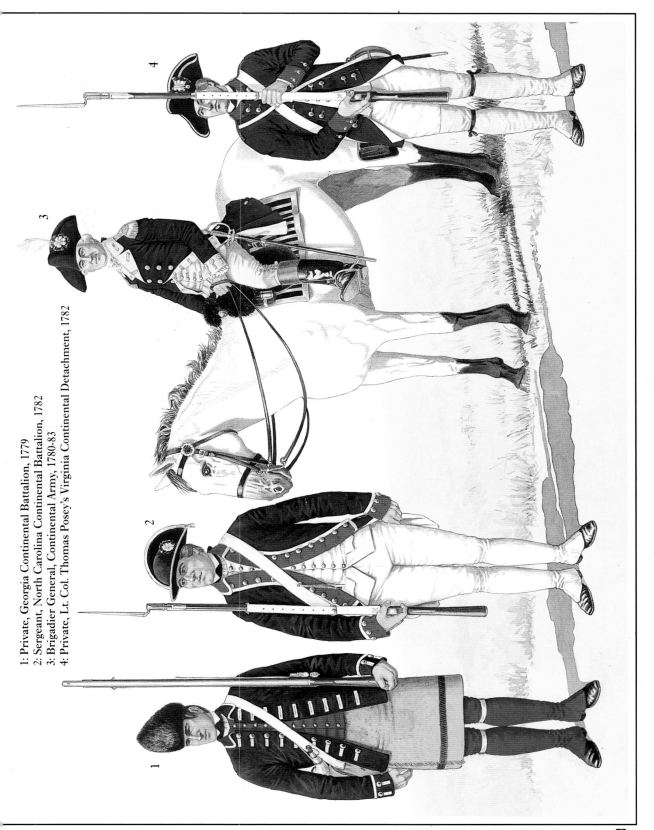

1: Private, Georgia Continental Battalion, 1779
2: Sergeant, North Carolina Continental Battalion, 1782
3: Brigadier General, Continental Army, 1780-83
4: Private, Lt. Col. Thomas Posey's Virginia Continental Detachment, 1782

E

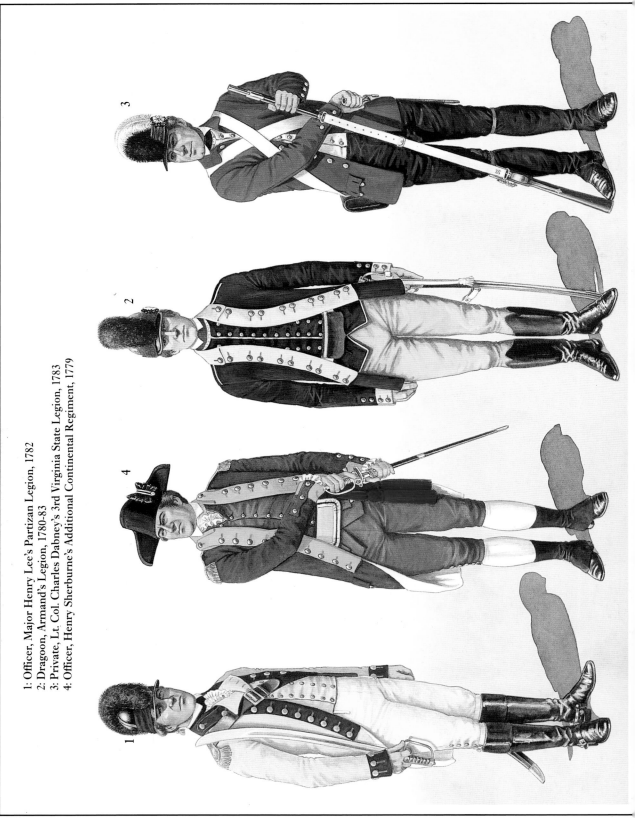

1: Officer, Major Henry Lee's Partizan Legion, 1782
2: Dragoon, Armand's Legion, 1780-83
3: Private, Lt. Col. Charles Dabney's 3rd Virginia State Legion, 1783
4: Officer, Henry Sherburne's Additional Continental Regiment, 1779

F

1: Private, 2nd New Hampshire Regiment, 1782
2: Sergeant, Light Infantry Company, 2nd Pennsylvania Regiment 1780–82
3: Drummer, 2nd New York Regiment, 1779–82
4: Officer, 2nd New York Regiment, 1779–81

WR/95

G

1: Private, 4th Massachusetts Regiment, 1782
2: Ensign, Rhode Island Regiment, 1782-83
3: Drummer, Rhode Island Regiment, 1782-83
4: Sergeant, 3rd Connecticut Regiment, 1782-83

H

tapered to 2⅗ at bottom, 10 large equidistant buttons and button holes. *Cuffs* Round, 4 large buttons and close worked button holes. *Pocket flaps* Across, 4 button holes, 2 interior open, 2 exterior close worked and suited to the button holes. *Skirts* Behind to be cut full, 2 button holes where skirts and waist unite, 2 large buttons on hips, 2 in centre of each skirt, at equal distance with lapel buttons and one at bottom. *Waistcoat* High in neck, 12 buttons, small flaring skirt with 4 buttons and holes as coat. *Breeches* Small fall, 4 buttons on each knee, 1½ inch wide band. *Hat* Large and fashionable, waistcoat button, small silver corded loop. *Buttons* To have the number of the regiment on it – see illustration. See also portrait of Colonel Van Cortlandt.

June 1782: inspection, regiment in superior order, clothing incomparably well made and consisted of 535 coats, 534 hats, 532 vests, 525 woollen overalls, 2 breeches, 656 shirts, 245 stockings, 530 shoes and 377 blankets.
3rd February 1779: regimental standard completed. July 1779: 274 pair white breeches and 400 pair white hose drawn. November 1779: white and blue cloth to be purchased for regimental uniforms.
State Regiment in Continental Service January 1783: received from David Brooks, Deputy Continental Clothier General, 383 coats, 383 vests, 153 woollen breeches, 230 woollen overalls, 670 shirts, 383 hose, 320 hats, and 250 caps for 383 rank and file. February 1783: received 300 pair moccasins; portrait of Colonel Marinus Willett by Ralph Earl (Collections of Metropolitan Museum of Art) shows a blue regimental coat with white cape, lapels and round cuffs, white waistcoat and breeches, silver buttons and epaulettes.

New Jersey

The four New Jersey Line regiments returned 1,076 rank and file fit for duty, who drew from the Continent 852 coats, 856 vests, 854 breeches, 856 shirts, 337 pair hose, 274 blankets and 842 shoes. To make up for the shortfall of Continental clothing the state appointed Enos Kelsey as Clothier for the State. In October 1779 Kelsey presented an estimate for 720 yards blue cloth to make 415 coats (which on later

inspection were found to be without linings, lapels sewn down and without button holes); 150 yards scarlet cloth for facings, 400 yards oznaburgs for sleeve linings, 300 yards shalloon for coat linings, 1,443 pair hose, 5,250 yards of linen for 1,500 shirts, and 2,175 yards oznaburgs for overalls.

Private, 6th Connecticut Continental Regiment, 1780–82. Blue coat; white facings, lining, buttons, waistcoat, breeches and stockings; white cypher and trim on black leather cap. (Peter F. Copeland, Smithsonian Photograph)

At the end of December 1780 the three regiments remaining in the New Jersey Line reported only 61 coats good, 628 bad, and 763 wanting; 65 waistcoats good, 627 bad, 759 wanting; 72 breeches good, 268 bad, 742 wanting; and hats 19 good, 799 bad, 805 wanting.

Regimental distinctions:

August 1779: Brigadier General William Maxwell,

commander of the New Jersey Brigade, advertised for a blue greatcoat with small velvet cape. Brigade standard, 1779–80: buff canton with white stars and blue field.

1st 1782. 24 January 1783: inspection report, coats turned, facings changed to the established uniform, hats neatly bound and a cockade in each.

2nd January 1781: blue overalls.

Pennsylvania

The Pennsylvania Continental Line retained the uniform prescribed for it in August 1779. However, because the uniform colours – blue faced with red – were the most sought-after in America, the Commonwealth of Pennsylvania and Continental authorities were in continual competition to obtain cloth of these colours and to have it made up into regimental uniform. Based on estimates submitted by a committee of Pennsylvania officers in January 1779, the General Assembly resolved on 13 March 1779 that every officer receive from the state a complete suit of regimental uniform at prices current at the beginning of the war. Because of the uncertainty of Continental supplies Governor Joseph Reed ordered the purchase of a large quantity of flour for export, to be returned in the form of cloth and other military stores. The appointment of Francis Swain as State Clothier on 30 July 1779 required him to post a surety bond of £20,000.

When the Pennsylvania Division, excluding the 4th and 8th Regiments, was inspected on 1 September 1779 Lieutenant Colonel Josiah Harmar of the 6th Regiment reported that the officers were armed with swords and espontoons, arms in shining order and almost complete with bayonets, tolerable accoutrements, uniform (received in the fall of 1778) was blue and red, but not a good hat in the division. In November 1779 the state sent red coats to camp for the drummers and fifers, and tried to obtain silver hat bands and epaulettes for the sergeants.

Later distributions and details of uniforms include: 1780, January: hats round and bound. 27 February: Swain delivered 2,194 coats of which 691

Drummer, 6th Connecticut Continental Regiment, 1780–82. White coat, waistcoat, breeches, and stockings; blue lapels, wings, cuffs, cape, and drum body. (Peter F. Copeland, Smithsonian Photograph)

blue and red, 69 red, and 84 blue and white; 1,409 vests, 872 pair overalls, 1,983 shirts, 6 pair leather breeches, 639 hats and 9 caps; 295 suits of officers' clothing, 259 officers' hats, 49 pair boots, 259 pair silk stockings, 259 pair worsted stockings, 137 pair shoes, and 768 stocks. 8 July: Extracts from an invoice of articles to be purchased on behalf of the State of Pennsylvania by James Searle for 350 officers and 6,000 privates: 30,000 yards deep blue coating for privates, 875 yards blue broadcloth for coats for officers, 24,000 pair white yarn stockings for privates, 6,000 pair plain steel shoe buckles for soldiers, 4,000 shoulder knots for corporals, 350 beaver hats for officers and 12,000 felt regimental hats for soldiers,

George Welles, captain of a Yale Students Company, 1779. After a contemporary drawing. (Peter F. Copeland)

1,750 yards of Russia drilling for officers' overalls and 30,000 yards coarse Russia drilling for soldiers. 26 July: soldiers' coats recently received are blue faced white, while officers in blue faced scarlet. August: hats to be cut down to caps ornamented with red hair; trousers to be altered into overalls. 1781, 25 March: the Music furnished with scarlet. 6 October: Colonel Farmer issued 485 coats, 1,395 linen vests, 3,576 linen overalls, 1,000 stocks, 100 pieces white binding, 1,078 yards drummers' lace, and 110 hats.

Regimental distinctions:

1st 1783: black cloth gaiters to be altered for wear with overalls.

2nd 1780: Colonel Walter Stewart ordered leather caps bound white for grenadier, light infantry and battalion companies, drummers and fifers. 1782: See Plate G2 for light infantry sergeant's uniform.

7th 1780: white hunting shirts and overalls.

8th 1779–80: Captain Samuel Brady's Company have faces painted red with three black stripes across cheeks, racoon skin caps with hawk feathers painted red fastened to the top of the cap, legs and thighs dyed with wild cherry and white oak bark, breechcloth, leather leggings and moccasins. 10 August 1783: Deputy Clothier General sends 320 uniform coats, blue faced red; 20 white faced blue for music.

10th July 1780: two sergeants, deserted, one in blue regimental coat faced red with buff edging, round hats.

State Regulars In February 1779 the Continental Congress authorized the Supreme Executive Council of Pennsylvania to raise five companies of Rangers on the Western frontier. Each man was to receive a hunting shirt, pair of leggings and shoes, or money in lieu thereof. The parties of white men and Indians employed as scouts needed 60 watch coats, 120 Indian shirts, and 60 small silk handkerchiefs. Company uniforms were: *Captain Thomas Robinson's* All riflemen, officers blue coats faced red, rank and file short coats or coatees of blue trimmed white. *Captain Spaulding's Wyoming Valley Company* December 1780: blue coat with buff lapels, gilt buttons, and cocked hat.

Philadelphia County Militia Horse Lieutenant colonel: two epaulettes, green turned up with buff.

1st Philadelphia City Troop 1779: leather caps, blue coats.

Brig. Gen. Enoch Poor,
after a drawing by
Thaddeusz Kosciuszko in a
private collection. Blue
coat, white lapels, cape,
waistcoat, stock and
ruffles; silver buttons and
epaulette. (Peter F.
Copeland)

State Officers Portrait of Lieutenant Colonel Robert Knox, see illustration.

Delaware

From 12 May 1779, when ordered by General Washington to join the 2nd Maryland Brigade, the Delaware Continental Regiment received clothing from both its home state and from Maryland. The Delaware uniform remained as ordered by the Continental Board of War in 1779. Regimental staff received clothing from George Craighead, Clothier General of Delaware, who also provided when possible for the rank and file.

Distinctions and distributions:
1779: 352 coats, 109 jackets, 22 pair breeches, 30 pair stockings, 20 pair socks, 700 pair shoes, 350 hats, and 647 linen overalls. Blankets – May, 4¾ yards of white nap cloth each. Hats – 16 March, to be bound with yellow. 1780: 196 coats, 225 hats. 1781: 28 pair shoes for officers. 1782: 48 pair boots for ditto.

Maryland

Between 1779 and 1782 Maryland's clothiers – Abraham Faw at Frederick, George P. Keeports at Baltimore, John Muir at Annapolis, and John Randall with the Maryland Line in the field – issued to the Line the following totals: 2,746 regimental coats, 119 linen coats, 3,695 regimental vests, 778 woollen and leather breeches, 10,791 pairs linen overalls, 2,022 pair woollen overalls, 4,522 hats, 13,654 shirts, 6 hunting shirts, and proportional quantities of shoes, stockings, blankets, and socks. During this period no change occurred in the basic uniform of blue coat faced with red and lined white, white 'vest' and breeches, white metal buttons. The scheme of military goods to be shipped to Maryland by Richard Harrison and Company, Merchants at Cadiz, in 1780 also specified: 3,000 pair white yarn hose, 2,000 pair copper buckles, 2,000 castor hats, 14,000 yards white linen for soldiers' shirts, and 600 yards white sheeting for lining. A similar order placed with Jean Holker, France's Consul in Philadelphia, in February 1781 added buff belts and large blankets to the list of specifications.

Dimensions and particulars of clothing supplied by Maryland include:
Hats June 1781, military form with button, loop, and linen binding. *Overalls* 1780, 2½ yards of ¾ cloth for a middle sized pair; 1781, lined to the knee. *Coatees* 1780, brown shalloon; 1782, 2 yards linen for Invalids. *Buttons* March 1781, officers' marked with number of regiment and letter M. *Blankets* 1781–83, 2 yards of ⁶⁄₄ bearskin cloth. *Coats* March 1782, 2½ yards cloth. *Breeches* March 1782, ¾ yard. *Shirts* March 1782, 3½ yards linen. *Jacket* 1783, 1¼ yards white kersey, red cape and cuff. *Colours* 22 April 1780, 7 pair delivered from Continental Quartermaster General.

Regimental distinctions:

Maryland Regiment Extraordinary, raised for Continental service in 1780 for one year, was clothed in brown faced with red, acquired from Continental stocks in New Jersey by Lieutenant Colonel Edward Giles.

4th Regiment May 1780: deserter described in blue coat edged yellow, lined white.

Militia Light Horse Volunteers Put into the field in 1781 to face General Arnold's forces operating in Virginia, and clothed at their own expense. Members of these county-based troops requested horse equipment and arms, 'according to the English model at present used by their Horse . . .'. The appearance of one of these troops is shown in an illustration herewith.

Virginia

The Virginia Line regiments with General Washington were, in 1779, well supported by John Moss, Virginia's Clothier at Philadelphia, who, that July, reported on hand 550 suits of ready-made soldiers' clothing, and brown linen for overalls, but needed additional hats, cloth, shirts, shoes and stockings to complete the 3,550 rank and file under his care. Moss

ordered James Irwin of Chestnut Hill, Pennsylvania, to make 1,540 soldiers' hats of the following dimensions: 5 inches behind, 4 inches before on the brim, quite before to be 3½ inches, the sides 3 inches. Captain John Peyton, the State Clothier who succeeded Moss, ordered in February 1780 768 soldiers' hats and 12 silver-laced for sergeants.

From 1779 onwards the prescribed uniform for the Virginia Line was worn by all its Continental regiments except the 9th, stationed in Pittsburgh, which had blue coats cuffed white, striped overalls and waistcoats. The Virginia Board of Trade imported superfine blue and scarlet cloth for regimental coats for the officers, with white or buff for one waistcoat and a pair of breeches for each. In 1780 Governor Thomas Jefferson changed the state uniform to blue coats with blue waistcoats and breeches. When Virginia became the major site of the war in 1781 the state's imports failed just as the need became most critical. Nevertheless, the state carried on

Commission of Jonathan Childs as a sergeant in the 5th Company of Infantry, 3rd Regiment, 2nd Brigade, Vermont Militia, dated 10 November 1780.

The figure wears a cocked hat bound red, brown coat and waistcoat, black breeches, and white stockings. (Smithsonian Institution)

Uniforms of Virginia State Troops and Militia, 1779–83

Unit	Coats	Facings	Headgear
Convention Guards Rgt.*, 1779–81	green	white	leather caps
Frointier Indep't. Companies*, 1779	brown	yellow	blue kilmarnocks
Illinois Regiment:			
1779	white shirts, blue leggings and breech clouts		bandannas
1780–82	See Plate C2		
1783	blue	red	hats
Crocket's Western Battalion:			
Officers	brown	blue	hats
Rank and file	brown	red	flapped hats
Slaughter's Western Corps	blue		
State Garrison Rgt.	state uniform		
Drums/Fifes	red	blue	
State Artillery Rgt.:			
1779–81	state uniform		
1782	blue	buff	buff lining
3rd State Regiment	state uniform, red lining		French hats
State Infantry	brown	buff	yellow lining
State Light Dragoons:			
1779	white canvas jackets		
1780–81	blue stable jackets		round hats
1782	green	red	fronted caps with chains and white hair
Illinois Light Dragoons	See Plate C2		
Magazine Guards	blue	buff	
1st and 2nd State Legions, 1781–83:			
Infantry	blue	white	leather covered with bearskin, black and white plumes
Cavalry	green	white	ditto
3rd State Legion, 1782–83:			
Infantry	state uniform with blue overalls. See also Plate F3		
Cavalry	green	red	
Fairfax Volunteer Light Horse Troop, 1781	jockey frock sheeting		light horsemen's caps

(*Continental units raised in and by Virginia.)

making military clothing after the capture of Williamsburg by setting up a depot outside the Albemarle Barracks under Commissioner of War Colonel William Davies. Utilizing German prisoners-of-war as artificers and tailors, the Albemarle facility functioned until, at the war's end in May 1783, operations and existing clothing stocks were moved to Point of Fork.

In October 1782 David Ross, State Commercial Agent, reported to the Governor that he had imported to Petersburg 1,000 suits of soldiers' clothing consisting of blue coats with blue capes and lapels lined with white serge, trimmed with white metal buttons marked USA, epaulettes of worsted for corporals and silk for sergeants; white waistcoats lined with serge, small USA buttons; breeches of stout twill lined with flannel; sergeants' coats of better quality; 20 drummers' coats of stout white cloth and blue serge linings; also 309 green horsemen's jackets, 1,470 pairs of shoes, 200 pair German hempen trousers with spatterdashes sewn on, and 961 pairs of blue worsted stockings. The supply, which included cloth and buttons in gross amounts, was utilized to provide the remaining Virginia state and Continental troops until demobilization in 1784. The table opposite summarizes uniforms of Virginia State Troops and Militia, 1779–83:

North Carolina

In March 1779 the Continental Congress authorized reduction of the North Carolina Line to six battalions, and the discharge of the North Carolina Light Horse. When the regiments were ordered to join Major General Benjamin Lincoln's Southern Army, operating in the Carolinas and Georgia, General Washington and the Continental Board of War extended themselves to clothe the troops for the campaign. By July 1779 Brigadier General James Hogun, commanding the Line, announced to Governor Richard Caswell that his officers were in want of clothing and requested the Governor to order Thomas Craike, Commissary of Purchases, to buy blue and white cloth, as that was the uniform ordered for them by the Continental Board of War. On 23 November 1779 Washington informed the Board of War that the North Carolina troops were ready to march having been supplied with uniform which consisted of 547 coats and vests, 361 pairs of

Maj. William Barber of New Jersey, aide-de-camp to Maj.Gen. William Alexander, Lord Stirling; after a miniature in a private collection. (Peter F. Copeland)

breeches, 182 pairs of canvas and linen overalls, 1,348 pairs of shoes, 304 shirts, 1 hat, and 109 blankets.

Numbering over 717 rank and file in September 1779, the troops needed additional support on arrival in North Carolina; purchases of officers' clothing were completed by Captain James Reed of the 1st Regiment. The entire Line were captured at Charleston; and as prisoners of war, these officers petitioned the Board of War on 31 January 1781 to change the uniforms of the Line to scarlet facings laced at button holes and edges with silver, the men to have white tape where the officers had lace. General Washington, receiving this petition on 14 May 1781, agreed with it in substance, but warned against the use of lace. Imports ordered in October 1781 for the account of North Carolina included large quantities of blue and scarlet cloth. Other supplies of cloth and clothing were purchased from local merchants or impressed by district lieutenants.

In 1783, 60 officers each receipted for 2½ to 2⅞ yards blue, ⅞ yard scarlet, ⅜ yard white cloth, 10½ to 14 yards of linen for shirts, 1 hat, 1¼ yards of ribbon, ¼ white taste, 2½ dozen large and 2½ dozen small buttons. For the pattern of facings, lace and collar of this uniform see the portrait of Lieutenant Colonel John Baptist Ashe. The uniform of the North Carolina Continental Detachment, received from the Deputy Clothier General with the Southern Army, is illustrated in Plate E4.

Between 1780 and late 1782 the North Carolina Militia provided drafts for the North Carolina State Legion and for the volunteer light horse troops and foot battalions. Under the Act of June 1781 for 'Raising Troops out of the Militia of this State for the defence thereof . . .', the district militia officers were responsible for clothing the light horse drafts with leather caps, boots, spurs, swords, saddles, and bridles to supplement the shirts, overalls, stockings, breeches, lined waistcoats and thick woollen coats with white capes and cuffs customarily supplied to the foot militia. For the Light Dragoon uniform of 1780, see Plate C2.

South Carolina

With the fall of Charleston in 1780 the South Carolina Continental Line was captured. While prisoners of the British, officers of the Line petitioned the Continental Board of War to change the authorized uniform to a coat without lapels, button holes on each side of the coat laced with gold, trimmed with yellow buttons and an edging of lace, collar and cuff of buff, with a double edging of lace, buff lining and 'under clothes' (smallclothes), the men to have yellow tape where the officers wore lace. General Washington approved the change on 29 May 1781 excepting for lace, which he found too expensive.

For the South Carolina officers still prisoners of war Governor Mathews ordered in March 1782 from James McDougall, a British merchant in Charleston, fine blue cloth for officers' coats, red cloth for facings and fine white or buff for waistcoats and breeches, for which a supply of rice would be smuggled through the lines.

For the rest of the war military operations were handled by State troops and Militia, most of whom were raised for mounted duty. Troopers were furnished at state expense with a coat, horseman's cap,

Uniforms of mounted units

Regiment	Coats	Facings	Turbans
Militia Light Horse 1781–82:			
Kershaw's	light blue	black	black
Giles	See Plate C3		
Richardson's	light blue	blue	blue
McDonald's	light blue	red	red
Kolb's	light blue	green	green
Light Dragoons 1781–82:			
Myddleton's	blue	red	red
Hampton's	blue	red	red
Hammond's	blue	red	red
Maham's	blue	white	white
Peter Horry's	See portrait of Peter Horry		dark blue
State Regiments of Light Dragoons:			
Daniel Horry's, 1779	dark brown	red	
James Greg's Company, 1779	dark brown	white	
James Conyer's, 1782	brown	red	red
Charleston Militia			
Artillery	blue	red	cocked hats

Sketch of regimental button, from original at foot of description of the uniform of the 2nd New York Continental Regiment, Swarthout Papers, New York Historical Society. (Peter F. Copeland)

pair of shoes and spurs, blanket, and two each of waistcoats, overalls, shirts, and pairs of stockings. Arms and accoutrements were to be obtained from captured stores. Uniforms of these mounted units are summarized in the table opposite.

Georgia

With the Georgia Continental Brigade of four regiments reduced to 98 rank and file fit for duty in April 1779, John Sanford Dart, Deputy Clothier General at Charleston, SC, reported to Major General Benjamin Lincoln, Commander of the Southern Department, that the Georgians could be amply clothed from stores available in Charleston. For this uniform, see Plate E1.

Regimental distinctions:

4th Regiment February 1779: deserter described in blue coat edged white, and pewter button with number 4.

Georgia Continental Battalion 1782: received from the Continental Board of War 500 yards of white cloth for 200 waistcoats and breeches.

Georgia State Legion 1782: deerskin coats turned up with blue cloth, horsemen's caps, overalls and boots.

Militia 1779: Major, blue coat, ruffled shirts and black silk breeches.

Supplementary bibliography

Only sources not used n *General Washington s Armies 1775–1778* are included in this bibliography.

Col. Philip Van Cortland, 2nd New York Continental Regiment, after a miniature by John Ramage in a private collection. Blue coat, buff cape and lapels; gold buttons and epaulette; white waistcoat, frills and stock. (Peter F. Copeland)

Printed sources Eerlyn M. Acomb, ed., *The Revolutionary Journal of B on Ludwig von C osen, 1780–1783* (Chapel Hill, NC, 1958); Samuel Haz rd *et al.*, editors, *Pennsylvania Archives* (Ph ladelphia, 1854 +); *New York in the Revolution as Colony and State* (Albany, 1904), Vol. II; Robert L. Klin er and Richard A.W. Wilder, *Sketch Book 1776* (Arlington, 1967); Fitzhugh McMaster, 'The Horse Troops', *Sandlapper*, October 1976; Ernest W. Peterkin, *The Exercise of Arms in the Continental Infantry, Being a Study of the Manual of the Firelock as set forth by Major-General von Steubin* (Alexandria Bay, 1989); Howard C. Rice and Anne S.K. Brown, eds., *The American Campaigns of Rochambeaus' Army 1780, 1781, 1782, 1783* (Princeton, 1972).

Manuscript sources
American Antiquarian Society: US Revolution Collection; Boston Public Library: Orderly Book of Thomas Grosvenor 1780 June 25 to September 12, MS.F.3.5; Chicago Historical Society: John Hardin, Quartermaster Supply Account Book, 1777–79; William L. Clements Library: *Papers of Nathanael*

Greene; Connecticut Historical Society: Records of the 3rd Connecticut Regiment; New Haven Colony Historical Society: Nathan Beers Papers; Massachusetts State Archives: Revolutionary War Rolls, Vol. 75; Morristown [New Jersey] National Historical Park: Morristown Manuscript Collection; University of Wisconsin: *Francis Marion Papers*, Draper Manuscript Collection; Harvard University, Houghton Library: Frederick M. Dearborn Collection; Pennsylvania Historic and Museum Commission: RG 4 Comptroller General, Commissary's Accounts Box 2; New York Historical Society: *Von Steuben Papers*, Orderly Books Collection; New York

Public Library: *Military Papers of Peter Gansevoort*, Vol. V; Rhode Island Historical Society: Orderly Book of the 1st Rhode Island Regiment, 1777 July 12 . . . to 1779 July 29; *Israel Angell Papers*; Rhode Island Council of War Minutes; Rhode Island State Archives: Military Papers.

THE PLATES

A1: Trumpeter, 4th Regiment Continental Light Dragoons, 1779–81
Trumpeters of the 4th Light Dragoons were distin-

Cl. Christopher Greene

Col. Christopher Greene, Rhode Island Regiment, after a portrait in the collections of Brown University. Blue coat, white cape, lapels, cuffs, waistcoat, stock and frills; silver buttons, epaulettes, and button holes. (Peter F. Copeland)

guished by scarlet turbans and brass letters '4LD' on their leather caps. Otherwise the uniform was that of the troopers: green cloak with red cape; green regimental coat lined and turned up at sleeves with red, brass buttons; red belted waistcoat; green breeches, boots, black stock, and brown shirt. (Portrait of Captain John Heard, private collection, *Pennsylvania Packet*, 3 April 1779; *Pennsylvania Journal*, 14 April 1779; Henry Papers, HSP; Pennsylvania Archives)

A2: Trooper, 2nd Regiment Continental Light Dragoons, 1782

White round-cut stable jacket with blue standing collar, cuffs, edging of shoulder straps, and rose on hip, one row of small white buttons; japanned black leather caps with black horsehair crests, white plume with red top not exceeding top of cap, black leather cockade; leather breeches, black stock and white shirt. (Orderly book of Heronimous Hoagland, New England Historic Genealogical Society; account book of Elisha Jane, US National Archives)

A3: Officer, 3rd Regiment Continental Light Dragoons, 1781

This regiment retained the same uniform from 1779 to 1783, but with variations in the fashion and the shade of blue of officers' facings. We show a white coat with dark blue lapels, lapets, cape and cuffs, silver buttons and epaulette; black sword belt; white waistcoat; black leather cap with officers' distinctive metal crest and black plume, white horsehair; white stock and frills; black horse furniture. (*MUIA Plate* 689)

A4: Trooper, 1st Regiment Continental Light Dragoons, 1781–83

The regulation uniform prescribed for Continental Light Dragoons, as adopted by the 1st Light Dragoons late in 1781, consisted of a short-skirted blue regimental coat with white cape, lapels and round cuffs, buttons, turn-back, and overalls, and a helmet crested with black fur. (Drawing by de Verger, Anne S.K. Brown Military Collection; Executive Papers, Virginia State Library)

B1: Sergeant, Philadelphia Department, Continental Corps of Invalids, 1781

Red watch coat over green regimental coat with

Col. Walter Stewart, 2nd Pennsylvania Continental Regiment, 1780, by Charles Willson Peale. Blue coat; scarlet lapels, cape, and waistcoat; silver epaulette, buttons and lace; black cravat, white shirt and ruffles. (Anne S.K. Brown Military Collection, Brown University)

yellow buttons; black stock; checked shirt; brown overalls; white waistcoat; and flapped round hat. (*Freeman's Journal and Weekly Advertiser* [Philadelphia], 27 September 1780 and 15 October 1781; USNA)

B2: Officer, Corps of Sappers and Miners, 1782–83

Blue coat faced buff and edged scarlet, gilt buttons and epaulettes; buff waistcoat and breeches; white stockings; cocked hat; white shirt, stock and frills. (Portrait of the Chevalier de Cambray-Digny by Charles Willson Peale, Collections of the Independence Hall National Historical Park)

B3: Waggoner, Quartermaster General's Department, 1779

Plain brown single-breasted coat, plain white buttons; green under-jacket; blue ribbed stockings; black

Capt. William Trueman Stoddert, 5th Maryland Continental Regiment, by Charles Willson Peale. Blue coat, red lapels, cape and shoulder strap; silver buttons and lace on strap; white waistcoat, ruffles and stock; black round hat turned up on left side and black feather or hair roach over crown. (The Society of the Cincinnati Museum, Anderson House, Washington, D.C.)

civilian hat with button, and black silk handkerchief around the neck. (*Pennsylvania Packet*, 30 March 1779, USNA)

C1: Private, Illinois Regiment, Virginia State Forces, 1780

Short blue coat turned up at cuffs with white, blue lapels, white Spanish-type collar; white buttons, waistcoat and overalls; brown shirt, no stock; Spanish cocked hat, musket and waistbelt cartridge box. (*MUIA Plate* 369)

C2: Dragoon, Captain John Rogers' Company of Illinois Light Dragoons, Virginia State Forces, 1780

Blue cloak; black stock; tanned moccasins; blue cloth cap with white binding; blue short coat with white binding; white overalls, and blue leggings; white belts. (George Rogers Clark Papers, Virginia State Library)

C3: Volunteer, North Carolina Militia, 1780

When reporting for active duty the foot component of the North Carolina Militia was to be fully clothed in 'cloth-coloured' short hunting shirts with blue capes. They also had cloth-coloured overalls and flapped black hats, and were to be fully armed and accoutred as riflemen. (North Carolina Archives)

C4: Trooper, South Carolina Regiment of Militia Light Horse, 1782

Belonging to Giles's Troop, this light horseman has yellow cape, cuffs and turban, as well as the standard light blue single-breasted short coat, black leather-fronted cap, plain white waistcoat and overalls. (*MUIA Plate* 473)

D1: Bandsman, 3rd Continental Artillery Regiment, 1782–83

Scarlet British sergeant's coat with blue lapels, yellow buttons; white waistcoat, breeches and stockings; black cocked hat with Union cockade. (Papers of William Heath)

D2: Sergeant, 2nd Continental Artillery Regiment, 1780–82

Blue coat, scarlet lapels with buttons in pairs, round cuffs with buttons in pairs, scarlet piping on wings and shoulder straps, yellow buttons; white waistcoat, overalls, sword belt; black cocked hat with round cockade. (*MUIA Plate* 665)

D3: Officer, 4th Continental Artillery Regiment, 1779

Blue coat, small standing collar, two lines of gold lace at edge, scarlet edged with gold, lapels and round cuffs with slashes, gold buttons and epaulettes; buff waistcoat and breeches; cocked hat with scarlet plume, gold band and loop; white shirt and ruffles, black stock. Small artillery flag with blue field, gold finial and cords and tassels. (Portrait of Thomas Forrest by Charles Willson Peale, Collections of Independence Hall National Historical Park; Cadwallader Papers, MdHS)

E1: Private, Georgia Continental Battalion, 1779

Blue short coat, faced blue, white buttons and lace; red waistcoat; grey kilt with black line; red overalls with white garters; black fur cap. (Papers of Benjamin Lincoln, Massachusetts Historical Society; Collections of the Georgia Historical Society)

E2: Sergeant, North Carolina Continental Battalion, 1782

Blue short-skirted coat, scarlet lapels, cuffs and cape with white tape edging, white buttons; white waistcoat and overalls; black stock and white shirt; fantailed hat edged with silver. (North Carolina Archives; George Washington Papers; Papers of Nathanael Greene, Clements Library)

E3: Brigadier General, Continental Army, 1780–83

Our model for this reconstruction is Brigadier General Anthony Wayne who obtained a blue coat lapelled, caped and cuffed buff, with gold buttons and laced button holes; buff waistcoat and breeches; gilt epaulettes, white or silver star on shoulder strap; cocked hat with white feather or plume. (Anthony Wayne Papers, Clements Library; Anthony Wayne Manuscripts, HSP; miniature of Brigadier General Anthony Wayne by John Ramage; Collections of Detroit Institute of Arts)

E4: Private, Lt.Col. Thomas Posey's Virginia Continental Detachment, 1782

Blue coatee, blue lapels, eight buttons in pairs on

Col. John Cropper, Virginia Militia, by Charles Willson Peale, 1792. Cropper resigned his commission in the Virginia Line on 16 August 1779, but returned as a colonel of Virginia Militia from 1781 to the end of the war. Except for the rise-and-fall collar which reflects the fashion at the time the portrait was made, the blue coat, scarlet facings and gilt buttons and epaulettes reflect the uniform of his last service. (Smithsonian Institution)

Maj. John Baptista Ashe, 6th North Carolina Continental Regiment, after an unattributed original in a private collection. Note placement of lace on cape and lapel, and plain button hole. (Peter F. Copeland)

each, red cape and red shoulder strap to support cartridge box belt, slash sleeve with three small buttons, one button on each hip; long Russia sheeting gaiters; white breeches and waistcoat; black stock, and white shirt. (Virginia War Office Papers, Virginia State Library; Papers of Christian Febiger, HSP)

F1: Officer, Major Henry Lee's Partizan Legion, 1782

Buff coat, green cape, lapels and cuffs, gilt buttons and epaulette; buff double-breasted waistcoat; black sword belt; leather breeches; leather cap with bearskin roach, green turban. (Portrait of Major Henry Lee by C.W. Peale, IHNHP Collections; USNA)

F2: Dragoon, Armand's Legion, 1780–83

Blue coatee, buff pointed lapels, cape and round cuffs, yellow buttons in pairs; blue waistcoat with buff edging and three rows of small yellow buttons; yellow breeches, black hussar boots; red stock, white shirt; brass French dragoon helmet with bearskin roach and brown fur turban; French hussar sword and waist cartridge box, white webbing. (Portrait of Colonel Armand by C.W. Peale, HSP; Papers of the Continental Congress; drawing by de Verger, Anne S.K. Brown Military Library)

F3: Private, Lt.Col. Charles Dabney's 3rd Virginia State Legion, 1783

Green sailor's jacket; white buttons, feather and waistcoat; blue overalls; black cap. (Account book of Henry Young, Virginia State Library, Executive Papers, Virginia State Library)

F4: Officer, Henry Sherburne's Additional Continental Regiment, 1779

Dark brown coat, yellow lapels, cape and cuffs, silver buttons, white lining; green vest and breeches; cocked hat bound silver. Waist cartridge box and sword attributed to Colonel Sherburne. (*MUIA Plate* 477)

G1: Private, 2nd New Hampshire Regiment, 1782

Brown-dyed British coat, faced and cuffed white, narrow white lace on outside of facings, collar and upper end of cuffs, blue diamonds with white binding at the corner of the turnbacks; British hat, white waistcoat, linen overalls; white star on the breast of coat; black stock and white shirt. (New Hampshire Archives; Orderly book 2nd New Hampshire Regiment, New Hampshire Historical Society)

G2: Sergeant, Light Infantry Company, 2nd Pennsylvania Regiment, 1780–82

Short blue coatee, scarlet cuffs, lapels, wings and cape, white buttons, white lining, yellow binding on lapels, cuffs and cape; brown linen vest and Russia drill overalls; red sash over shoulder, black sword plume, white binding on front with white triangle on front plate to indicate rank. (Pennsylvania Archives; Andrew Peters Papers, American Antiquarian Society)

G3: Drummer, 2nd New York Regiment, 1779–80

Buff coat, blue lapels, cape and cuffs, white buttons, white turnbacks with blue heart, blue tape on seams and blue shoulder knots; white waistcoat and breeches; grey stockings; black stock, white shirt, plain cocked hat. (*New York in the Revolution As Colony and State*, Vol. II)

G4: Officer, 2nd New York Regiment, 1779–81

Blue coat lined white, buff lapels, cape and cuffs, silver buttons and epaulette; white waistcoat, breeches and stockings; black half-gaiters; crimson sash. (Miniature of Colonel Philip Van Cortlandt, by John Ramage)

H1: Private, 4th Massachusetts Regiment, 1782

Blue coat, white lapels, cape, cuffs and 3-year faithful service chevron; white buttons, linings, waistcoat; buff breeches; black knee straps and half-gaiters, grey stockings; cocked hat with white feather, tape, loop and button, tassels; round black cockade with white relief. Bayonet fixed to musket, therefore no bayonet belt. (*MUIA Plate* 601)

Silk coatee associated with the Pinckney family of South Carolina. It may have been worn by Gen. Thomas Pinckney, a captain in the 1st South Carolina Continental Regiment, later aide-de-camp to Generals Lincoln and Gates. The body of the coat is 'cloth-coloured'; light blue lapels, cuffs, heart in the turnback and inside of modified standing collar; white lining and turnback. (The Charleston Museum)

Col. Peter Horry, South Carolina Light Dragoons, 1781–82, after an original portrait by Henry Benbridge. White coatee, waistcoat, shirt, ruffles, and stock; blue lapels, lining, cape and cuffs; silver buttons and epaulettes; buff breeches; black sword belt and horse equipment. (Private collection, Peter F. Copeland)

H2: Ensign, Rhode Island Regiment, 1782–83

Blue coat, white lapels, pointed cuffs, waistcoat, cape and overalls; silver RIR buttons in pairs with laced button holes; brown overcoat; black leather cap trimmed in silver, with silver anchor, black feather. Regimental standard. (*MUIA Plate* 559)

H3: Drummer, Rhode Island Regiment, 1782–83

White coat, blue lapels, cape and pointed cuffs, blue lace on seams; black leather cap with white anchor and white fringe along edge of cap; white waistcoat and overalls. (*MUIA Plate* 559)

H4: Sergeant, 3rd Connecticut Regiment, 1782–83

Blue long-skirted coat and cape, white cuffs, lapels, and waistcoat, ticken overalls; cocked hat bound white; black stock, brown shirt. (Webb Papers, Deacon Nathan Beers Papers, Yale University)

*Lt.Col. Robert Knox,
Pennsylvania Militia, c.
1783, by Charles Willson
Peale. Medium blue coat,
scarlet lapels, cape and
cuffs; silver edging,
epaulettes, and buttons,
white stock and ruffles,
buff waistcoat. (Fort
Ticonderoga Museum)*

*Trooper, Baltimore Troop
of Light Dragoons,
Maryland Militia, 1781.
Composed of members of
the local gentry, this unit's
volunteer horsemen wore
modified fox-hunting
garb, such as short
country-cloth coats with
blue cuffs and cape, white
under-jackets and white
leather breeches, and
beaver caps bound with
silver lace with the letters
LH on the front. (Peter F.
Copeland)*

INTRODUCTION

The 18th-century British soldier might easily have been excused for suspecting that he had very few friends. To most contemporary politicians the Army was no more than an unwelcome necessity in wartime and an unjustifiable extravagance in peacetime. Nevertheless, the overall impression which is to be gained from a close study of the Army's own records, and from the surviving letters, diaries and memoirs left behind by its officers (and occasionally by its men), is that by and large the British Army of the 18th century was very little different in character or in spirit from today's British Army. It was, above all, an army which was led, not driven, into battle.

Curiously enough there was, in a very real sense, not one British Army but two: a British or English Establishment, and an Irish Establishment. The former was of course the senior of the two, but constitutionally rather precarious, and always liable to swinging cuts whenever a case could be made for declaring units surplus to requirements. However, by an Act of 1699 Ireland was allocated a separate military establishment of 12,000 officers and men (raised to 15,325 in 1769), paid and administered from Dublin Castle. Obviously Ireland could occasionally be stripped of men in times of crisis – sometimes embarrassingly so, as at the time of Thurot's raid on Carrickfergus in 1760 – and in response to a European war the establishment might temporarily be increased; but the important point was that in peacetime it was not to be reduced below 12,000 men.

The Irish Army – made up of units raised in Scotland or England – was primarily intended for the defence and internal security of that country. Never-theless, apart from the Viceroy's ceremonial Battle-axe Guards (dressed similarly to the English Yeomen of the Guard), no regular units were permanently assigned to the Irish Establishment – though the four regiments of 'Irish' Horse might have been forgiven for thinking otherwise; and on being ordered over-seas or on service a battalion automatically reverted to the English Establishment.

However, because the strength of the Irish Establishment was fixed and therefore not susceptible to Treasury interference, the Duke of Cumberland and his successors at the Army's administrative headquarters, Horse Guards, came to regard it as a safe haven for regiments which might otherwise be

A typical soldier's grenadier cap of the type worn by those units which had no distinctive badge. The rather battered and shapeless appearance is probably rather more typical than the neat caps depicted by David Morier. (Author's Collection)

disbanded in Treasury-led defence cuts. Unfortunately, attractive though it might have appeared, the concept of using the Irish Establishment as an Imperial reserve was greatly hampered by two factors.

In the first place the constitutional independence of the Irish Establishment, which was so vital in protecting it from interference by the English government, also worked to restrict the control which could be exercised over it by Horse Guards. Instead it was run by a quite independent staff in Dublin Castle. This lack of any real control, and Dublin's understandable preoccupation with employing the army as a rural constabulary, led to its becoming a byword for inefficiency. (In 1752 officers in Limerick had to be rather sharply reminded to wear their swords, and not to slouch about in slippers and nightcaps . . .)

Secondly, in order to cram as many regiments as possible on to the 12,000-man establishment, it was necessary to reduce them to little more than cadres, which needed to be hastily filled out with drafted men and new recruits whenever a battalion was ordered on service. This particular problem was compounded by the fact that for security reasons units carried on the Irish Establishment were traditionally forbidden to do any recruiting in Ireland – except in wartime, when they could be expected to be shipped overseas without undue delay.

For instance, when the badly understrength 44th and 48th Foot were ordered abroad in 1755 they had to wait until they reached North America before beating up for the recruits which they desperately needed to fill out their depleted ranks. (Nevertheless, it was apparently not unknown for some of the more enterprising units to enlist Ulster Protestants, ship them across to Stranraer in south-west Scotland, and there clap Scots blue bonnets on their heads before ostentatiously bringing them back on the next ferry.)

Scotland, or North Britain as it was sometimes called, also had its own Commander-in-Chief based in Edinburgh Castle; but unlike his Irish counterpart

Private, 1st (or Royal) Regiment, as depicted in the 1742 Cloathing Book. This is one of the most famous images of the 18th-century British soldier, yet the rather old-fashioned order of dress depicted here would be superseded within a year or two; none of Morier's paintings show belts being worn over the coat when the lapels are displayed. (Trustees of the National Museums of Scotland)

he reported directly to Horse Guards, and his troops for all practical purposes belonged to the English Establishment.

Rear view of an infantryman, after a sketch by Thomas Sandby, 1746. As usual on campaign the coat skirts have been unhooked; less usually, the thigh-length gaiters appear to have been discarded. The duffle-bag-style knapsack can be seen quite clearly. (Author's Collection)

ORGANISATION

Regimental strength and organisation varied throughout the 18th century according to military necessity and short-term financial policy. At the outset regiments were known only by the name of their colonel, but in 1742 regimental numbers were fixed in place of the informal order of seniority which had hitherto existed.

During the War of the Austrian Succession (1743–48) no fewer than 79 numbered regiments of foot were carried on the Army List, but the 67th–79th Regiments were temporary corps hastily raised during the Jacobite emergency and just as hastily disbanded once it was over in the summer of 1746. Two years later, at the end of the war, a further 17 infantry battalions (including ten battalions of Marines ranking as the 44th to 53rd Foot) were disbanded as surplus to requirements.

Normally seniority counted for everything in deciding which units would survive and which would not. However, although he failed to have Bragg's 28th broken for their notorious inefficiency, the Duke of Cumberland did succeed in retaining the 43rd Highlanders, and 54th to 59th Foot, on the grounds that they were good regiments. Consequently their numbers changed to become the 42nd to 48th Foot respectively; and Trelawney's 63rd, by virtue of forming the Jamaica garrison, also survived to become the 49th.

Cumberland's abrupt dismissal after the disastrous Hanoverian campaign of 1757 saw a reversal of this attempt to retain regiments on the grounds of merit rather than mere seniority; at the close of the Seven Years' War in 1763 the inevitable reduction in the Army's strength was achieved simply by disbanding all regiments junior to the 70th (Glasgow Greys), the only exceptions on this occasion being five Invalid Regiments, temporarily renumbered the 71st to 75th Foot before they too were disbanded as an economy measure in 1769.

Infantry regiments normally mustered only a single battalion, although the 1st Foot or Royal Regiment (later the Royal Scots) had two battalions, and the 60th Royal Americans normally had four. From time to time other units did muster second battalions, but generally speaking these were either

ROYAL REGᵗ   QUEEN'S REGᵗ   3 REGIMENT

Grenadiers of 1st, 2nd and 3rd Foot. The well-known paintings by the Swiss artist David Morier are commonly dated to 1751, but a close analysis suggests that they may actually have been painted in 1748, at the end of the War of the Austrian Succession. Stylistically the grenadier paintings can conveniently be divided into three groups, and this is representative of group A, which comprises six rather stiff paintings depicting the 1st to 15th Foot and the 28th, 29th and 30th Foot. An

early date is suggested for this group by the fact that only three out of the 18 grenadiers in the group have wings on their shoulders, as against slightly less than half in groups B and C. It would also appear that this group was painted in winter – probably 1747/48 – since 13 out of the 18 have their lapels buttoned over for warmth. Out of the 26 soldiers in the other groups (discounting four lacking lapels), only two have their lapels buttoned over. (The Royal Collection © Her Majesty the Queen)

disbanded within a short time or else taken into the line as independent units. In 1755 and 1756, for example, a number of regiments were authorised to raise second battalions, but in 1758 these battalions were detached from their parent units to become the 61st to 75th Foot. To all intents and purposes the two battalions of the Royals were also regarded as separate units; it would appear that the only occasion during the 18th century on which they were brigaded together was at Coxheath Camp in 1778.

Other units were more fortunate. During the Seven Years' War both battalions of the 42nd Highlanders served together in North America, as did both battalions of Fraser's 71st Highlanders during

Grenadiers of 31st, 32nd and 33rd Foot.

Group B of the Morier series comprises five paintings depicting the three Regiments of Footguards, the 16th to 24th Foot, and the 31st, 32nd and 33rd Foot. In marked contrast to group A these paintings are full of vitality, and the grenadiers are depicted against a backdrop of camp scenes apparently painted from life. Morier evidently had a well-developed sense of humour: note the soldier disappearing over the fence with a chicken under his arm. It is significant that all but three of the regiments comprising this group were serving in Flanders in 1748. They appear contemporary with a large canvas, also by Morier, depicting officers and men of the Royal Artillery at Roermond in April 1748. The 'odd three out' – 16th, 17th and 18th Foot – all appear on one very well known canvas, which oddly enough has for its centrepiece an Austrian soldier contentedly puffing on his pipe as he watches the artist at work. Upon closer examination, however, it is apparent that the three grenadiers do not fit very comfortably on to the canvas, and must have been added at a later date. (The Royal Collection © Her Majesty the Queen)

the American War. In the latter conflict, however, the second battalion of the 42nd served in India and subsequently became the 73rd; while the two battalions of the original 73rd were similarly separated, 1/73rd in India and 2/73rd at Gibraltar.

In peacetime infantry battalions could sometimes muster as few as eight companies, but on service generally mustered ten, on paper at least. In wartime a number of regiments also had 'Additional Companies' which were not intended to go on active service but instead functioned as recruit depots. This at least was the theory, but in 1745 the Jacobite emergency saw the 'Additional Companies' of the Royals, 21st, 25th and 43rd, then stationed in Scotland, pitchforked into action against the rebels, while the companies in England were hurriedly formed into three Provisional Battalions commanded by unemployed Marine officers.

Three of the battalion companies were notionally

REGIMENT · REGIMENT · REGIMENT

This useful study of soldiers in full marching order belongs to Group C. This comprises seven paintings depicting the 25th, 26th, 27th and 34th through to 49th Regiments of Foot.

Although rather less stiff than group A they are depicted against a studio backdrop; and the numbering of certain units (e.g. the 42nd Highlanders) indicates that at least some of the regiments were painted or reworked after the reductions which followed the Peace of Aix-la-Chappelle in 1748.

It is often remarked that Morier could not actually have used a man from each regiment as his models since some units were serving overseas at the time; but in fact, given the presence of the rudimentary depots maintained by each regiment in Britain or Ireland, there is no reason why he should not have been able to obtain a man from each regiment. (The Royal Collection © Her Majesty the Queen)

commanded by field officers. The senior of these was the colonel himself. In the 1740s some officers, such as Peregrine Lascelles, might still occasionally be found commanding their regiments in the field (he did so at Prestonpans in 1745), but increasingly they were general officers and consequently rarely to be seen. By the end of the century they had simply become 'colonel proprietors'. Throughout the period most regiments were in fact commanded on a day-to-day basis by their lieutenant colonel, or even, in his absence, by the third field officer – the major. The latter, assisted by the adjutant, was also particularly responsible for training and discipline.

Since the colonel, even when he was present, usually had rather more pressing matters to attend to, his company was actually commanded for all practical purposes by a captain-lieutenant. This officer ranked as the regiment's senior lieutenant, but by courtesy was addressed (though not paid) as captain. However, should he subsequently be promoted to captain his seniority was accounted according to his captain-lieutenant's commission rather than to the date of his promotion.

The remaining companies were commanded by captains, each assisted, like the field officers, by a lieutenant and an ensign, except in the case of the elite 'flank' companies – the grenadiers and later the light infantry – who had second lieutenants in place of ensigns.

Apart from the company officers each battalion also mustered four commissioned staff officers; the adjutant, quartermaster, surgeon and chaplain.

The first was normally an additional (and purchasable) appointment held by one of the keener subalterns, but there are occasional cases of individuals holding the post without the benefit of a lieutenant's or ensign's commission – these were probably meritorious NCOs promoted to the job without purchase.

The quartermaster's commission could, in the early days, be purchased just like any other, but it was an important appointment demanding a considerable degree of experience and acumen; conse-

quently, by the end of the century it could only be given to capable quartermaster sergeants. However, although an officer could not therefore acquire a quartermaster's commission the reverse was not true, and there was nothing to prevent a quartermaster from subsequently bettering himself by purchasing an ensign's commission.

The surgeon, by the nature of his office, was of course a specialist, and often a very good one at that. When Surgeon John Wright of 1/Royals was appointed by General Williamson to be Purveyor of the Hospitals on San Domingo in 1794 he was described as 'an excellent character & has great Professional merit'.

Unfortunately the same could not be said of the chaplain, who was normally an absentee. Neither the

The grenadier company was organised into two platoons, one of which was usually posted on each flank of the battalion when drawn up in line. Alternatively the grenadier companies of several units might be brigaded together in provisional battalions. This particular recreated platoon are at the 'Make Ready' position, holding their firelocks upright as they cock them. (Author's Collection)

Reverend Miles Beevor, nor his brother George, who were appointed to the 1st and 2nd Battalions of the Royals in 1786 and 1790 respectively, are ever recorded as having turned up at battalion headquarters: monthly returns invariably record the pair of them as absent (by the leave of the Commanding Officer) since the day of their appointment.

Each company normally mustered three sergeants, three corporals and two drummers, although the colonel's company had five sergeants, including the sergeant major and the quartermaster sergeant. The grenadier company also boasted two fifers – normally replaced by pipers in Highland regiments. The senior of the three sergeants in each company also held the appointment of pay-sergeant.

Otherwise the theoretical strength of each company varied considerably according to whether an individual unit was on the English or Irish Establishment at the time. In peacetime a company on the former establishment was supposed to muster 70 rank and file (always assuming that sufficient recruits could be found in the first place), but only 30 men were allowed for each company in battalions on the Irish Establishment.

On active service battalion companies were invariably understrength, and there was generally little attempt made to ensure that they were maintained at a uniform size. Nevertheless, the élite flank companies were normally kept up to strength at the expense of the battalion companies. When 1/Royals were sent from Jamaica to San Domingo early in 1794 the two flank companies accounted between them for a quarter of the battalion's strength. This imbalance was further exacerbated by the fact that both companies were actually detached from the regiment and assigned to a provisional Flank Battalion at the time.

THE OFFICERS

The British Army's officers came from a wide variety of backgrounds and were characterised by a surprising degree of upward social mobility; but by and large it was only the aristocrats and landed gentry who made it to the very top. The gentry had the money with which to purchase promotion and, much more importantly, could also command the necessary 'interest': that is, they could rely upon patronage and

A representative group of 'hatmen' – contemporary Army slang for men belonging to the ordinary or battalion companies. These men wear the blue facings and plain white lace of the Royals. The white gaiters seen here were normally replaced by black, brown or grey on campaign. (Author's Collection)

the influence of friends and relations in high and sometimes not so high places to facilitate their upward progress.

By far the greater number of ordinary regimental officers, however, were simply 'private gentlemen' (invariably a rather elastic term in the 18th century): generally of good family, but seldom possessed of very much in the way of either money or prospects. Captain Robert Bannatyne, one of three soldier brothers, doubtless spoke for many when he wrote shortly before his death at Conjeveram in 1759: 'My Father had no great Estate and dying whilst his Children were young you May guess whether five of us did not find use for small inheritance.' Bannatyne's father was the minister of Dores in Inverness-shire, but doctors and other professionals, and indeed even a fair sprinkling of tradesmen contributed their sons as well, while a fair proportion were, quite naturally, themselves the sons of soldiers.

Amongst the latter were the sons of a rather neglected, but nevertheless quite significant, class of officer: the promoted ranker. Contrary to popular belief, merit was recognised and often rewarded in the 18th-century British Army. Able NCOs were perhaps most frequently promoted into newly raised corps where their experience was obviously at a premium. Naturally some of them were getting on a bit by comparison with their fellow subalterns, but younger individuals could also win what were in effect battlefield promotions. Many of the commissioned NCOs served as adjutants. This was an important post with considerable responsibility for training as well as administration, and it was clearly much better filled by an able veteran soldier – such as Sergeant Major George Edington of 1/Royals, promoted in 1794 – than by an inexperienced subaltern.

A quite disproportionate number of officers were Irish or Scots. It has been estimated that in the 1760s something between 20 and 30 per cent of officers were Scots, and this proportion was constantly rising. There was in fact a decided feeling in some quarters that by the latter part of the century the British Army was in the grip of something akin to a Scottish mafia. While such an ungenerous view was undoubtedly coloured by the influence enjoyed by officers such as David Dundas, it is also borne out by an analysis of the infantry regiments in the Army List for 1794.

Officer's grenadier cap of an unbadged regiment – in this case the 43rd Highlanders prior to their adopting furred caps. Apart from the obviously superior quality of workmanship and materials, the design is far more elaborate than that used for common soldiers' caps, and the stiff front is separate from the softer bag or 'stocking' behind. (Author's Collection)

In all at least 845 out of 2,470 officers serving in 82 battalions of the line can be identified as Scots – a proportion of 34.2 per cent, although the true figure may have been as high as 40 per cent. Moreover, only 204 of the officers concerned – just 8.2 per cent of the total – were serving in Highland regiments, and a further 79 in other recognised Scottish units such as the Royals (later the Royal Scots) and the Cameronians. These accounted for 11.5 per cent all told, leaving the remaining 22.7 per cent – nearly a quarter of all the officers then serving in the line – scattered amongst 'English' regiments.

Only a single battalion (the 8th Foot) appears not to have had a single Scots officer among the 30 on its rolls in 1794. On the other hand the 19th Foot (The Green Howards) had at least 19 – an astonishing 68 per cent of its officers; while the 9th and 57th were

Privates of 119th (Prince's Own) Regiment of Foot, 1762–3, as painted by David Morier. See Plate D3 for details of colouring. Apart from the crested helmets the resemblance to contemporary Croat or Pandour uniforms is quite striking. Note particularly the Hungarian breeches and ankle boots. The helmet plates bear the G.R. cypher. The man on the left has fixed his unusual sword bayonet on a staff to form a pike, while the man on the right still carries his in its scabbard. Blankets (or more probably cloaks, since the Croat model is being followed) are carried because light infantry units were expected to move with the minimum of regimental baggage. (The Royal Collection © Her Majesty the Queen)

not very far behind, with sixteen and seventeen Scots officers respectively. Nineteen battalions had five Scots officers or fewer; 34 had between six and ten; and 15 battalions boasted between 11 and 15 Scots. The remaining 13 battalions, including of course the Highland regiments, numbered considerably more, although the 42nd (Black Watch) appears to be the only battalion with an all-Scottish officer list.

Formidable though these figures are, they still do not tell the whole story. Thirty-one regimental colonels, amounting to 40 per cent of the total, were Scots – and all of them were general officers with considerable powers of patronage. With few exceptions they appear to have wielded this patronage almost exclusively to the benefit of their fellow countrymen. The fact that General David Graeme had commanded the 19th Foot for upwards of 25 years doubtless accounted for the large number of Scots officers in that battalion, but others bid fair to achieve similar results in less time. James Grant's

11th Foot, for example, had eight Scots officers besides the colonel in 1794, all of them gazetted to the battalion since Grant's appointment in November 1791; and by 1798 that number had doubled, so that Scots accounted for 40 per cent of the 11th's officers. Similarly the 8th Foot, which in 1794 had not a single Scots officer, boasted at least nine by 1798: 21 per cent of the total, and all gazetted since Ralph Dundas took over the regiment in July 1794.

It has been estimated that in peacetime up to two-thirds of all commissions were purchased, though it is hard to say what the true cost of the transaction actually was to the individual. Although there was an officially regulated scale the cost sometimes varied from regiment to regiment, and no doubt according to its geographical proximity at the time to London. Regulations specifically forbade officers to pay additional sums 'on top', but there is no doubt that it happened in the more fashionable regiments. Sometimes the prohibition was evaded by paying the additional sum to a 'friend' of the officer concerned. However, apart from such *douceurs*, the actual sums which changed hands tended in practice to be less than a superficial perusal of the official scales might suggest. Samuel Bagshawe explained it thus in a memorandum written sometime in 1742:

'... When a Capt. has to leave to quitt the Service & dispose of his Commission 'tis generally done in this manner, the Lieutenant recommended either gives him his (own) Commission and the difference between the Commissions of a Capt. & Lt. or a certain sum of money in which last case the Lt. has the disposing of his own Commission which if sold to an Ensign, that Ensign acts in the same way that is, gives the Lieutenant his Ensign's Commission and the difference or else a certain Sume & sells the Colours himself, So that the price of a Captain's Commission is either a certain Sume, or is compos'd of the difference between a Capt. and a Lieutenant's Commission, the difference between a Lieutenancy and a pair of Colours & the Colours. Now suppose a Company is dispos'd of in this last way & sold for eleven hundred pounds the Case stands thus

The Difference between the Captains & the Lt's Commission	£600
The Diff. between ye Lieutenancy & ye Colours	£100
The Colours	£400
	£1100'

Once the initial investment had been made in an Ensign's commission (and of course in the additional cost of his not inconsiderable kit) it was therefore fairly easy to find the £100 necessary to purchase the next step to lieutenant, though the jump to captain might sometimes be a little more difficult. However, if an officer died in harness, or was dismissed from the service by the sentence of a court-martial, his successor – normally the most senior officer in the rank below – stepped into his boots gratis, and everyone else gratefully shuffled up behind.

In theory officers were supposed to spend a minimum period in each rank before obtaining fur-

ther promotion, and generally speaking it normally took about ten years to make captain. Nevertheless there were of course some spectacularly quick promotions, and in times of crisis the inevitable expansion of the Army (and the equally inevitable casualties) provided considerable opportunities for ambitious officers and would-be officers.

Not only could aspiring officers more easily find non-purchase vacancies at subaltern level; but more senior commissions could also be offered to gentlemen who had the right connections, and fair prospects of raising the requisite number of recruits for a company or even a regiment. Under an able Secretary at War, such as Viscount Barrington, the inevitable abuses of the system were kept within reasonably acceptable bounds; but in the breakneck race to expand the Army in 1793 the aged and quite ineffectual Lord Amherst presided over a scandalous

Infantryman c. 1760, after Paul Sandby. This useful sketch provides a better picture of the British soldier at the time of the Seven Years' War than do Morier's paintings of c. 1748. Note particularly the **new, shorter gaiters with leather tops, linen breeches, and what appears to be an early version of the goatskin knapsack, worn square on the back. (Author's Collection)**

Highland officer, c. 1760: a reconstruction largely based on entries in the orderly book of Captain Stewart's company, 42nd Highlanders. On active service a plain 'frock' was worn in place of the expensively laced full-dress 'regimentals'. Note also the very popular, but at this stage unauthorised, white waistcoat. (Author's Collection)

state of affairs. A key figure in the process, if a sometimes shadowy one, was the regimental agent. The agent was a civilian who was appointed by the regimental colonel to act for him as a business manager-cum-banker. His various functions were admirably described by the then Deputy Secretary at War in 1798:

'To apply for, receive, disburse and account for public money advanced to him under general regulations or by particular orders. He is the ordinary channel of communication between the Regiment and the Public Departments and is resorted to not only for providing and forwarding of arms, clothing and other regimental supplies, but also in the business, public or private, of the individual officers.'

Most agents acted for a number of different units, though London-based agents could not act for regiments on the Irish Establishment or vice versa. Therefore, if an officer desirous of advancement found that no vacancy was available in his own corps, it was a relatively easy matter for the agent to arrange his exchange into another one on his books. In 1795, for example, the recently promoted Captain John Urquhart (late of 1/Royals) arrived in Cork to find his new regiment, the 106th Foot, about to be disbanded and its personnel drafted into other units. Nothing daunted, he contacted the 106th's agent, Humphrey Donaldson and promptly obtained a company in one of the latter's other regiments, the 85th Foot. Only a couple of months later he exchanged with Captain Hugh Campbell on to the Half Pay of the disbanded Royal Glasgow Regiment, managed by a Mr. Lawrie, who had taken over much the ailing Donaldson's business.

This sort of transaction was harmless enough, and most exchanges were carried out between officers of equal rank or involved only a single step; but if the money answered and the agent, like Donaldson, was unscrupulous enough, the process could be carried on almost indefinitely. This was exemplified by an Anglo-Irish baronet named Vere Hunt who appears to have been commissioned ensign in the 2nd (Queen's) Foot on 12 April 1793. Just over a year later, on 3 July 1794, he was appointed colonel commandant of his own (and happily short-lived) 135th Loyal Irish Volunteers.

It was little wonder, therefore, that the acerbic Major General James Craig was to write from Hol-

Grenadier, 25th (Edinburgh) Regiment, c. 1771. One of a series depicting units in the Minorca garrison, this painting contains a number of interesting features, not the least of them being the non-regulation fur cap. The traditional grenadier's matchcase attached to the cartouche box belt shows up quite clearly, but the waistbelt has been replaced by what can only be described as a strap over the right shoulder. (NMS)

land in November 1794: 'Out of fifteen regiments of cavalry and twenty-six of infantry, which we have here, twenty-one are literally commanded by boys or idiots – I had the curiosity to count them over.'

Craig might grumble about boys, but although the minimum age limit of 16 was frequently flouted in the granting of commissions, under-age officers were generally expected to stay at school until they were ready to join their regiments. The real problem was not one of adolescent subalterns, but rather that by the time they did condescend to turn up at regimental headquarters they had gained sufficient notional seniority to quality for such immediate promotion as they, or perhaps a doting relative, could afford to purchase. Nevertheless, although naturally seized upon by the Army's many critics, such examples were actually quite rare.

Very few of the higher-numbered regiments ever saw active service; instead, their recruits were almost invariably drafted to bring veteran units up to strength. This was naturally resented by the more ambitious officers since it meant that they had to begin recruiting afresh, and compensation for the drafted men could often be a long time in coming. Some units, such as Bagshawe's short-lived 93rd Foot and Johnstone's 101st Highlanders, were repeatedly milked of men in this way in the 1760s, and to all intents and purposes were treated simply as recruiting depots for better established units.

In 1795 the process was carried a stage further when the hitherto unprecedented step was taken of drafting entire battalions (such as the Royal Glasgow) and after a decent interval placing their remaining officers on the Half Pay list. This might have seemed harsh at the time, but it was obviously preferable to fielding untried regiments commanded by inexperienced officers.

At the end of his service an officer was normally expected to provide for his retirement by selling his commission. This step, however, was obviously not open to those officers who had not purchased their commissions in the first place. Nevertheless such officers, who had often earned their rank by hard work and ability, were still provided for. By way of a reward they could be appointed to the Half Pay establishment of a disbanded regiment, leaving behind a free vacancy in their original corps. In 1765 Lieutenant William Bannatyne of the 13th Foot retired in this way by transferring on to the Half Pay of Monson's 96th Foot, disbanded two years previously. The vacancy left by his departure from the 13th was then filled internally.

It was also possible for the system to work in reverse. An ambitious officer left unemployed by the disbandment of his regiment could easily return to the active list by exchanging with a 'purchase' officer who wanted to retire but also to retain his links with the Army and draw Half Pay. Ordinarily an officer who sold his commission was expected to provide for himself out of the proceeds and could not subsequently purchase another commission. However, if he exchanged with a Half Pay officer – as in the case of Captains Urquhart and Campbell – he was entitled to receive the difference in value between his existing

Breastplate, 80th (Royal Edinburgh Volunteers), c. 1780 – brass with a very high copper content. Despite their 'Royal' title the 80th bore yellow facings, and were disbanded at the end of the American War. (NMS)

Lieutenant Robert Hamilton Buchannan, 21st Royal North British Fuziliers, 1776–9: an important portrait depicting a number of interesting features, the most notable being the absence of a sword. Judging by a number of paintings, orders and memoirs a surprising number of officers seem to have considered swords an unnecessary encumbrance. The grenadier cap bears the universal pattern plate without the distinctive badge authorised for this regiment in the 1768 Warrant, although the small breastplate has an indistinguishable circular feature on it which is most probably a thistle within the circle of St. Andrew. (NMS)

commission and the less valuable Half Pay equivalent, as well as drawing his pension. Moreover, should he then choose to do so, there was nothing to prevent his returning to active duty at a later stage.

In fact, an officer who had retired on to the Half Pay at the end of one war and returned to active service at the beginning of another could usually expect to be offered a free step in rank if he was willing to recruit himself a company or battalion.

Far from being aristocratic dilettantes, most British officers were highly competent professionals – a fact amply testified by the plethora of drill manuals and other military works which appeared throughout the 18th century. Strategy seems to have been little studied, except by reference to the obligatory classics, but minor tactics clearly excited passionate interest. The results were plain for all to see; and as the Jacobite Adjutant General, John William O'Sullivan, remarked in 1746: 'there are no troops in the world but what they overcome in fireing, if yu don't go in Sword in hand, or the bayonett among them.'

THE SOLDIERS

Not until 1782 were regiments formally associated with particular localities; in theory, apart from the restrictions imposed on regiments on the Irish Establishment, all regiments were permitted to find recruits anywhere within the British Isles and British North America.

The Industrial Revolution and the coincidental unemployment created by agrarian reform did not begin to swell the ranks of the urban poor to any notable degree until towards the end of the century, and consequently most of the Army's recruits were still countrymen or discontented tradesmen picked up at markets or hiring fairs. In 1740 the Duke of Argyll claimed, perhaps a little too harshly, that they were for the most part men who were 'too stupid or too infamous to learn or carry on a Trade'; but their

recorded behaviour rarely bears out the frequently expressed contention that the army was the last refuge of the desperate and the criminal classes.

During the expedition to L'Orient in 1746, to quote just one example from amongst many, a party of grenadiers crept on their hands and knees behind a wall to rescue the badly wounded Major Samuel Bagshawe under heavy fire. Having done so they then carried him on their shoulders eleven miles through the night to safety.

The written instructions regularly issued to all recruiting parties solemnly warned them against enlisting Catholics (technically illegal, though often winked at), foreigners, boys, old men, idiots, the ruptured and the lame. There was also a certain understandable reluctance on the part of recruiting officers to entertain 'strollers, vagabonds, and tinkers', who were of course the very individuals whom magistrates were keenest to dump on the Army. Indeed, the instructions issued to recruiters for the 93rd Foot in early 1760 ruled that they should only take such men 'as were born in the Neighbourhood of the place they are Inlisted in, & of whom you can get and give a good Account'. It was not always possible or expedient to be so choosy, and in times of rapid expansion recruiters tended to be less discriminating – and never more so, perhaps, than in the period

Furred caps of the 1768 pattern. Actually belonging to the 97th Highlanders c. 1795, the cap in the centre bears the 'universal' plate used by all unbadged regiments. The cap on the left is the variant used by drummers and bears trophies of colours, drums and drumsticks. The cap on the right is the version worn by pioneers. Unlike the other two the enamel 'ground' is red rather than black, and is predictably decorated with axes and saws, the traditional tools of a pioneer. (NMS)

1793–95. Nevertheless, these and similar injunctions clearly contradict the casual view of the 18th–century British Army as some kind of penal institution.

The majority of recruits also seem to have been comparatively young men when they enlisted – ser-

The front and side views of a coat belonging to Lieutenant John Dalgleish, also of the 21st, provide a useful comparison with Buchannan's portrait. Note the elaborate design of the epaulettes. Company officers normally wore a single epaulette on the right shoulder, but fusiliers and grenadiers wore two. (NMS)

Ruthven Barracks, near Kingussie, Scotland. Built in 1721 as a patrol base for troops guarding General Wade's Highland roads, it was gallantly defended against the Jacobites by

Sergeant Molloy and 12 men of the 55th Foot in 1745/46. Molloy was subsequently commissioned. (Author's Collection)

vice generally being at that time for life, or in other words until such time as a man was too 'crazy' or worn out to soldier any longer. Out of the 67 men who joined Captain Hamilton Maxwell's company of the 71st Highlanders during the winter of 1775–76 the oldest was aged 40, while two others, including a sergeant, were 38 and 39 respectively; but the overwhelming majority of his recruits were aged between 17 and 25 years – in other words, most of them were young men who had not yet settled down to a trade or calling, and were without family or other ties.

Not all soldiers were given the opportunity to volunteer. In 1745 the Jacobite emergency produced two hasty Acts encouraging magistrates to impress all 'able-bodied men who do not follow or exercise any lawful calling or employment' and 'all such able-bodied, idle and disorderly persons who cannot upon examination prove themselves to exercise and industriously follow some lawful trade or employment, or to have some substance sufficient for their support and maintenance'. These Acts were naturally greeted by the local authorities as a heaven-sent opportunity to dispose of all the rogues and vagabonds which recruiting parties normally declined to entertain. Since £3 per man was paid into the vestry account in order to provide for any dependants which these reluctant heroes might leave behind as a burden on the parish, they were generally referred to as 'Vestry Men'.

Quite unwanted by the Army and of decidedly dubious military value, they were undoubtedly responsible for some of the few verifiable atrocities which followed the suppression of the 'Forty-Five' rebellion; many of them were also relegated to the despised but undemanding job of prisoner-handling, before being discharged as swiftly as possible. Notwithstanding this rather unhappy experience, similar Acts appeared during the later crises of 1755–57 and 1778–79.

Occasionally prisoners of war might also be induced to enlist in the British service. Hundreds of captured Jacobites were given the opportunity to 'volunteer' for service in West Indian garrisons, or with Boscawen's Independent Companies, recruited for an expedition to Pondicherry in 1747. A good many of this particular batch of recruits 'volunteered' from amongst the prisoners belonging to the French Army's Irish Brigade. Most of those captured at Culloden were either summarily dealt with as deserters from the British Army, or, if considered to be French subjects, were repatriated as prisoners of war. However, those captured at sea en route to join the rebels were treated slightly differently. 'Frenchmen' were repatriated under the existing cartel or exchange agreement, but those found to have run from the British Army or otherwise considered to be British subjects were drafted into units serving in the West Indies, including Dalzell's unfortunate 38th Foot. Two of Boscawen's companies were specifically earmarked to be raised from Jacobite prisoners in Scotland; but prisoners held in England, including members of the ill-fated Manchester Regiment, were also drafted into the other companies.

These were not the only prisoners to find themselves donning red coats. Other examples were to be found in the American War, and an Edinburgh man named James Aytoun who enlisted into the 58th Foot in 1786 mentions a comrade named Belair, who was 'a native of France and had served in a Spanish regiment called Walloons. He was one of the men who was saved from the Spanish sunk ships at the siege of Gibraltar. A great many of these prisoners inlisted into British regiments'.

Apart from the enlistment of prisoners, whether voluntarily or otherwise, the British Army had very few foreigners serving in its ranks during the 18th century. Negro slaves were sometimes enlisted as drummers, and German musicians turn up from time to time, but few appear amongst the rank and file. The muster rolls of the Royal Artillery also reveal Dutchmen and Germans, but otherwise the great majority of foreign recruits appear to have been officers.

There was certainly no permanent equivalent of the Dutch Army's Scots Brigade, or of the large German, Swiss and Irish contingents in the French and Spanish armies. This was in part a reflection of the prevailing view in society that if soldiers were a bad thing, then foreign soldiers must consequently be worse. Prejudice aside, however, financial constraints were just as effective: it was difficult enough persuading Parliament to pay for British soldiers. (The 60th Royal Americans did, however, include substantial numbers of Swiss and German officers and men. Nevertheless, even from the outset Scots, English and Irish officers and soldiers also served in the unit, and it was not officially recognised as a foreign corps.)

In wartime the situation was sometimes slightly different. Hessian regiments were employed in Scotland in 1746, again in southern England during the invasion scare at the outset of the Seven Years' War, and most famously during the American War. However, although these contract units obviously came under the direct command of British officers, and were often supplied and paid by British commissaries, they remained very much a part of the Hessian, Brunswick, or whatever other army might have hired them out, and returned home again as soon as hostilities were concluded.

Soldier's breastplate, 42nd Highlanders, c. 1779. Originally Highland units carried both cartridge box and bayonet on a narrow belt around the waist, but the replacement of the belly-box some time during the American War with a larger cartridge box slung more conventionally on the right hip also necessitated the introduction of a new bayonet belt slung over the right shoulder. This rather crude copper breastplate appears to have been a locally produced item. (Author's Collection)

WEAPONS AND TACTICS

Linear tactics predominated throughout the 18th century, and centred around the application of firepower. The noted British superiority in this field, alluded to by O'Sullivan, can principally be attributed to three factors.

The first was the employment of the platoon firing system. Before 1764 the administrative organisation of the battalion into companies and the tactical organisation into platoons and grand divisions were quite separate – although the grenadiers were always left to their own devices. Immediately before a battalion went into action the major and his assistant the adjutant rode along the line telling the men off into platoons and grand divisions. The precise organisation varied according to the number of men present and fit for duty, and sometimes upon the major's interpretation of the drill book; but essentially the idea was to divide the battalion as evenly as possible into four grand divisions, each made up of about three, four or five platoons – about 30 men being reckoned to be the optimum for each platoon.

In 1764 the process was considerably simplified by formally dividing each company into two platoons and pairing off the eight battalion companies into four divisions, thus harmonising tactical and administrative organisation.

When the command was given to open fire only the first platoon in each of the grand divisions did so, being followed by the second, which in turn was followed by the third and so on. In theory, by the time the last platoon in the division had fired the first had reloaded and was ready to begin the cycle anew. In practice, what began as a well-conducted sequence soon degenerated into a free-for-all, with first each platoon and ultimately each individual loading and firing at will; but the effect was the same – a relentless meat-grinding barrage of fire.

The second factor was the general lack of proper training facilities for complete battalions and larger formations, which meant that such training as was carried out necessarily centred around the manual exercise (basic weapon handling) and platoon firing to a far greater degree than on the Continent.

Corporal, Warley Camp, 1778: after de Loutherberg. Identified as a soldier of the 25th, he lacks that regiment's bastion-shaped lace loops, although the foliage in his hat may recall its service at Minden – in the 18th-century laurel leaves or, failing that, any other available greenery seems to have been worn in preference to the 'Minden Roses' of more modern times. (Author's Collection)

Thirdly, and not to be despised, was the acknowledged superiority of the Land Pattern firelock and its derivatives, commonly known as the 'Brown Bess'. This flintlock musket had a calibre of 0.75 in. (12 bore) firing a 1¼-ounce soft lead ball. Initially it had a barrel length of 46 in., but this was officially superseded in 1768 by the 42 in.-barrelled Short Land Pattern. Although contemporary French fire-arms are generally held up as being of a superior quality, testimony from British officers is unanimous in stressing the real edge which they reckoned to have from the heavier weight of ball – though just as important, perhaps, was the equally superior quality of British gunpowder, which was made using salt-petre imported from Bengal towards the end of the century by the East India Company.

A preoccupation with the lethal application of firepower may also have encouraged the development of light infantry. This was probably in part a result of North American experience, but it also very largely reflected other European practices. Generally such troops were expected to serve as a lightly equipped striking force, capable of undertaking rapid marches and redeployments, rather than actually

Light infantrymen of the 69th Foot: after de Loutherberg, 1778. The rather odd-looking headgear has sometimes been interpreted as a cut-down hat, but this drawing fairly clearly shows it to be the ordinary stiff leather light infantry cap with the addition of a small peak at the front to shade the eyes, and a larger flap at the back capable of being turned down to protect the neck in bad weather. The bullet bag and large powder horn were found to be of little use during the American War and were officially discarded afterwards. The soldier on the right also appears to have a tomahawk case – another item discarded during the post-war reorganisations (Author's Collection)

serving as battlefield skirmishers. They were certainly encouraged to make use of cover when it was available, and good marksmanship was stressed, but there were few formal light infantry drills as such. If it came to a fight in the open they generally seem to have formed up shoulder to shoulder like everyone else.

The introduction of light companies in infantry battalions was, it is true, originally intended to provide some flexibility; but in practice the light companies were almost invariably creamed off, together with the grenadiers, to form provisional 'flank battalions'. If numbers permitted – as during the principal campaigns of the American War – separate battalions of light infantry and grenadiers might be formed, but otherwise the two categories would simply be brigaded together in mixed units. In practice this made little difference since their actual, as opposed to theoretical, roles were virtually identical.

Despite the existence of official drill books, prior to the adoption of Dundas's famous manual in 1792 there was little consistency in their interpretation, and most regiments had their own ways of doing things. Indeed, the satirical *Advice to Officers* published ten years earlier cheerfully recommended its readers: 'When promoted to the command of a regiment from some other corps, show them that they were all in the dark before, and overturning their whole routine of discipline, introduce another as different as possible.'

Inefficient though this might seem, it did not prevent British infantrymen from proving themselves to be the best in the world. Indeed, the very lack of rigid consistency highlights the fact that far from being a stiffly pipeclayed automaton, the British soldier of the 18th century was tough, resourceful and above all adaptable.

THE PLATES

A: Scotland
A1: Grenadier, 21st Foot; Culloden, 1746
The two 'Additional' companies were recruiting for this regiment in Scotland when the last Jacobite rising began, and it was also one of three regular Scottish battalions to fight at Culloden on 16 April 1746. Fusilier Edward Linn afterwards wrote a vivid account of the battle in a letter to his wife:

'They fired 2 pieces of Cannon first upon us; we Returned them 6, & so they came up very boldly & very fast all in a Cloud together, sword in hand; they fired their pieces & flung them away, but we gave them so Warm a Reception that we kept a Continuall Closs ffireing upon them with our Small Arms; besides 2 or 3 of our Cannon gave them such a Closs with grape shott which galled them very much & so in ane instant they Retreated. . . . I never Saw a Small field thicker of Dead.'

Coats were worn with lapels buttoned over and skirts unhooked at Culloden – Linn recalled how he and his comrades kept their firelocks dry with their coat skirts. White gaiters were reserved for peacetime parade grounds and on campaign grey, black or brown were worn instead – a Morier painting of Cumberland at Culloden very clearly depicts the 13th Foot wearing black. As a grenadier this man is distinguished from lesser mortals by the now ornamental matchcase on his cartridge box sling, and by his elaborately embroidered mitre cap. As fusiliers all ranks of this regiment should have worn them, but in practice the battalion companies may have worn cheaper tricornes on active service. Most regiments simply bore the royal cypher on the front of their caps, but as a Royal regiment the 21st were permitted a badge, in this case the thistle enclosed within a strap bearing the old Scottish motto NEMO ME IMPUNE LACESSIT. The caps worn by the battalion company men, as depicted in the 1742 Cloathing Book, differed slightly from that shown in that the white horse of Hanover was replaced on the little flap by another thistle.

A2: Sergeant Terry Molloy, 55th Foot; Ruthven Barracks, 1745
In August 1745 General Sir John Cope left Ruthven Barracks, near Kingussie, in the charge of 'a very good Serjeant and twelve Men'. On the 29th Sergeant Molloy's little command was surrounded by a force of rebels which he estimated to be upwards of 300 strong; but upon being summoned to surrender he stoutly replied that 'I was too old a Soldier to surrender a Garrison of such Strength, without bloody noses'. At this point the rebels 'threatened hanging me and my Men for Refusal [but] I told them I would take my Chance'. He then proceeded to beat off the assault which followed; and Cope after-

Scotland 1745/6
1: Grenadier, 21st Foot;
   Culloden, 1746
2: Sergeant Molloy, 55th Foot;
   Ruthven Barracks, 1745
3: Private, 64th Highlanders;
   Culloden, 1746

A

North America and the Caribbean
1: Private, 2/Royals; Havana, 1762
2: Private, 44th Foot; Monongahela, 1755
3: Private, 60th Foot; Niagara, 1759

B

Europe
1: Corporal, Battalion Company, 5th Foot; Wilhelmstal, 1762
2: Corporal Todd, 12th Foot, 1761
3: Lieutenant William Bannatyne, 13th Foot; Gibraltar, 1762

Light Infantry
1: Private, 85th Royal Volunteers, 1760
2: Officer, 90th Light Infantry, 1762
3: Private, 119th Light Infantry, 1762

D

25th Foot, Minorca
1: Grenadier, 1770
2: Private, Summer Guard Order, 1771
3: Private, Highland Company, 1771

E

1768 Regulations
1: Lieutenant John Dalgleish, 21st Foot, 1782
2: Sergeant, Light Company, 5th Foot, 1780
3: Corporal, 26th Foot (Cameronians), 1780

F

North America
1: Marksman, 21st Foot; Ticonderoga, 1777
2: Private, 40th Foot; Germantown, 1777
3: Private, 42nd Highlanders; Halifax, 1784

G

1/Royals, Caribbean, 1790's
1: Lieutenant John Urquhart,
 San Domingo, 1794
2: Grenadier, San Domingo, 1794
3: Sergeant Major George Edington,
 Jamaica, 1793

H

wards passed his report on to the Secretary of State for Scotland with a recommendation that Molloy 'be made an officer for his gallant behaviour'. It is pleasant to record that he is next heard of as Lieutenant Molloy, although by that time a second attack in February, this time with artillery support, had forced his surrender on very good terms.

Sergeant Molloy is depicted in his regimentals, with the gaiters left off – a common practice in barracks. As a Sergeant he would normally carry a halberd, though he was undoubtedly using a firelock on 29 August. Nevertheless, he is still distinguished by plain white lace on his uniform and a worsted sash around his waist. As it would obviously have been impossible for him to obtain an officer's regimentals while at the barracks his promotion was probably marked simply by shifting the sash from his waist to over his shoulder. He is depicted here wearing a hat, but as he was promoted to lieutenant rather than ensign it is possible that he and his men were grenadiers.

Originally raised in Scotland in 1741, Lee's 55th Foot became the 44th after the disbandment of Oglethorpe's 42nd and ten regiments of Marines in 1749.

A3: Private, 64th Highlanders; Culloden, 1746
Besides the three regular Scottish battalions, the British army at Culloden included a Highland unit – the Argyll Militia. Many of its company commanders were actually regular officers, and some further stiffening was found in the shape of three companies of Loudon's 64th Highlanders. One of these companies, led by Captain Colin Campbell of Ballimore, played an important part in the battle, although Ballimore himself and half a dozen of his men were killed in a rather one-sided firefight towards the end of the battle with the retreating 'French' regulars of the Royal Ecossois. After Culloden the 64th were

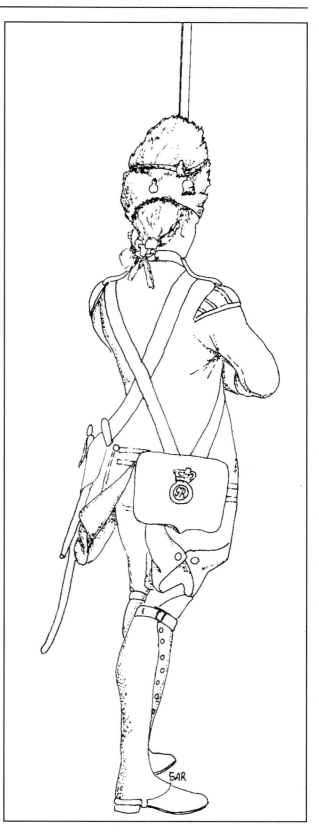

Good rear view of a grenadier of the 69th: after de Loutherberg, 1778. Note the small grenade badge on the rear of the bearskin cap, and the crowned cypher on the cartridge box flap. The cartridge box itself is also of interest in that no large buckles are visible on the sling, which is presumably directly attached instead to small buckles on the bottom of the box. The use of swords at this period is unusual and was probably confined to dress parades. (Author's Collection)

sent to Flanders, and served at Bergen op Zoom before being disbanded in 1748.

A surviving invoice from 1746 relates to the provision of a green sett with red and yellow overstripes – apparently very similar to 'Hunting MacLeod'. This reconstruction, however, is based on two surviving portraits of officers and what looks like a pair of red-tartaned Highlanders in the background of Morier's painting of the Royal Artillery at Roermond in early 1748. The red tartan appears to be the Stuart of Bute sett (see MAA 261), and particularly noteworthy is the simple red-checked waistcoat.

B: North America and the Caribbean

B1: Private, 2/Royals; Havana, 1762
The 2nd Battalion of the Royals spent most of the war in North America, but after the conquest of Canada they were redeployed to the Caribbean. This figure is taken from a painting by Domenic Serres, an artist who accompanied the expedition against Havana. The only concession to the climate appears to be the short ankle-length gaiters worn instead of the usual thigh-length variety, although 1/Royals were ordered in 1762 to wear white waistcoats, and presumably white breeches as well. Swords were still officially supposed to be worn by battalion companies, but in fact were increasingly left off as a useless encumbrance. By the 1750s the hair, which had previously been brushed up under the soldier's hat, was being tied back; but it was common in the American campaigns at least to have it cropped short, and standing orders for the 78th Highlanders specifically laid down that hair should be tied back only if it was long enough to do so.

B2: Private, 44th Foot; Monongahela, 1755
In September 1754 Halkett's 44th (formerly the 55th) were despatched to North America under General Braddock. At the time they were carried on the Irish Establishment and could only muster 350 rank and file, but a further 350 men were added through

A front view of another grenadier, again after a de Loutherberg sketch. Note the vandyke arrangement of the lace on the wings. Although as a grenadier he wears a sword, it was noted in 1784 that none had actually been carried in action during the American War and they were accordingly recommended to be dispensed with. (Author's Collection)

drafting from other battalions and by beating up for new recruits on their arrival in America. The drafted men were probably absorbed without too much difficulty – it was, after all, a common practice – but the large number of new recruits must have been more of a liability than an asset, and probably contributed to the regiment's poor performance at the Monongahela on 9 July 1755. After the battle the battalion was again brought up to strength by recruiting in the colonies, and consequently by the end of the war it was to all intents and purposes an American regiment.

This figure is based upon General Braddock's entirely sensible instructions issued before beginning his fateful march. The usual red wool breeches and waistcoat were replaced by cooler linen ones, and most items of equipment – belts, pouches and swords, were left in store.

B3: Private, 60th Foot; Niagara, 1759

As an alternative to the expensive and inefficient process of deploying regiments from the English and Irish Establishments across the Atlantic, tentative attempts were made in the middle of the 18th century to create an American Establishment. General Oglethorpe raised the 42nd in England in 1738 for service in his colony of Georgia, and at the end of the following year Colonel Spotwood received letters of service for the 43rd, this time to be raised in America. In 1744 and 1745 two New England regiments were added, the 65th and 66th. The 43rd (better known as Gooch's) were disbanded as early as 1743, but the others survived until 1748. However, the two New England regiments were re-raised in 1754 as the 50th and 51st respectively. Neither, unfortunately, survived the capture of Fort Oswego in 1756, and they were formally disbanded on 25 December 1756. In the meantime letters of service for the four battalions of the 62nd, later 60th Royal American Regiment, were issued on 25 December 1755.

In May 1757 Colonel Prevost recommended that as their service would very largely be in the woods they should wear a ranger-style uniform with a short jacket, simple kilt, Indian leggings and a stiff leather cap – a 'bonnet l'Allemand' as he called it. This uniform can be seen worn by two soldiers in the background of a painting of Sir William Johnson, head of the Indian Department. Neither man wears a kilt, but their unlaced coats have been cropped short, *mitasses* or Indian leggings are worn in place of gaiters, and they have black leather caps bearing the Royal cypher.

C: Europe
C1: Corporal, Battalion Company, 5th Foot; Wilhelmstal, 1762

This figure, largely based on a watercolour sketch by Sandby, illustrates how the basic infantry uniform was evolving. He is distinguished as a corporal by the looped 'knot' of white worsted tape behind his right shoulder. Unlike the similar knots or aiguilettes worn by officers and some cavalrymen, the corporal's knot appears to have originated in the extra skein of slow match issued to corporals of musketeers during the 17th century.

The old duffle-bag-type knapsack, virtually unchanged since the days of the Great Civil War, has now been replaced by a rectangular one, worn square on the back. The gaiters are also quite different from those worn in the 1740s, being made of waterproofed black linen with stiff leather tops. Red breeches were still prescribed for non-Royal regiments, but increasingly white or off-white cloth or linen ones were being worn instead, since they were more comfortable and much easier to keep clean. This widespread practice would soon be sanctioned for all regiments by the Royal Warrant of 1768.

The bearskin cap being worn by this battalion company soldier was an unofficial distinction peculiar to the 5th Foot. At Wilhelmstal on 24 June 1762 they forced the crack Grenadiers de France and Grenadiers Royaux to surrender, and promptly celebrated the victory by appropriating their fur caps. They also took a colour which somehow failed to get handed in to the proper authorities, and was paraded ever after (despite official disapproval) as a third or 'Drummer's Colour' – a tradition still maintained by the regiment today, although the original trophy, sadly, perished in a fire long ago.

C2: Corporal Todd, 12th Foot, 1761

Each infantry battalion had a pioneer section comprising a corporal and eight men, made up of one man from each company except the grenadiers. In addition to their ordinary infantry equipment they carried axes and saws, and wore russet leather aprons. In 1768 the cloth forage cap depicted here was ordered to be replaced by a leather cap trimmed with fur, probably not unlike those worn by the Highland Company of the 25th – see Plate E3; but by the 1790s they generally had grenadier caps with distinctive plates.

A notable pioneer was Corporal Todd of the 12th Foot, who left an interesting journal of his service with the army in Germany. On 18 November 1761 he and some of his men were taken prisoner by the French while cutting wood, and no fewer than seventeen pages of his journal are devoted to the nine days which he spent in captivity before being exchanged on the 27th. On the whole he and his men were treated reasonably well, but they had to contend with some determined attempts to entice them into joining the French army's Irish Brigade. Ten ducats a man and rapid promotion were offered, but Todd and his pioneers refused to budge, even after a heated exchange which ended when one of the Irish 'drew his sword and made a lunge at me and cut me over the eye in a shocking manner'.

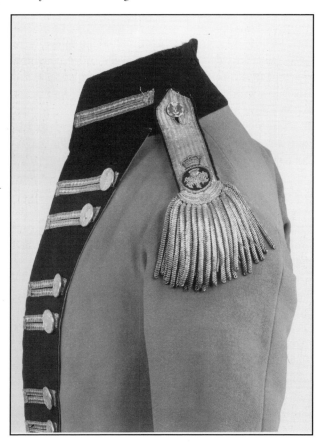

Ivory-hilted dirk marked up to an officer of the 72nd Highlanders, post 1785. Such dirks were popular secondary or 'undress' weapons in many units, but it is interesting to find this particular style carried in a Highland regiment. (NMS)

Another coat worn by John Dalgleish, while serving in the 21st c. 1790. The embroidered button loops of the earlier coat have been replaced by gold braid, and the epaulette has altered quite markedly, though it still retains the regiment's thistle badge. (NMS)

C3: Lieutenant William Bannatyne, 13th Foot; Gibraltar, 1762

William Bannatyne was a typical example of that class of officer characterised by a contemporary as private gentlemen 'without the advantage of birth and friends'. Born at Dores near Inverness in 1738, he was the son of a Presbyterian minister. His elder brother Robert served in the East India Company's Madras Army with some distinction before his death at Conjeveram in 1759; and his stepbrother, Forbes MacBean (another minister's son) commanded a battery at Minden and died a general. One of his sisters married an Army officer, and he himself married the daughter of one.

Despite its strategic importance Gibraltar remained a backwater throughout the Seven Years' War, and Bannatyne therefore found no opportunity for rapid advancement. Entering Pulteney's 13th Foot as an ensign on 3 January 1756 at the age of 17½, he obtained his Lieutenancy on 1 August 1759, but was still a lieutenant when he transferred on to the Half-Pay of Monson's 96th Foot at the beginning of September 1765.

The Gibraltar garrison was normally renowned for its spit and polish, but some concessions must have been made to the climate, for a 1766 inspection (by which time they had returned home) revealed that the 13th were already wearing white waistcoats and breeches, and had white linings to their coats instead of the required philemot yellow facing colour. Gaiters were normally worn by infantry officers on parade, but as adjutant, a post which he held from 29 September 1760 until his retirement, Lieutenant Bannatyne was required to be mounted and therefore wore boots.

D: Light Infantry
D1: Private, 85th Royal Volunteers, 1760

Inspired by the exploits of the Croats and Pandours in the Imperial service and their opponents and imitators in France and Germany, Britain too raised a number of regiments of light infantry during the Seven Years' War. The 85th, which took part in the successful Belle Isle expedition, was one of the earliest, and this reconstruction is based on both a contemporary drawing and a report of an inspection carried out at Newcastle upon Tyne on 10 March 1760:

'The officers and men had swords, the officers armed with fuzees, and have cross buff belts. They wear their sashes round the waist. . . . Uniform a red coat without lapels, with blue cuffs and capes, silver

Gilt and ivory hilt of the elegant spadroon. This infantry officer's sword is often said to have been introduced in 1786, but portraits show it carried during the later stages of the American War. (Author's Collection)

loops lined white – double breasted short waistcoats of white cloth and breeches of the same – hats cocked in the manner of King Henry VIII with a plume of white feathers. The arms much lighter than those of the infantry. Officers and men have hangers – the men short but young – accoutrements new, pouch belt much narrower than what is used by the infantry, the waistbelt worn across the shoulder. The men have red coats without lapels, blue cuffs and capes with white loops lined white – double breasted short waistcoats of white cloath, breeches of the same – hats cocked in the manner of King Henry VIII with a narrow white lace, and plume of white feathers, no white or black gaiters but a black leather gaiter which comes half way up the leg.'

The firelock was presumably the 0.67 cal. Light Infantry Carbine first set up in 1758. Curiously the drawing shows what at first appears to be an elegant walking stick, but given the continental influences this is much more likely to be a *Jäger*-style aiming rest.

D2: Officer, 90th Light Infantry, 1762

Although the 85th sported rather rakish hats, most British light infantrymen wore caps or helmets of

some description. This figure is based upon a portrait by Reynolds of Lieutenant Dan Holroyd, killed at Havana in 1762. This particular style of cap, with minor variations, was to be one of the most popular. Holroyd's coat is also interesting. Although conventional enough in having prominent lapels, albeit negligently fastened as seems to have been the fashion, the cuffs are much smaller than usual and cut in light dragoon style. Reynolds neglected to depict Holroyd's lower legs, but it is likely that the 90th's officers wore short ankle-length gaiters on Cuba.

The choice of a spontoon for a light infantry officer is at first sight surprising since it was much more usual to find them equipped with fusils or 'fuzees'; but there was actually a good case for insisting that an officer should devote all his attention to leading his men rather than becoming involved personally in the firefight.

D3: Private, 119th Light Infantry, 1762

While the uniform and equipment of the 85th was clearly based upon that worn by German *Jägers*, one of Morier's paintings shows that the short-lived 119th wore a curious uniform which, with the exception of the helmet, was very largely copied from the *Jägers*' opponents, the Croats in Imperial service. The classically styled helmet was the most distinctive feature, but perhaps rather more noteworthy are the white Hungarian breeches or pantaloons and ankle boots. The pike is another indicator that the commanding officer, Colonel Hon. Charles Fitzroy, was influenced by the practices of the Austrian *Grenztruppen*. The pike used by the latter had a small hook set in the side in order to serve as an aiming rest as well as a useful defence against cavalry. That carried by the 119th, however, was a simple staff on the end of which could be 'fixed' a fairly long sword-bayonet. The hilt of this sword was a simple tube which slotted on to the end of the staff, but it is not

Officer's breastplate, 1st or Royal Regiment. Gilt with silver beading and star, this masterpiece of the jeweller's art is unlikely to have been worn in action. The thistle badge was peculiar to officers of the regiment; rankers had St. Andrew in *the centre of the collar and no crown. In 1799 the British Military Library noted: 'The ornaments on the breastplate being variously arranged to denote the Battalion.' This example is thought to be from the 1st Battalion. (NMS).*

clear from Morier's painting whether it was also capable of being fixed on to the firelock.

A set of drawings in the Royal Collection, dated to about 1770, shows a slightly different uniform for a light infantry unit – perhaps the projected light companies – with ordinary gaiters and no lapels on the coat, although the helmet appears very similar to this one. The light infantrymen in the drawings are armed with half-pikes or spontoons, but while Morier depicts ordinary firelocks – presumably the 0.67 cal. Light Infantry Carbine – those shown in the drawings seem to be armed with rifles or carbines with folding 'spear' bayonets, again perhaps fired using the pike as an aiming rest.

E: 25th Foot, Minorca

The 25th (Edinburgh) Regiment is particularly well documented in two series of paintings and sketches depicting officers and men serving on Minorca in about 1770. Although the 1768 Warrant should in theory have taken effect by that time, their uniforms display some quite marked divergences from it. Some are perhaps explicable by the men wearing out their old clothing, but others appear to be unauthorised regimental distinctions.

E1: Grenadier, 1770

The grenadiers are a case in point. In theory they should have been wearing the regulation pattern bearskin cap with a black metal plate in front bearing the King's crest and motto, NEC ASPERA TERRENT. In fact two variants are shown in the paintings, neither of which conforms to this pattern. Commonest is a plain black bearskin without a plate, although two men are shown wearing the very distinctive variety seen here. Bearskin caps had been noted in inspection reports as far back as 1766 and their 'plain fronts' were remarked upon in 1768. This white metal plate may therefore have been a short-lived regimental pattern introduced after that date. At any rate a portrait of a grenadier officer named Charles Watson shows that the regulation pattern had certainly been adopted by about 1780.

Dirk carried by Lieutenant John Urquhart, 1/Royals, on San Domingo. The grip is a replacement – the original was reeded black ebony – and the blade is 8 inches long. (Author's Collection)

The grey blanket appears to be a substitute for the hussar cloak recommended by Cuthbertson for sentries, while the white garters supporting the gaiters are a regimental distinction noted as early as 1768. The red waistcoat should of course have been replaced by a white one long since; and two years after the promulgation of the 1768 regulations this man is still wearing the old pattern of regimental lace.

E2: Private, Summer Guard Order, 1771

Although it is common to portray 18th-century British soldiers sweating in their heavy red woollen coats in the hottest of climates, more sensible measures were frequently employed in practice. At the very least coats could be lined with linen or even have no lining at all; but this unusual, if not unique, white linen uniform is depicted in one of the Minorca paintings.

No bayonet belt is shown, so the soldier presumably fixed it before mounting guard and unfixed it again on returning to his quarters. The grenadiers wore a very similar jacket, distinguished only by small red square-cut wings (trimmed on the outside with regimental lace), and they still wore their fur caps – the plain variety – although they had no matchcases on the rather narrow slings of their cartridge boxes.

E3: Private, Highland Company, 1771

Anticipating the permanent creation of light companies, the 25th had a 'Highland Company'. The cap was of red lacquered leather trimmed with bearskin, but otherwise the uniform was very similar to that of the battalion companies, with both long and short gaiters being worn according to circumstances. There was in fact a feeling in many regiments that the short jackets prescribed for light infantrymen spoiled the symmetry of a battalion on parade. In this case the 'jacket' is simply an ordinary soldier's coat with cropped skirts – a recommended expedient – and the bastion-shaped lace loops prescribed for this regiment in 1768 have at last come into use.

Officers belonging to this company are shown in a large group painting wearing a very similar uniform, with short gaiters, and carrying basket-hilted broadswords suspended on white belts worn over the right shoulder. A regimental distinction which appears in a number of portraits and sketches of both officers and men of the 25th, at least until the 1790s, is the addition of white piping to the cuffs and lapels of the coat, and red piping to the waistcoat.

F: 1768 Regulations
F1: Lieutenant John Dalgleish, 21st Foot, 1782

Like William Bannatyne of the 13th Foot, John Dalgleish was a professional soldier with neither money nor influence to recommend him. Born in Fife in 1755, he was unable to purchase a commission in the British Army, and so began his career by joining one of the regiments in the Dutch Army's

76	First (or the Royal) Regt. of Foot (1st. Bat.)			
			Rank in the	
Rank.	Name.	Regiment.	Army.	
Colonel - -	Lord Adam Gordon	9 May 1782	Gen.	12 Oct. 91
Lieut. Colonel -	Francis Dundas	31 Mar. 1787	Col.	12 Oct. 93
Major - -	Jeffly Watfon Green	18 July 1791		
Captain	William Duncan	29 Sept. 1785	24 Dec.	77
	Francis Manunch	23 June 89		
	Christopher Morfhead	30 Jan. 90		
	W. Ja. Cockburne, Br.	9 Mar. 91		
	John Clayton Cowell	12 Sep.	24 Jan.	57
	Gordon Skelly	16 Oct. 92		
	Samuel Sinne	7 Aug. 93	26 Mar.	91
Captain Lieut. and Captain	Wm. Hutchinfon	7 Nov. 1792		
Lieutenant -	Robert Nicholfon	28 Feb. 1787		
	John Puxley	30 June		
	John Clunes	25 June 89		
	William Duncan	30 Sep.	4 Aug.	81
	James Blair	24 Mar. 91	9 Feb.	51
	Neil McKellar	30 Nov.		
	James Garth	24 Jan. 92		
	Henry Erskine	20 July		
	John Urquhart	16 Oct.		
	Hutton Rowe Spencer	1 May 93		
	David Rattray	2 do.		
Enfign -	Thomas Seaver	5 Sept. 1791		
	James Campbell	30 Nov.		
	Alexander Davifon	20 July 92		
	Hugo Robert Arnot	9 Oct.		
	Matthew Smith	16 do.		
	John Garfion	1 do.	18 Sept.	92
	J. Stewart Robertfon	15 May 93		
	—— Hed	2 do.	15 May	95
Chaplain - -	Miles Beevor	14 Feb. 1785		
Adjutant - -	Robert Nicholfon	16 Oct. 92		
Quarter-Mafter -	Alexander Davidfon	28 May 82		
Surgeon - -	John Wright	13 Mar. 93		

Agent, Meffrs. Meyrick, Parliament Street.

Officers of the 1st Battalion, Royal Regiment – better known as the Royal Scots – in the Army List for 1794. Published annually, the List was (and still is) an invaluable 'who's who', recording not only the names of all the officers serving in the Army but also their dates of seniority. (Author's Collection)

Scots Brigade in 1774, before eventually obtaining a lieutenant's commission in the 21st Royal North British Fuziliers in 1776. Unfortunately, in the following year the 21st were amongst the regiments forced to surrender at Saratoga, and he remained a prisoner until 1780. Thereafter the rest of his career was spent in regimental duties at home and in the West Indies; he became a captain on 19 August 1789 and a major in September 1795, before retiring as lieutenant colonel in October 1797.

This figure has been reconstructed using one of two surviving coats belonging to Dalgleish and a portrait of another officer named Robert Hamilton Buchannan. As a fusilier officer he wears epaulettes on both shoulders, a distinction otherwise shared only with field officers, flank company officers and Highlanders. For the same reason he carries a fusil and, less commonly perhaps, has a bayonet for it but no sword. According to the 1768 regulations the 21st were to have the King's crest on the front plate of their bearskin caps and a thistle within the 'circle' of St. Andrew – their 'ancient badge'; but Buchannan's portrait simply shows the standard version, presumably because it proved too difficult to fit both badge and crest on to the same plate. In fact the bearskin cap was probably only worn by fusilier officers in full dress, and the ubiquitous Tarleton helmet became a popular substitute from the 1780s onwards. The 21st had leopardskin turbans on their helmets and a large silver thistle badge on the right side.

F2: Private, Light Company, 5th Foot, 1780

The 5th played an active part in the early campaigns of the American War. The flank companies fought at Lexington and Concord and the whole battalion was engaged at Bunker Hill; afterwards they formed part of the 2nd Brigade on Long Island and in the Pennsylvania campaign before being posted to the West Indies.

Despite a number of recommendations and regulations there appears, to have been no real consensus as to the best form of headgear to be worn by light infantrymen. At first a simple leather skullcap with a low front plate, like the 'bonnet l'Allemand' worn by the 60th in the 1750s, was advocated; but although examples are seen in use as late as 1790 this was generally rejected in favour of a variety of regimental patterns. This particular variant is also known to have been worn by the 9th Foot (with a Britannia badge on the front), and by a number of militia units seen at Warley Camp *c.* 1779–80. The brass crest provided protection against sword-cuts, and the peak to shade the eyes was a frequently demanded feature.

F3: Corporal, 26th Foot (Cameronians), 1780

The 26th, or Cameronians, were scattered in small detachments between Montreal, Trois Riviéres, Chambly, St. John's, Crown Point and Ticonderoga at the outbreak of the American War. It was Captain William Delaplace and 45 men of the 26th who formed the garrison of Ticonderoga when it was captured by Ethan Allen and his 'Green Mountain Boys' on 10 May 1776. The regiment did not subsequently play an important role in the war, and was eventually drafted in 1779, having spent nearly 14 years in North America.

This soldier, representing the archetypal infantryman of the American War, is dressed largely in accordance with the 1768 regulations, and armed with the 42 in. barrel Short Land Pattern firelock. His bayonet belt is now worn over the right shoulder,

Grenadier, 1st or Royal Regiment, by Edward Dayes, c. 1790. This watercolour is particularly interesting in depicting a grenadier – identified by the wings on his shoulders – wearing a cocked hat instead of a furred cap.

The old embroidered cloth grenadier cap seems to have been cheerfully worn in and out of season, but the bearskin cap which replaced it appears to have been much less popular and generally reserved for formal occasions. (NMS)

and in place of the knot formerly worn by corporals on that shoulder he wears a small white fringe on the end of a shoulder-strap as his mark of rank.

G: North America
G1: Marksman, 21st Foot; Ticonderoga, 1777
The brigading of flank companies into *ad hoc* battalions naturally deprived the parent units of their own skirmishers, and in order to cover this deficiency the practice arose of designating the best shots in each battalion company as 'marksmen' or 'flankers'. Ironically these unofficial skirmishers may sometimes have been better at their job than their counterparts in the regimental light companies, and were often creamed off in their turn. In 1776 General Burgoyne assembled a ranger unit of such marksmen under Captain Alexander Fraser of the 34th Foot, only to lose most of them at Bennington.

One man was demanded from each company for this unit. Each was to be selected for his strength, activity and marksmanship, and provided with a good firelock. It was further directed that they were to ascertain the best loads for their individual weapons and make up their own cartridges accordingly.

This figure is based upon a small group of figures in the foreground of a contemporary watercolour depicting Fort Ticonderoga. Like most light infantrymen they wear short jackets, but can be identified as marksmen by an absence of wings and the distinctive red waistcoats still worn by light company men. Also noteworthy is the fact that all the regimental lace has been stripped off their jackets. One man wearing yellow facings (perhaps of the 34th Foot) wears blue *mitasses* in place of the more usual gaiters, but the soldier in the blue facings of the 21st has buckskin leggings. All three wear peaked light infantry caps of slightly varying styles, and the marksman of the 21st has a small badge on the front of his; this is presumably his regiment's thistle within the star of St. Andrew, and probably came from the 'flap of his cartridge box. None of the caps bear a crest, but a well-known painting depicting the burial of General Fraser shows his nephew Captain Fraser with a cap surmounted by a luxuriant red mane.

G2: Private, 40th Foot; Germantown, 1777
Two important paintings by Xavier della Gatta depict men of a light infantry unit and battalion companies of the 40th Foot during the Pennyslvania campaign of 1777. Both wear substantially similar uniforms, although the 40th are distinguished by the buff facings on their cuffs (the light infantry appear to have none) and buff rather than black equipment. En route to Pennsylvania General Howe had ordered the bayonet belt to be discarded and the scabbard attached to the cartridge box sling instead, but this seems to have met with some resistance, and Gatta shows the bayonet belt still worn over the right shoulder. This may have been due in part to a

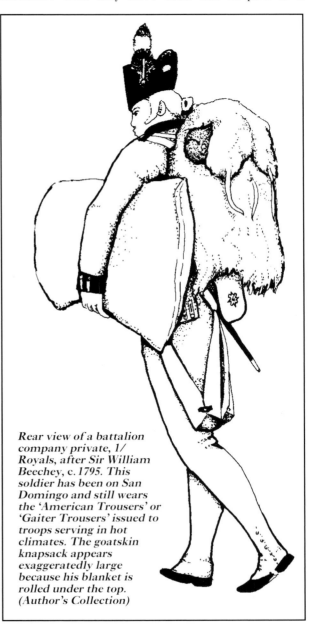

Rear view of a battalion company private, 1/Royals, after Sir William Beechey, c.1795. This soldier has been on San Domingo and still wears the 'American Trousers' or 'Gaiter Trousers' issued to troops serving in hot climates. The goatskin knapsack appears exaggeratedly large because his blanket is rolled under the top. (Author's Collection)

reluctance to part with the regimental breastplates which were now replacing the old frame buckles on this belt.

While the light infantry wear white gaiter-trousers the men of the 40th wear the usual black ankle gaiters with white stockings and breeches. The latter should have been buff, like the regiment's facings, but those depicted are presumably linen or duck alternatives worn in warm weather. Also notable are the uncocked round hats worn by both units.

G3: Private, 42nd Highlanders; Halifax, 1784

The rigours of campaigning naturally took their toll on Highland dress. As early as 1775 it was noted that broadswords were considered 'incumbrances' and had largely been abandoned in favour of bayonets (although some, perhaps just those belonging to the grenadier company, had been handed into store at Halifax as late as 8 December 1783). This figure is based upon the report of a later inspection carried out at Halifax, Nova Scotia, on 9 June 1784:

'The 42nd could not appear in their full uniform for want of plaids, etc., which the C.O. thought proper annually to dispose of during the late War, to purchase a more commodious dress for the American service, with the approbation of the Commander in Chief [presumably Sir Guy Carleton]. The regiment appeared remarkably clean dressed . . . the men had on white strong ticken trousers with short black cloth gaiters.'

This soldier still wears the old 'belt order' comprising a belly-box and bayonet worn on a narrow waist belt, but by 1784 this had very largely been superseded by a more conventional set of black leather equipment comprising a large cartridge box on the right hip and the bayonet, suspended from a shoulder belt, on the left.

H: 1/Royals, Caribbean, 1790s

The 1st Battalion of the Royals, the senior infantry regiment in the British Army, were stationed in Ireland in the 1780s; but on 20 January 1790 they embarked 349 effectives at Cork on the *Chichester* (44) for Jamaica. With a further 21 rank and file left behind as a rudimentary depot, they were fully recruited up to the Irish establishment of 370 rank and file. On embarking they reverted to the English Establishment. In consequence the agency passed from Fraser and Reed of Dublin to Messrs. Meyrick of Parliament Street, London, and the depot was then allowed to beat up for recruits in Ireland.

They remained on Jamaica for the next four years, but at the beginning of 1794 were sent to San Domingo (Haiti) and served there until February 1797.

Officer, battalion company, 1st or Royal Regiment, by Edward Dayes, 1790. Dressed for 'duty' i.e. on guard or picquet, he has gaiters in place of boots. Note the black- or dark blue-tipped white hackle in his hat. (NMS)

H1: Lieutenant John Urquhart, San Domingo, 1794

Most first commissions were obtained by purchase in peacetime but it was also possible for an aspiring officer to serve in the ranks until a non-purchase vacancy occurred. John Urquhart (1768–1848) originally enlisted as a private in 1/Royals in 1789 but obtained an Ensign's commission two years later and was subsequently promoted to Lieutenant on 16 October 1792. By the beginning of 1794 he was serving in the grenadier company and went with it to San Domingo. On 1 May he was captured after an abortive dawn attack on a fort at Bombarde, but released shortly afterwards. Subsequently he was attached to an émigré unit, Contade's Legion, before being promoted into the short-lived 106th Foot, and eventually becoming Assistant Military Secretary to the East India Company.

Besides their expensive 'regimentals' officers were advised to provide themselves with two 'frocks' or unlaced coats for everyday use, particularly on active service. Lieutenant Urquhart is depicted wearing a typical officer's campaign uniform comprising a round jacket, of the style popularised in the American War, without epaulettes or lace, and a round hat with a grenadier's white hackle. Although gaiters were supposed to be worn on parade or on duty, boots were *de rigueur* on service; the plain black boots shown are more likely to be the 'regimental' type referred to in orders than the rather soft pair worn by Captain Cowell.

Another officer of the Royals, Thomas St. Clair, describes a very similar uniform still being worn as late as 1806: 'Round hat, cockade, a small feather at the side, regimental jacket, Russia duck pantaloons, with sash and small dirk hanging by a waist belt to

Captain John Clayton Cowell, 1/Royals, after Sir William Beechey; Cowell appears to have been painted on his return from San Domingo in 1795. According to the battalion's monthly returns he was assigned to command one of the flank companies, but has only the single epaulette of a battalion company. Since he wears both his gorget and sash the soft boots may be the 'regimental' ones referred to in standing orders, but they are so clearly impractical that they are more than likely a personal affectation. Another unexplained personal foible is the tying of his sash cavalry-fashion on the right side, rather than on the left as was proper for infantry officers. (Author's Collection)

Scott sculp.t

PACIFICATION with the MAROON NEGROES.

our sides.' The regimental pattern sword carried by officers in the Royals at that time had an uncommonly heavy blade – it was virtually a broadsword – so Urquhart's decision to carry a dirk for the bush-fighting on San Domingo is entirely understandable.

H2: Grenadier, San Domingo, 1794

On 8 July 1791 it was ordered that soldiers going to the West Indies should have a red jacket buttoning as a waistcoat – i.e. a single-breasted garment – distinguished by collar, cuffs and shoulder straps of the regimental facing colour, with gaiter trousers and a round hat. No mention was made of regimental lace; but the unusual use of a button loop on the shoulder strap is shown in a sketch by Dayes, and as a grenadier this man has wings on his shoulders. The wings were of course a traditional grenadier distinction, and both they and the fur crest on the round hat are shown in contemporary illustrations of troops in the West Indies. A painting of Captain John Clayton Cowell of 1/Royals *c.* 1795 shows that this particular battalion was equipped with white goatskin knapsacks.

The Royals' grenadier company, largely made up of long-service veterans, fared quite badly in the débâcle at Bombarde on 1 May 1794, with Corporal Thomas Hammond and five men killed, five more wounded, and 16 others besides Lieutenant Urquhart taken prisoner. Despite this they continued to serve creditably, most notably in storming a battery at Fort Bizeton in March 1795.

H3: Sergeant Major George Edington, Jamaica, 1793

Promotion of meritorious NCOs was surprisingly common in the 18th-century British Army, and an Irishman named George Edington was a fine example. First appearing as an 'acting ensign' in the monthly return for 20 May 1794, he was properly commissioned on 9 September, and became adjutant a month later. The latter appointment was not an uncommon one, since former NCOs generally knew the workings of a battalion inside out; but Edington later went on to become a lieutenant on 13 May 1795, and a captain on 6 December 1798, before retiring a year later.

Although short, single-breasted jackets were prescribed for all troops serving in the West Indies there is considerable evidence that some units, including the Royals, also took their full dress regimentals with them. Indeed the Royals were generally admitted to be the 'neatest, best-looking men in Port au Prince'. This figure is therefore closely based on a contemporary print by Bunbury. Apart from the white duck gaiter-trousers he is dressed pretty well as he would have been at home. As the battalion's senior NCO he wears what is effectively an officer's 'regimentals', being distinguished only by the substitution of silver lace for gold. The white hackle with the black or dark blue tip is a regimental variant which can be seen in both Dayes' sketches and a contemporary portrait.

Recommended Reading:

Alan J. Guy, *Oeconomy and Discipline* (Manchester, 1985)

J.A. Houlding, *Fit for Service: the Training of the British Army 1715–1795* (Oxford, 1980)

H. Strachan, *British Military Uniforms 1768–96* (London, 1975)

Left: Contemporary sketch 'from the life' by Bruyas, depicting British officers on Jamaica. All wear full regimentals. The curious animal badge on the grenadier's cap appears to be the antelope of the 6th Foot. (Author's Collection)

INTRODUCTION

The organisation and character of the 18th century British Army is discussed in the first part of this study; *King George's Army 1740–1793 (1)* [MAA 285]. The purpose of this volume is to look in rather more detail at infantry uniforms, and also to cover the various auxiliary infantry formations, such as Militia, Volunteers, Marines and the troops of the East India Company.

The 18th century was marked by a steady growth in central control of the British Army and a corresponding decrease in the influence enjoyed by individual commanding officers. The most obvious sign of this process was the increasing uniformity of the clothing issued each year to the soldiers. Nevertheless, as far as those who devised the Clothing Regulations were concerned, it was a constant, and invariably quite uphill struggle to enforce compliance.

The individual soldier's entitlement to clothing during this period was laid down in 1729 and only slightly amended by subsequent regulations. According to the 1729 Warrant each infantryman was supposed to receive:

'A good full-bodied Cloth Coat, well lined, which may serve for the Waistcoat the Second Year
A Waistcoat
A Pair of good Kersey Breeches
A Pair of good strong Stockings
A Pair of good strong Shoes
Two good Shirts and Two good Neckcloths
A good strong Hat, well laced.
For the SECOND YEAR:
A good Cloth Coat, well lined, as the First Year
A Waistcoat made of the former Year's Coat
A Pair of New Kersey Breeches
A Pair of good strong Stockings
A Pair of good strong Shoes

King's Colour, Barrell's 4th Foot. Carried at Culloden, this colour was briefly taken by the Jacobites, but recaptured by the end of the battle. Lieutenant Colonel Sir Robert Rich and Ensign Brown were both badly wounded defending this colour and it bears obvious signs of damage. (Trustees of the National Museums of Scotland))

A good Shirt, and a Neckcloth
A good strong Hat, well laced
For the Fusilier Regiments, Caps once in Two Years
The new Waistcoat in the First year, is only to be given to Regiments new-raised, and to additional men, who are likewise to be furnished with Two Pair of Stockings and Two Shirts.'

Coat, waistcoat and breeches were all to be red, lined and turned up with the regimental facing colour. Royal regiments, by way of a distinction were permitted blue rather than red breeches though this privilege was not universally observed.

In 1768 the soldier's entitlement was varied slightly in that in the second and every succeeding year only a waistcoat front would be provided, the back part being made from the previous year's front (or to judge from surviving articles, any other handy

piece of material). This alteration was necessary because the 1768 Clothing Warrant had also required the replacement of the old red waistcoat and breeches with white 'small clothes'. At the same time regiments with buff facings were authorised to adopt buff small clothes. It was no longer possible therefore for old coats to be converted into waistcoats, or breeches for that matter. Such at least was the theory although mention of red breeches sometimes crops up during the subsequent American War and red waistcoats were also still being worn, perhaps unofficially for some years after 1768. Red waistcoats were also re-introduced, along with short jackets, for the newly-authorised light companies in 1771.

The 1768 Warrant also saw the official replacement of the cloth mitre cap worn by grenadiers with a black fur version. Previous to this date fur caps should only have been worn by the grenadiers of highland regiments. In actual fact the grenadiers of the 30th Foot also seem to have had them as early as 1755, while the 13th, 20th, 25th and 33rd were all reported to have been wearing them in 1766. An even more notable, or perhaps blatant case was the 5th Foot. For some time the battalion company men as well as the grenadiers defiantly wore the fur caps which they had captured from the French at Wilhelmstal in 1761.

Ironically, no sooner was the use of bearskin caps officially sanctioned than grenadiers began to become increasingly reluctant to wear caps at all except on formal parades, and even then only if they had to. All manner of excuses were advanced at inspections to explain the absence of caps. It would appear that

Private, 37th Foot, as depicted in the 1742 Cloathing Book.

This regiment was wearing a rather old-fashioned style of uniform in 1742. Particularly noteworthy are the rather large plain cuffs and an absence of lace looping on the lapels. Although the lapels and turnbacks are yellow, the regimental facing colour, the cuffs are red. All lace is plain yellow. This uniform appears to have been modernised in 1743, when a number of regiments still wearing single breasted coats were ordered to adopt lapels. By 1746, when they fought at Falkirk and Culloden, the 37th ought to have been wearing yellow cuffs of conventional style. The practice of wearing the belt on top of the coat with lapels displayed had also been abandoned by that time. Ordinarily the belt was worn under the coat in German fashion, except when the lapels were buttoned over and skirts unhooked in bad weather. (NMS)

while the old cloth pattern was shabby and lacked style, it was also well nigh indestructible, was little affected by bad weather and could at the end of the day be jammed on any old how. The new bearskin variety in comparison was less comfortable and much less robust. In 1790 an inspecting officer casting his jaundiced eye over the 3/60th noted (no doubt with a straight face) that the hair had fallen off the pioneers' bearskin caps. Instead, grenadiers were increasingly seen wearing ordinary cocked hats distinguished only by a white hackle.

There appears to have been little or no uniformity in the style of cap worn by the Light Infantry Companies. The official pattern, a leather skull cap with an upright frontlet, was evidently unpopular and a considerable number of inspection reports on regiments note that the caps were 'not regulation'. By the end of the period the Tarleton style helmet may very largely have replaced the 'Chain Cap', as it was sometimes known, although a number of regiments had their own distinctive patterns.

Corporals were at first distinguished only by a white shoulder knot on the right, made either from cord or white worsted tape, but by the 1770s this was increasingly being replaced by an epaulette with a white worsted fringe.

Sergeants also wore substantially the same uniform as the rank and file although invariably of a superior quality – the coat being much nearer to scarlet than brick red. As a further distinction all sergeants had a red worsted sash tied around the waist with a central stripe in the regimental facing colour. Further distinctions were generally governed by regimental custom, but in the best regulated corps silver lace was substituted for the usual worsted variety and silver hilted swords were also common – the latter often being bought at the sergeants' own expense. Towards the end of the period the Sergeant Major could also aspire to a silver epaulette. Whether or not canes were carried by NCOs depended very much on regimental custom and practice.

It was the colonel's responsibility to contract, through his regimental agent, for most of this clothing at the best price which he could obtain. It was actually paid for, however, out of the 'Off-Reckonings' – that portion of the annual pay due to each soldier in the battalion, over and above his 'subsistence'. It was recognised that the colonel would

Regimental Colour, Barrell's 4th Foot. Also carried at Culloden, this blue colour appears to be rather unusual in having no Union in the canton. Like the King's colour it bears a crown and sceptre in the centre, though oddly enough in this case without the lion passant on top of the crown seen on that colour. (NMS)

usually be able to make a profit or 'dividend' on the transaction and although there were occasional queries over the size of this dividend, it was generally accepted to be one of his legitimate perquisites.

A similar practice was followed by the East India Company, except that since there were no 'Colonel Proprietors' in that service the 'dividends' were split between all the field officers and captains.

In practice the colonel only provided what was called the 'Large Mounting'; that is the major items such as the coat, waistcoat and breeches. The shirt, neck-cloth or stock, pair of shoes and pair of stockings due to each soldier annually, was referred to as the 'Small Mounting' or 'Half Mounting' and could either be provided along with everything else by the colonel, or else the equivalent value might be paid or credited to the individual soldier. The various items might then be bought either by the company officers, or by the soldiers themselves.

Hard cash was also supposed to be paid, or at the very least credited to the soldier when the clothing supplied was deficient in any way.

From 1790 sergeants of regiments bound for the

West Indies were to receive compensation of four shillings and sixpence (22½p), being the difference in value between the short single-breasted jacket worn in the islands, and the fairly substantial coat normally provided. Privates and Corporals did not fare quite so well, being allowed only one shilling and ninepence (9p) in compensation, though all also received money in lieu of breeches and stockings, which were to be replaced by trousers. This money was to be 'carried to the credit of each man's accompt, and laid out for him to the best advantage, under the direction of the Colonel of his Regiment'.

In most cases this money will have been used to offset the cost of what were referred to as 'Necessaries'. These were additional items of clothing and equipment, such as gaiters, knapsacks, brushes, boot-polish, extra shirts, stockings, spare pairs of breeches and so on. A rather notable omission from the mountings and necessaries, is any official mention of underwear and in particular drawers. Since they are known to have worn them the soldiers presumably had to make their own arrangements. The only official provision of drawers was made after 1791 when a pair of flannel ones was allowed to soldiers serving in the West Indies, to wear under their thin ticken trousers at night.

Otherwise, necessaries were normally paid for by deductions from the subsistence portion of the soldier's pay although a 1792 Warrant also allowed each soldier the cost of a second pair of breeches, a pair of gaiters, and some other small items including the cost of making up a forage cap from scrap material. In any case the charges made or deducted for necessaries were normally a paper transaction since most (the knapsack being an obvious case in point) were actually provided through the quartermaster. Otherwise the individual soldier was again sometimes given a cash allowance and permitted to acquire the items himself at the best price he could find.

Fusilier, 21st Foot (Royal Scots Fusiliers), as depicted in the 1742 Cloathing Book. The cap worn by this battalion company soldier differs somewhat from the version worn by a grenadier of the regiment, as depicted by David Morier in 1748. This one has a blue front (the regiment's facing colour), the star of St. Andrew is white with a yellow collar enclosing a red thistle on a green roundel. The little flap or frontlet is also blue and bears a thistle in its natural colours. The title 'ROYAL FUZILIERS' is picked out in black on a white strip. The grenadiers, according to Morier, had a thistle encircled by a collar bearing the motto 'NEMO ME IMPUNE LACESSIT', surmounted as usual by a crown. The frontlet is red, rather than blue, and has the usual running horse device and motto 'NEC ASPERA TERENT'. The tuft on the top was of mixed white and blue threads. (NMS)

Greatcoats were not provided, since the full skirted regimental coat was in effect a greatcoat. Bennet Cuthbertson, writing in 1768, recommended however that a 'proper number of Huzzar-cloaks' should be provided for sentries. These had large falling capes or hoods and he recommended that blue 'is the most lasting colour'. Company numbers were to be marked in red under the hood. Practice obviously varied from regiment to regiment. Cuthbertson was serving in the 5th who clearly had more than one watchcoat per company. The 37th on the other hand had only a single watchcoat per company, though it was at least of the 'hussar kind' and made of blue cloth turned up with red. Perhaps more typical was the 54th Foot. When the clothing of five companies was lost in Long Island Sound in 1781, it included 52 watch coats – 10 per company.

The clothing warrants proceeded on the assumption that coats, waistcoats and breeches would require to be replaced annually – given ordinary wear and tear. However most regiments very sensibly retained the old clothing as long as possible in order that the new clothing could be reserved for inspections and other formal parades.

It was also customary during the 18th century for the new clothing to be issued in time to be properly fitted to the soldier and worn for the first time on the king's birthday parade in the summer – officially 4 June. Obviously this was not always possible during wartime and considerable delays were often experienced in providing new clothing to regiments in foreign parts.

Some regiments in the West Indies seem to have gone for years without a proper clothing issue. The most notorious case was the 38th Foot, exiled to the Caribbean for 59 years between 1706–65. In March 1745 the Governor of the Leeward Islands complained: '. . . from the distance between one clothing and another, which amounts at most to three clothings in four years, the men now, instead of being tolerably clothed are in rags, most of them bear [sic] headed, recruits in ragged sea frocks, trousers and not a cartouch box among the latter, as some of the others, not a sword in the whole regiment'.

The regimental colonel, Major General Robert Dalzell, was eventually called to account for this state of affairs, but it was by no means unique and James Aytoun of the 30th Foot, serving on Dominica in 1788–91, complained that the regiment had not received its clothing regularly for several years.

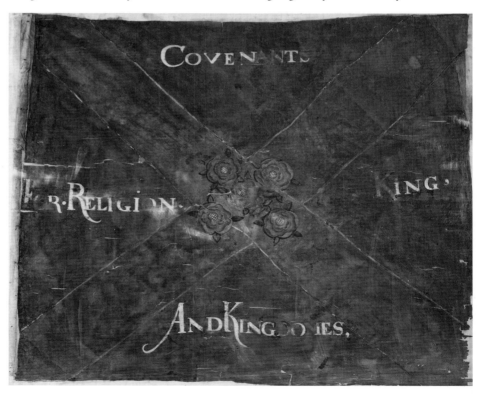

Advocate's Colour'; this relic of the Great Civil War of the 1640s and 1650s was apparently carried by the loyalist Edinburgh Volunteers at the battle of Falkirk in 1746. It is blue with a white saltire, five red roses in the centre (originally denoting the 5th Captain's company of an unidentified regiment) and gold lettering. (NMS)

The West Indies

Prior to the American War there was little concession made to the climate in which the soldier was expected to serve. Uniforms for warmer regions were normally lined with linen rather than wool and if at all possible linen small clothes were also substituted for wool. Beyond that, further modifications were left to the discretion of officers on the spot. Discarding the waistcoat was one option, wearing canvas smocks or sea-frocks as the 38th did was another. The 25th Foot wore a white linen uniform for a time when they were stationed on Minorca but that appears to be unique, although it is quite possible that other units in the Minorca garrison had similar clothing.

The lack of proper tropical clothing was not necessarily as short-sighted as might at first appear. There is evidence that the climate was generally colder in the 18th century although the tropics can still be very cold indeed at night.

Two well-known paintings by an artist named Gatta do show what appears to be a special uniform worn by troops in Pennsylvania in the summer of 1777. All wear single breasted red jackets, some with breeches and others with the increasingly popular gaiter-trousers, also known as American trousers or mosquito trousers. Whether this dress was an experiment or a widely used alternative to the regulation uniform is unknown, but it was evidently successful, for in 1790 this clothing was officially adopted for all troops serving in the West or East Indies.

Nevertheless, it is clear both from the instructions regarding the clothing to be issued to recruits bound for the Indies and contemporary descriptions that many regiments serving overseas managed to take their full regimentals with them as well as the prescribed tropical clothing, in order to make a suitable impression on important occasions.

Recruit clothing

The policy on clothing recruits varied from regiment to regiment. Most units carried a certain amount of surplus clothing for this purpose – although too large a surplus might bite into the colonel's expected dividends. It was evidently the practice in at least some units to issue recruits with a very basic suit of 'frock' clothing which would serve until the next annual issue. This usually appears to have consisted of the Small Mounting, plus a pair of breeches, and a coat or jacket devoid of the expensive regimental lace. No doubt second hand and cast-off clothing was also used for this purpose.

The Standing Orders for the 70th Foot in September 1788 laid down that:

> 'All soldiers enlisted between 4th June, and the 4th of December, are to be entitled and receive their full complement of clothing. etc.
> All inlisted between the 4th of December, and the 4th of March, are to be entitled to a coat, breeches and hat.
> All between the 4th of March, and 4th of June are to be entitled to a jacket and hat only.
> All recruits inlisted at any period of the year, are always, upon joining the Regiment, to be furnished with jackets'.

John Calcraft (1726–72). Perhaps one of the most famous of all the 18th century regimental agents, Calcraft began his career as a deputy paymaster under the Duke of Cumberland in 1745 and eventually had no fewer than 63 regiments of the line, 16 independent companies, two fencible regiments and four militia regiments on his books at the close of the Seven Years War. The end of hostilities saw this number reduced by half and in 1765 the day-to-day running of the Agency passed to his sometime clerk James Meyrick. (Author's collection)

A view of the ditch and the main gate, Fort George Ardersier.

Since these jackets did not form part of the official mountings they were presumably supplied at regimental expense. It is not clear, however, whether these were new garments or cut down from old coats as the same Standing Orders laid down a set of standard prices for tailoring which included a charge for altering old coats into jackets.

Although a full-length coat remained the army's official uniform until 1797, there was an increasing tendency during and after the American War to replace this with some form of short jacket.

Recruits passing through the depot at Chatham, en route for battalions stationed abroad in the 1790s, were ordered to be issued with a single breasted jacket, distinguished by a collar, cuffs and shoulder straps in the regimental facing colour, a pair of gaiter trousers and a round hat, unless the appropriate colonel specifically ordered the man to be given his full clothing.

PERSONAL EQUIPMENT

Accoutrements included a buff leather belt which until 1768 supported a sword and a bayonet. In theory this was worn around the waist and until about 1743 was invariably worn over the coat. After that date infantrymen seem to have picked up the continental practice of wearing it under the coat except in bad weather. By 1768, with the sword largely abandoned an unofficial practice had grown up of wearing the belt slung over the right shoulder and across the body instead. As usual this eventually received official sanction and as a result the old open frame buckle became replaced by a rectangular or oval 'breastplate' bearing the regimental number, badge or title according to taste.

Slung over the left shoulder was another belt supporting a 'cartouche' or cartridge box. Both items

Personal kit was carried in a knapsack which in the early period was a cow-hide duffle-bag slung on a single strap over the right shoulder. By the 1760s this had generally been replaced by a variety of rectangular styles worn square on the back by means of a strap over each shoulder. Goatskin knapsacks were popular, but the price allowed by the government was based on the cost of the more practical canvas 'folding' style.

Other equipment, such as water canteens and haversacks was provided at government expense only on active service. On 22 February 1793 the 'Camp Necessaries' for a battalion of 10 companies were laid down to be:

12 Bell Tents
12 Camp Colours
20 Drum Cases
10 Powder Bags [presumably for company reserve ammunition]
142 Hatchets
142 Tin Kettles
654 Wooden Canteens
654 Haversacks
142 Private tents will be issued from the Board of Ordnance and 284 blankets from Messrs. Trotter.'

Officers were expected to provide their own tents – one each for captains and one between two for subalterns – and the 12 Bell Tents, other wise known as *Bell of Arms* were for the storage of firelocks and bayonets. Each company would have had 14 'private tents' (wedge type?). The allocation of blankets seems rather meagre if they were intended as bedding, but at two per tent it is more likely that they were to be used as groundsheets, or at least laid over the straw usually provided.

Firelocks and bayonets were also provided at government expense. Originally colonels were responsible for actually buying the arms and then recharging the cost, but by the 1740s they were instead issued to regiments on demand. The effective life of a firelock was reckoned to be about twelve years, though neglect and rough handling could reduce this somewhat. Inspection reports were frequently critical in this respect.

Sergeants in line companies were supposed to have halberds, though these were generally allowed

Reconstruction; Highland Officer, c. 1760, demonstrating the drill position 'Charge Your Bayonets Breast High'. On the next command 'Push Your Bayonets' the soldier was to thrust the musket forward with the heel of his right hand upon the butt. The marked resemblance to 17th century pike drill is quite obvious. (Author's collection)

of equipment were contracted for by the colonel and, although broadly similar throughout the army, there were usually some minor differences at a regimental level. This was most evident in the equipment issued to the light companies.

In 1768 all belts were ordered to be whitened – except in those regiments with buff facings who were permitted to retain buff accoutrements – but light companies were ordered to have blackened tan leather accoutrements and belly boxes rather than large cartouche boxes carried by a belt over the left shoulder. It is clear from inspection reports that a great many regiments disregarded this instruction – probably in order to keep the light company as uniform as possible with the rest of the battalion.

Reconstruction; Highland Officer, c. 1760, detail. This officer is wearing an unlaced frock jacket – commonly worn in everyday use in place of the expensive full dress uniform. According to regulations his waistcoat should still have been red, but white or pale buff waistcoats also seem to have been pretty universally worn by this period. The equipment of belly-box, bayonet, broadsword and musket is also typical. Highland officers were generally allowed to carry dirks in place of bayonets, but in practice only did so on parade, or else substituted them for the heavy broadsword. (Author's collection)

to be 'heavy and unwieldy' weapons and replaced by half-pikes or spontoons in 1792. Grenadier and light infantry sergeants carried fusils or light firelocks instead, although the grenadiers were ordered to take up the newly introduced pike in 1792 – whether they actually did so on active service is open to question. Battalion company sergeants are also known to have carried firelocks on campaign, particularly in North America and in the Caribbean, though the practice was generally an unofficial one.

Swords were supplied by the regiment until officially abolished in 1768, and paid for by deductions from the individual soldier's subsistence – a factor which no doubt contributed to their unpopularity and effective abandonment during the Seven Years War.

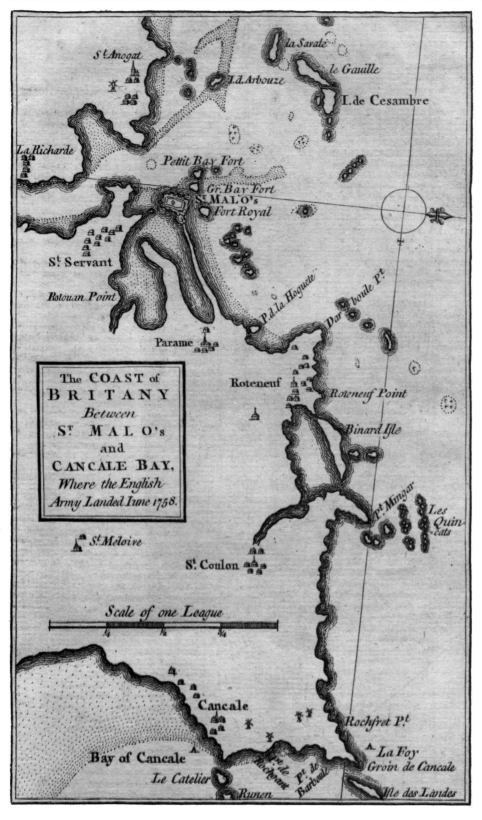

The COAST of
BRITANY
Between
St. MALO's
and
CANCALE BAY,
*Where the English
Army Landed June 1758.*

Scale of one League

Contemporary map, from the Gentleman's Magazine, depicting the area around St. Malo and Cancale bay. This was the scene of one of the less than glorious amphibious operations against the French coast in 1758. Although derided as 'breaking windows with guineas' these raids did successfully tie down large numbers of French troops who might otherwise have been deployed to Germany. While the initial adventures varied from disappointing fiascoes to outright disasters, the later raids and in particular the capture and occupation of Belle Isle, produced some very solid results. (Author's collection)

OFFICERS

Officers were responsible for purchasing their own clothing and equipment. A young officer was expected to arrive at his battalion with a complete outfit, made to measure by his tailor. This would have included a regimental coat, conforming to the current clothing warrant and any regimental idiosyncrasies, and more importantly a couple of much simpler frock coats for everyday wear. These were almost invariably unlaced and frequently had plain red cuffs and lapels. The cut of these frock coats might also differ from that laid down in the warrants.

It must be stressed that, while considerable variations certainly existed, variations in dress were almost always 'regimental' (except on campaign when everyone got away with murder) and did not necessarily reflect the whim or the purse of the individual officer. Unfortunately, although there are numerous references in standing orders to certain items of clothing or equipment being 'regimental', there is little to indicate the precise form which these distinctions took. One identifiable example, however, is the practice in the 25th of adding red piping to waistcoat and sometimes white piping to the coat as well. This can be seen in a number of paintings but is not otherwise referred to. Doubtless there were many other similar distinctions which are now lost.

Officers also had greatcoats, usually blue in colour and often turned up with red irrespective of the regiment's facing colour, although the 106th in 1795 had their black velvet facings on the collar.

Apart from the superior quality of materials used, officers' regimental coats and hats were distinguished by the use of gold or silver lace. Prior to 1768 this was used to edge cuffs, lapels and some seams, as well as forming button loops in some regiments. After 1768 it was used only for button loops and in contrast to earlier practice these loops were invariably square, irrespective of whether the regiment's rank and file wore square or bastion shaped loops. Some regiments such as the Royals permitted those officers who could afford to do so to have their buttonholes embroidered instead of using loops of gold or silver lace.

Prior to 1768 aiguillettes or shoulder knots of the appropriate 'metal' were also used and after that date epaulettes. Except in fusilier and highland regiments,

Officer, Norfolk Militia 1759, after a sketch in Wyndham's drill book. Scarlet coat, faced black with gold lace – see Plate E2 for details. (Author's collection)

Private, Norfolk Militia, after Wyndham. This left side view provides useful views of the French style vertical pocket flap, and the way in which the waistbelt carries only a sling for the bayonet, with no provision being made for the carrying of a sword. (Author's collection)

company officers wore one on the right shoulder while field officers wore two. Otherwise the principal badge of rank was a gorget and a crimson silk net sash. Prior to 1768 the sash was worn over the right shoulder, but afterwards worn around the waist with the knot tied at the left side. Gorgets, tied around the neck with silk ribbon of the regiment's facing colour should have been worn by all officers when on duty, but increasingly 'duty' seems to have been interpreted as applying only to the officer of the day or the guard commander.

As there was no regular entitlement to clothing, an officer replaced garments as and when they were needed and the expensive regimental coat might well have to serve most of his career. Minor alterations in style could be carried out by any competent tailor, but substantial alterations such as those called for by the 1768 Warrant were clearly unpopular since they

Private, Norfolk Militia, after Wyndham. A useful illustration of cuff detail. Note the absence of gaiters and how the waistcoat is very much smaller than the style worn by regular soldiers. See Plate E1 for details. (Author's collection)

required all officers to obtain new regimentals or substantially alter their existing ones. Suits of new clothing generally appear to have been ordered through the usual offices of the Regimental Agent.

On the 9 April 1759 officers of the 42nd Highlanders were somewhat illiterately informed; 'Such officers as bespoke cloathes at Halifax may rece it from the Qr. Mr. upon paying him for the same & whatever remains uncaulld for to be desposed off to the best advantage.' Similarly in 1774 supplies sent to the 49th Foot in Ireland included 10 embroidered regimental suits.

A fair amount of second hand clothing was also in circulation since the kit belonging to dead officers was normally auctioned off to their comrades, and those retiring or exchanging into other corps might also sell off any unwanted clothing.

Battalion company officers were supposed to be armed with swords and spontoons or half pikes, but the latter were very unpopular and it was noted in 1784 that they were not used in North America. Consequently they were officially abolished in 1786 and officers were told to make use of their swords alone.

Flank company and fusilier officers were supposed to carry fusils, and when they did bayonets were often carried in place of swords. In 1792 fusils, in Ireland at least, were ordered to be laid aside and swords carried instead. Less officially dirks seem to have been popular substitutes for swords, and pistols were also made use of on campaign.

REGIMENTS

In 1740 the British Army comprised 43 numbered regiments of infantry, besides the Foot Guards. By 1793 there were 77, although the intervening period had seen wild fluctuations, most notably during the Seven Years War when no fewer than 124 were carried on the Army List. Most of these were, of course, disbanded at the end of the war, but others were renumbered. Little is known about the uniforms of many of these short-lived units and the schedule below is restricted to the 70 regiments comprised in the Royal Warrant of 1768.

Prior to 1768 buttons were quite plain and usually domed in appearance, but from then they were required to bear the regimental number. Units bearing the same facing colours were normally distinguished by the patterned loops of worsted lace on buttonholes – a system which appears to have been unique to the British Army. In the 1740s a number of units had plain white lace without any distinguishing features, but by 1768 plain lace was pretty well confined to the Foot Guards and to the sergeants of line regiments.

Unless otherwise noted, any regimental badges authorised for the grenadier caps were also borne on the drums and colours. Prior to 1768 these badges were embroidered in full colour on the cloth caps, after the adoption of the bearskin cap they should have appeared in white on the red patch at the rear of the cap, but some units, including the 1st (Royals) and the 6th incorporated them on the new cap plate.

Light infantry caps were evidently less well regulated and sometimes unauthorised badges appeared on them; such as the 9th's figure of Britannia. Otherwise, regiments without badges simply bore a crowned GR cypher.

All coats were of course red, except for drummers and fifers of non-royal regiments, who wore reversed colours. Only the facing colour as laid down in 1768, an indication as to whether officers wore gold or silver lace, and any regimental badges or other peculiarities are noted below. Additional information is generally drawn from inspection reports, identified by date in parenthesis.

1st Royals: Blue facings, gold lace
Buttons in pairs. Officers had steel-hilted swords for most of the period. Officers permitted embroidered button-holes if they chose; otherwise rectangular loops. Battalion coys had white hackles with blue tips c. 1790. 1st Bn. in West India dress 1790 onwards. Grenadiers; cypher within green collar of St. Andrew. Light Coy: Figure 1 on front of cap. Green hackle. (1782) White belts and non-regulation caps (1789). Portrait shows Tarleton type helmet c. 1795.

2nd Queens: Blue facings, silver lace
Prior to 1768 facings were sea green (sometimes shown as sky blue). Grenadiers: Queen's cypher CaRa on red within garter. Caps 'almost worn out' (1789). Light Coy: White belts (1779) – still not regulation in 1781 and 1789.

3rd Buffs: Buff facings, silver lace

Grenadiers: Green Dragon – still wearing cloth caps in 1770. Light Coy: buff belts (1774).

4th King's Own: Blue facings, silver lace

Officers with embroidered button holes (1769). Battalion Coys had scalloped lace on hats (1774). Grenadiers: Cypher within garter. Light Coy: Dragoon style helmet with red mane. Lion badge on frontlet. White belts (1774).

5th: Gosling green facings, silver lace

Officers' coats faced pale green with silver binding (1755). White small clothes (1766). Bastion shaped loops (1768). Grenadiers: St. George & Dragon. Caps edged with fur (1768). Light Coy: Dragoon style helmet with red mane. St. George & Dragon badge on frontlet.

6th: Yellow facings, silver lace

Grenadiers: White antelope. Fur caps not adopted until 1770. Light Coy: Regulation cap with cypher – no badge.

7th Royal Fus.: Blue facings, gold lace

Battalion coys in caps. Badge: Rose within crowned Garter – only worn by grenadiers. Fur caps not adopted until after 1770. Light Coy: Black leather cap with peak and rear flap as for the 69th. Transverse black fur crest – overlaid with white feather.

8th: Blue facings, gold lace

1742 Cloathing Book shows yellow facings. Grenadiers: White horse on red within crowned garter.

9th: Yellow facings, silver lace

Officers had embroidered button holes (1774). Battalion wearing trousers in Caribbean (1790). Light Coy: Dragoon style helmet with red mane. Britannia badge on frontlet.

10th: Yellow facings, silver lace

Hats not regulation (1785).

11th: Green facings, gold lace

Bastion loops authorised 1768. Officers had embroidered button holes (1775). Same inspection complained of soldiers' hats with white cords and tassels. Light Coy: Regulation style cap with black fur trim. White belts (1771).

12th: Yellow facings, gold lace

Sergeants had gold laced hats (1758). White small clothes (1766). Bastion loops authorised 1768. Officers had embroidered button holes (1768). Grenadiers: Brass grenades on pouches (1755). Fur caps with yellow plated fronts (1768).

13th: Philemot yellow facings, silver lace

White small clothes (1766). Officers had embroidered button holes (1768). West Indies clothing (1790). Grenadiers: Fur caps with yellow plated fronts (1768). Light Coy: Cropped hat, white belts (1771).

Reconstruction: interior of belly-box as worn by officers of highlanders, light infantry and grenadiers. Comprising only a wooden block, painted red, with a simple leather flap, this particular example is drilled with holes for nine rounds. Those worn by private soldiers were sometimes larger. (Author's collection)

14th: Buff facings, silver lace

Reviewed in West Indies clothing 1791. Officers 'not dressed with much uniformity.' Grenadiers: Fur caps with red fronts, motto and horse in white metal (1765). No caps (1791).

15th: Yellow facings, silver lace

Officers' uniforms old but good (1768). Embroidered button holes (1774). West Indies clothing ordered 1790.

16th: Yellow facings, silver lace

Reviewed in jackets and round hats 1784.

17th: Greyish-white facings, silver lace

Greyish-white small clothes (1768). Grenadiers: Fur caps not adopted until late 1769. Plain hats 1791. Light Coy: Caps similar to 69th (1773). Plain hats in 1791.

18th Royal Irish: Blue facings, gold lace

No lapels until 1743. Grenadiers: Harp and Crown. Light Coy: White belts (1777).

Edinburgh Castle, c. 1775; home of the Commander in Chief in Scotland. If the date is correct the highlander in the foreground with light coloured facings may be a member of Fraser's 71st Highlanders. Note the comparatively flat bonnet. Since he has a cane but no sash over his left shoulder he is probably a senior NCO. (NMS)

19th: Green facings, gold lace

Inspection reports consistently note officers' coats unlaced. Light Coy: Officers wearing white waistcoats (1775). Caps and accoutrements 'not regulation' (1777).

20th: Pale yellow facings, silver lace

No lapels until 1743. Grenadiers: fur caps allowed 1766. Light Coy: White belts (1774).

21st Scots Fus.: Blue facings, gold lace

Battalion coys in caps. Badge: Thistle on red with St. Andrew's cross – grenadiers only. Gold embroidered button holes for officers (1782). 'Clothed and armed as fusiliers' (1791) i.e. carrying fusils and bayonets instead of swords. Light Coy: Tarleton Helmet with leopardskin turban.

22nd: Buff facings, gold lace

Bastion loops authorised 1768. Officers had embroidered button holes (1768). White hackles worn by soldiers (1788).

23rd Welch Fus.: Blue facings, gold lace

Battalion coys in caps. Badge: Prince of Wales feathers – only worn by grenadiers. Portrait *c.* 1790 shows officer wearing cap with Prince of Wales badge but no plate. Cloth caps still worn 1770. Most inspection reports note officers wearing hats. Reports in 1784 and 1788 also note battalion coys wearing plain hats with three white feathers arranged as Prince of Wales Crest – referred to as 'undress'.

24th: Willow green facings, silver lace

Light Coy: Accoutrements and caps not regulation (1775). Dragoon style helmet with red mane (1777).

25th: Yellow facings, gold lace

Bastion loops authorised 1768, previously square ones. White summer uniform worn on Minorca in early 1770s. Red edge on waistcoat and white edge on facings seen in various illustrations after 1768. Grenadiers: Fur caps (1766). No plates (1771) but note depiction of one with white metal plate *c.* 1771. Light Coy: Red leather cap with fur trim. Thistle on frontlet. Waistcoat and belts white. Officers armed with highland broadswords.

26th: Pale yellow facings, silver lace

Light Coy: Bunbury shows chain cap with star badge on frontlet.

27th Inniskilling: Buff facings, gold lace

White belts (1775) 'to be changed'. Grenadiers: Castle on blue disc.

28th: Yellow facings, silver lace

Officers had embroidered button holes 1768 and 1775.

Private Soldier, c. 1760, after Sandby. Like most infantrymen he no longer carries a sword on his waistbelt but the fact that he is wearing white gaiters and unhooked coat skirts suggests that he is taking part in a formal guard mounting, and indeed is almost certainly a member of the Foot Guards. An intriguing detail is the lace pattern clearly visible on the waistcoat skirts. This herringbone pattern was common on coat skirts, but what little evidence we do have suggests that it was usually stripped off when the coat was converted into a waistcoat. (Author's collection)

29th: Yellow facings, silver lace

'Negro' drummers from 1759. Bastion loops authorised 1768. Peaks fitted to grenadier and light infantry caps. Tufts in imitation of feathers worn in hats – officers had real ones (1791).

30th: Pale yellow facings, silver lace

Bastion loops authorised 1768. Hackles noted 1791 – reviewed in trousers on return from Dominica. Grenadiers: Fur caps (1755). Reviewed in hats on Dominica (1791). Light Coy: White belts (1777).

31st: Buff facings, silver lace

Knapsacks worn out 1779, men carrying provisions in their blankets.

32nd: White facings, gold lace

No lapels until 1743. Light Coy: Chain caps (1775). White belts (1777). Tarleton helmet in 1790s.

33rd: Red facings, silver lace

Bastion loops authorised 1768. Grenadiers: Fur caps authorised 1766 but fronts not regulation (1770).

34th: Yellow facings, silver lace

Officers noted to have hackles in 1790 and soldiers too in the following year. Light Coy: Caps too small and lacking flaps (1791).

35th: Orange facings, silver lace

Officers had embroidered button holes (1768). Officers reviewed in frock uniforms on return from West Indies (1786). Grenadier coy in hats at same inspection.

36th: Green facings, gold lace

Grenadiers: Home shows hats with white over red over black hackle 1791 – also moustaches! Light Coy: Home shows a crested helmet similar in style to Tarleton in 1791 with a brown crest and a green turban. Also white accoutrements.

Soldier, 25th Foot, c. 1771. One of an important series of watercolour sketches depicting members of this and other regiments in the Minorca garrison. This one is particularly interesting in showing what appears to be a soldier in battle-order. He wears his previous year's coat, shabby and cropped short for convenience, and stripped of its lace. His hat is worn in a manner which must have induced apoplexy in inspecting officers, and very unusually indeed a blanket roll is also depicted. The 18th century British soldier looked very different on active service from the rather stiff figure seen on the parade ground. (NMS)

37th: Yellow facings, silver lace

38th: Yellow facings, silver lace

No lapels until 1743. Bastion loops authorised 1768. Officers had embroidered button holes (1768). Hair dressed German style (1787). Grenadiers: Caps edged with fur (1768).

39th: Green facings, gold lace

40th: Buff facings, gold lace

Short jackets and round hats worn at Germantown during American war. Inspection reports note officers' coats unlaced. Hackles in officers' hats (1789). Grenadiers: Caps edged with white fur (1768). Light Coy: Felt caps in 1786 – regimental ones 'in store'.

41st: Blue facings, gold lace

Single breasted coats until 1768. No lace and blue small-clothes. Grenadiers: Rose and thistle on red ground within crowned garter. New **41st** raised 1788 with red facings.

42nd: Blue facings, gold lace

Highlanders – see MAA 261.

43rd: White facings, silver lace

Officers originally had gold lace. White belts (1764). Grenadiers: Fur caps (1767).

44th: Yellow facings, silver lace

Officers had embroidered button holes (1768). Silver appliqué button-loops (1775).

45th: Green facings, silver lace

Bastion loops authorised 1768. Officers had embroidered button holes (1769). In 1780 the buttonholes were noted to be evenly spaced, not paired like rank and file. Light Coy: Dragoon style helmet (1780).

Ensign Thomas Currie, South Fencibles, c. 1780. A typical battalion company officer on home service armed with sword and spontoon or half-pike – on active service most officers carried muskets or simply relied on their swords, and wore boots in place of gaiters. He wears a scarlet coat with green facings and gilt buttons. (NMS)

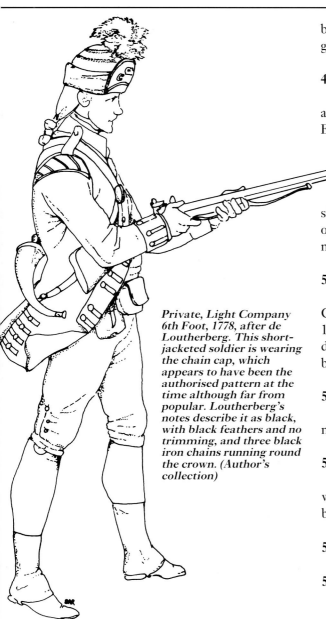

Private, Light Company 6th Foot, 1778, after de Loutherberg. This short-jacketed soldier is wearing the chain cap, which appears to have been the authorised pattern at the time although far from popular. Loutherberg's notes describe it as black, with black feathers and no trimming, and three black iron chains running round the crown. (Author's collection)

buttons unnumbered. Inspected in trousers on Antigua (1790), grenadier caps then described as 'bad'.

49th: Green facings, gold lace

Bastion loops authorised 1768. Officers' coats and waistcoats edged with green velvet (1768). Embroidered buttonholes. Battalion reviewed in trousers on Barbados 1790.

50th: Black facings, silver lace

White small-clothes 1758. Coats 'remarkably too short' 1769. Grenadiers: Caps issued in 1777 'worn out' by 1789. Light Coy: Accoutrements and caps not regulation (1789).

51st: Green facings, gold lace

Originally Sea Green but changed to Deep Green by 1768 Warrant. Bastion loops authorised 1768. Officers consistently noted to have embroidered buttonholes. Grenadiers: Caps covered with black goatskin (1777).

52nd: Buff facings, silver lace

Portrait of officer *c.* 1766 shows gold lace on hat, none on coat.

53rd: Red facings, gold lace

1768 inspection notes officers' uniforms edged with narrow gold lace and coats lined yellow. Embroidered buttonholes noted in following year.

54th: Popinjay green facings, silver lace

55th: Dark green facings, gold lace

Yellow lace on soldiers' coats and hats until 1768.

56th: Deep crimson/Purple (1764) facings, silver lace

White belts and breeches (1764). Officers had embroidered button holes (1768), vellum in 1777. Soldiers' coats too short (1771). Red feathers in hats (1787).

57th: Yellow facings, gold lace

Accoutrements 'bad' in 1769 – still wearing kit received in 1756. Inspection in 1791 also complained that accoutrements not regulation.

46th: Yellow facings, silver lace

No lapels until 1743. Light Coy: Felt caps noted 1788 but leather caps in the following year.

47th: White facings, silver lace

Grenadiers: Officers had red leather sword-belts (1768).

48th: Buff facings, gold lace

Inspection reports consistently note plain coats for officers and plain hats as well in 1780s. Officers'

58th: Black facings, gold lace

Black facings, buff linings and yellow lace (1756). Excessively short coat skirts and hats too small – but adorned with red and white tuft (1767). Officers wearing buff small-clothes and buff coat lining. Black velvet edging to waistcoat (1768). White small-clothes and linings by 1771. Grenadiers: No caps 1784.

59th: Purple facings, silver lace

Facings originally light crimson but altered in 1768, and then again in 1776, to white. Light Coy: Tan belts whitened 'which made them look very ill'.

60th R. American: Blue facings, silver lace

Unlaced until 1768. Caps, short jackets and blue or green mitasses worn in early days. Complaint by officer inspecting 3rd Bn: 'The hair's come off the Pioneers' caps' (1790). 1st Bn. Flank Coy officers carrying sabres 1792. Grenadiers: King's cypher within crowned garter.

61st: Buff facings, silver lace

Grenadiers: Caps covered in goatskin (1777).

62nd: Yellowish buff facings, silver lace

Coats described as too short – 'jackets' in 1771, 1773, 1775. Hats also too small. Officers had plain ones 1785. Light Coy: Dragoon style helmet with white mane 1777.

63rd: Deep green facings, silver lace

Buff (linen) lining until 1768. Officers had embroidered button holes in that year, but laced by 1771.

64th: Black facings, gold lace

Sergeants had yellow lace and officers none 1767. Officers' coats and waistcoats edged with black vel-

vet, buttonholes embroidered on coat. Plain hats (1768).

Private of an unidentified unit, 1778, after de Loutherberg. This soldier is almost certainly a militiaman as evidenced by such oddities in his dress as the vertically placed pocket flaps. The presence of some kind of lace trimming on the coat turnbacks suggests that they display the regimental facing colour rather than a plain white lining as worn by regulars, a feature sometimes also seen on the jackets of militiamen during the Napoleonic period. Oddly enough there does not appear to be any lace binding on the hat. Regulars invariably had plain white bindings but Loutherberg's notes refer to the binding on militiamen's hats being the same as their facing colour. (Author's collection)

65th: White facings, silver lace

Buff (linen) linings 1759. 'Hats cocked in a foreign manner' (1784).

66th: Yellowish green facings, gold lace

Buff small-clothes for officers until 1768. Lace changed to silver 1778. Battalion reviewed in trousers on St. Vincent 1790.

67th: Pale yellow facings, silver lace

Battalion reviewed in trousers on Grenada 1790. Light Coy: Chain cap. Black belts (1790).

68th: Deep green facings, silver lace

Light Coy: Brown leather cap with reinforced comb. Frontlet with Colonel Lambton's crest cypher, and motto 'FAITHFUL' (c. 1772).

69th: Willow green facings, gold lace

Light Coy: Loutherberg shows caps with peak and rear flap in 1778. Caps not according to regulations 1788, reported as felt in 1789, but leather ones, conforming to regulations, in 1790.

70th: Black facings, gold lace

Grey facings when first raised 1756 – 'Glasgow Greys'. Light Coy: Green hackle in cap (1786).

THE PLATES

A: Volunteer units 1745
A1: Scots Loyalist Volunteer

The Jacobite Rebellion of 1745 encountered widespread opposition in Scotland and a number of Loyalist Volunteer units were raised in various parts of the country. The most effective of these were the Argyll Militia and a brigade raised in the Lowlands by a Guards officer, Lord Home. The brigade comprised three battalions; one each from Edinburgh and Glasgow and a third, smaller battalion from Paisley raised by the Earl of Glencairn. This brigade did good service in helping to hold the line of the Forth in late 1745, preventing French regulars and other reinforcements led by Lord John Drummond from marching south to join the main rebel army. Afterwards the 'Glasgow Enthusiasts', Glencairn's battal-

ion and at least one company from Edinburgh fought at Falkirk on 17 January 1746. Ridden down by fleeing dragoons and then overrun by Jacobite highlanders, the 'Glasgow Enthusiasts' lost 22 killed, 11 wounded and 14 prisoners. Other volunteer units were raised in Stirling and Aberdeen and loyalist partisans from the Forfar area assisted in the rescue of some captured British Army officers from Glamis Castle.

None of the Scots volunteers were issued with uniforms (though Lord Home presumably wore his Guards regimentals) and equipment, too, was often in short supply. The Aberdeen Volunteers complained on 14 April 1746: 'There are already about three hundred Volunteers of and belonging to this town, including the men engaged in pay, and besides sixty of the old town Militia, we called for arms from Captain Crosby, who has delivered one hundred and thirty-seven firelocks with bayonets, so that you see we will need at least two hundred and fifty stand of arms more than we have got, otherwise our people cannot do duty, and it will be a great discouragement for any of them to want arms; besides there are no cartouche boxes to be got in this place, which you know are very necessary for the service, we wish these were likewise ordered.'

This volunteer wears his own clothing – short jackets being rather commoner than long coats in Scotland at this period – and is distinguished from his Jacobite counterpart only by the wearing of a black cockade rather than a rebel white one. Typically he carries a Land Pattern firelock and bayonet and has acquired an old cartridge box for his ammunition.

A2: Grenadier, Lord Harcourt's 76th Foot

During the 1745 rebellion a number of so-called 'provincial' regiments were raised in England by the nobility. At first there was some resistance to the officers of these units being given regular commissions, but eventually the urgency of the situation saw the Horse Guards giving in and the 13 such regiments of foot ranked as the 67th to 79th. Two regiments of horse; Montagu's 9th and Kingston's 10th were also raised at the same time.

Most of these regiments served in various garrisons, but the Earl of Halifax's 74th and Montagu's 69th (also known as the Ordnance Regiment) took part in the siege of Carlisle under the Duke of

Coat worn by Captain
John Hamilton, 73rd Foot.
A typical example of an
officer's coat as worn in
the 1780s, this one is
rather unusual in that it
was worn by an officer of
a highland regiment.
Officers of the 73rd, then
stationed in India and
about to become the 71st,
should have worn short
jackets, but throughout

the 18th century highland
officers were always
curiously reluctant to wear
the kilt and this coat may
have been considered
more appropriate wear to
accompany breeches. A
similar one is shown in a
contemporary portrait of
Lieutenant Colonel
Norman McLeod of the
2nd Battalion of the 42nd –
see MAA 261. (NMS)

Cumberland. Their services were soon dispensed
with and on 10 June 1746 nine of them were ordered
to be disbanded. The remaining four, Bedford's,
Halifax's, Montagu's and Granby's were kept on a
short time longer, guarding rebel prisoners. The men
were each given a bounty of six days pay. This was
admitted to be a meagre reward but it was considered
that giving them more might deter them from re-
enlisting in regular regiments, for which a bounty of

Volunteer Units, 1745
1: Scots Loyalist Volunteer
2: Grenadier, Lord Harcourt's 76th Foot
3: Captain William Thornton,
   Yorkshire Blues

3

1

2

A

Independent Companies
1: Independent Company, North America, 1740s
2: Independent Company, West Indies, 1740s
3: Officer, Independent Company, 1781

Invalids
1: Invalid, 1748
2: Invalid, c1780
3: Invalid Officer, Edinburgh Castle, 1773

C

Marines
1: Private 6th Marines, 1740s
2: Sergeant 5th Marines, 1740s
3: Grenadier Company, Marines 1775

English Militia
1: Private, Norfolk Militia, 1759
2: Officer, Norfolk Militia, 1759
3: Officer, Durham Militia, 1760s

E

Scottish Fencibles
1: Officer, Sutherland Fencibles, 1759
2: Private, Light Infantry, South Fencibles, 1778
3: Subaltern, Hopetoun Fencibles, 1793

F

Edinburgh Units
1: Private, Edinburgh Defence Band, 1781
2 & 3: Edinburgh Town Guard

G

The East India Company
1: Captain Robert Bannatyne, Madras Army, 1759
2: Private, Madras Europeans, 1776
3: Bengal Sepoy, 1790's

H

two guineas was offered. The officers fared better, having obtained regular commissions they were entitled to be placed on half-pay and two of them, Captain William Shirreff of Bedford's and Lieutenant John Gibson of Montagu's were still drawing it more than half a century later in 1798!

Little is known of the uniforms worn by these regiments, but as they were, however grudgingly, officially considered to be regulars rather than volunteers, they presumably wore red coats. Two grenadier caps survive. One belonged to the Marquis of Granby's 71st, who served in Newcastle Upon Tyne, and a very similar one to Lord Harcourt's 76th, who garrisoned Harwich and the Landguard Fort. On the evidence of these caps the two regiments appear to have had blue and yellow facings respectively.

A3: Captain William Thornton, Yorkshire Blues

Besides the provincial regiments a number of volunteer regiments were raised in England in 1745 and unlike their Scottish counterparts were generally fortunate enough to be provided with uniforms. These invariably appear to have been blue in colour in order to distinguish them from the regulars. The Volunteers raised in Devon were given blue coats lined and faced with red, hats edged with white worsted lace and a pair of white gaiters to each man. Other 'Blues' included a company of gentlemen volunteers in London called the 'Loyal Blue Fusiliers', and Colonel Graham's 'Liverpool Blues' who did good service in breaking down the Mersey bridges ahead of the advancing Jacobites before retiring to join Lord Cholmondley's 73rd garrisoning Chester.

The best known were perhaps the 'Yorkshire Blues'. Companies raised in the West Riding of Yorkshire in 1745 had double-breasted coats of blue

Light Company officer, Glamorgan Militia, 1778, after de Loutherberg. De Loutherberg's notes refer to a red coat turned up with black and ten white button-holes in pairs on the lapels. The rank and file had long black gaiters but for some unexplained reason this particular officer apparently wore white ones with black garters. The cap front shown here is plain, but another sketch of a private soldier rather predictably shows the Prince of Wales' feathers with the motto 'ICH DIEN', and the accompanying notes, speak of a 'black helmet Cap trimmed with white, red worsted in the top of the helmet a black upright feather, the ornaments in front silver.' (Author's collection)

kersey faced with red kersey, baize lining and two dozen buttons to a coat. The clothing for the East Riding companies was described as being: 'exactly the same as the Swiss and Dutch troops are clothed, but with the linings considerably better'. (Both the Dutch and Swiss troops then serving under Field Marshal Wade wore blue coats lined with red.)

Captain William Thornton from Knaresborough raised one of the West Riding companies at his own expense and joined Wade's army at Newcastle. There they were attached for a time to Pulteney's 13th Foot, which was then only about 300 strong, though whether they actually stood with them at Falkirk or were guarding the artillery that day is uncertain. At any rate about 20 of them, together with Lieutenant Crofts and Ensign Patrick Simson (who also happened to be the minister of Fala, near Dalkeith) were taken prisoner and Thornton escaped by hiding behind the wainscotting in his quarters.

This reconstruction is based upon a portrait of Thornton, wearing what appears to be the uniform of his corps. The blue coat faced with red certainly agrees with other descriptions but the hussar type boots are rather remarkable and it is worth noting that a volunteer cavalry regiment also raised in the area at this time, the Yorkshire Hunters, wore pretty much the same uniform with 'light boots'. They also had green cockades in their hats and it is possible that the 'Blues' did likewise.

B: Independent Companies
B1: Independent Company (North America) 1740s
Independent Companies were scattered throughout the colonies in the 1740s in order to stiffen locally raised militias. Normally they were employed in areas where it would be both militarily and economically impractical to deploy complete battalions. Instead of purchasing their commissions Independent Company officers were 'raising for rank'. In other words, provided he recruited the requisite number of men, an officer would be rewarded with a permanent commission. The official allowance for each recruit

was not very great and in the circumstances there was little incentive to ensure that the recruits were of a particularly high standard. Moreover, since those officers who had any ability or ambition exchanged into the line as quickly as possible, the military efficiency of these units was generally quite dismal.

This figure is reconstructed from a plate in the

Soldier of an unidentified unit, 1778, after de Loutherberg. The sword and the wings on his shoulders suggest a grenadier wearing a hat instead of the apparently unpopular fur cap. His hair however appears to be tied back and clubbed rather than plaited in grenadier fashion, so he may well be a militiaman. (Author's collection)

1742 Cloathing Book, depicting a soldier of an unidentified Independent Company. The dull green facing colour appears to have been common to all these units.

B2: Independent Company (West Indies) 1740s

Some of the Independent Companies depicted in the Cloathing Book have the usual green cuffs and lapels, but light brown turnbacks to their coat-skirts. These are presumably intended to represent the unbleached linen linings ordered for soldiers serving in the West Indies and other hot climates. In an effort to improve the efficiency of some of these companies the six serving on Jamaica and four others at Ruatan were ordered to be formed into a proper regiment; Trelawney's 63rd (later the 49th) on 2 February 1744. Nevertheless, in June 1747 when Admiral Boscawen was ordered to take a naval squadron to Madras, the land element of his expedition comprised 12 newly raised Independent Companies. Presumably the army was unwilling to risk a complete battalion on such a potentially hazardous expedition. Once again the quality of these companies left much to be desired and at least two of them were recruited from Jacobite prisoners who had been languishing in jail for upwards of a year.

B3: Officer, Independent Company 1781

By the time of the American War, Independent Companies were used simply as recruiting depots for regular corps and ambitious young officers could use them as a means of obtaining accelerated promotion:

'For a company – a lieutenant on full pay is to raise 50 men, including three corporals, to be allowed five guineas levy-money, and the pay of three serjeants and two drummers, during the levy, and to receive £150 from the successor to his lieutenancy.
A lieutenant on half pay to raise the like number, but to be allowed eight guineas levy-money.
For a lieutenancy – an ensign on full pay is to raise 20 men, including a corporal, and to be allowed five guineas levy money, with the pay of a serjeant and drummer during the levy.
An ensign on half pay to raise the like number,

Reconstruction: goatskin knapsack with blanket roll secured under the flap, largely based on the excellent rear view of a soldier in the background of Beechey's portrait of Captain Cowell of the 1st Battalion, The Royals (1795). Bennett

Cuthbertson writing in 1768 considered goatskin knapsacks to be particularly smart, but recommended leather straps, 'well whitened' rather than buff ones, probably because buff is rather prone to stretching. (Author's collection)

but to be allowed seven guineas levy-money.
No officer on full pay to engage in the above service without the approbation of his colonel or commanding officer.'

Once it was completed the men of the company would then be drafted as a reinforcement for a needy battalion – not infrequently the one from which the new captain had lately come. The fate of the officers was rather more uncertain. Most went on to half pay, but some units such as the 25th seem to have operated a policy of giving young officers the opportunity to raise Independent Companies and allowing them

This portrait is traditionally identified as Major Hugh Fraser, an officer who had served with the 27th (Inniskillings) at Culloden in 1746. However, the Army List shows that he was only promoted to lieutenant on 4 September *1754 and still held that rank when he dropped out of sight at the end of the Seven Years War. Moreover, although his uniform bears the buff facings of the 27th, its style, and particularly the epaulettes, clearly belong to a later period. (NMS)*

to exchange back into the regiment at the first opportunity. Lieutenant John Stewart for example, having raised his company, was gazetted captain on 24 January 1791 and immediately placed on the half pay list as his men were drafted. Two years later he exchanged back into the 25th in the place of Captain Richard Gardiner who retired on to the half pay list of the 1791 Independent Companies.

The quality of the recruits obtained in this way appears to have been depressingly bad and despite the fact that only three months were allowed in which to complete a company, in 1793 the standard letter to those officers authorised to do so sternly warned:

'Least the latitude, which from the particular circumstances of the case, was admitted in passing the men raised for the Independent Companies in the year 1790 should create an Expectation that the like will be allowed on the present occasion, I think it necessary to make you aware, that no Recruit will be approved who is not in every respect conformable to the terms prescribed.'

The uniform depicted here was described in instructions issued to all Captains of Independent Companies on 23 March 1781:

'The Independent Company raised by you, and which you command, is to be furnished only for the present, with the firelock, bayonet and cartouche box, as delivered from the Tower. You are immediately to clothe them with a plain red coat lappelled and white waistcoat and breeches equal to the clothing of the Army, and plain white buttons, long gaiters and a well cocked laced hat.'

C: Invalids
C1: Invalid 1748

Then as now the Army looked after its own, and soldiers who were disabled or worn out in the service could be granted one of the limited number of places in Chelsea Hospital, or Kilmainham Hospital, for the English and Irish Establishments respectively. Those unable or unwilling to be accommodated there could still be admitted as 'Out-Pensioners', receiving a small allowance instead. This rather inadequate sum was intended to do no more than supplement whatever income the former soldier could earn in civilian life. As a third alternative, men who were unfit for active service but were otherwise in possession of their faculties could volunteer for service in one of the numerous Invalid units: sedentary battalions and Independent Companies of old soldiers employed in garrison duties.

This figure is based upon David Morier's painting of a private of the 'Invalid Regiment', presumably Wardour's 41st Foot, who had been formed in 1719 and spent most of the 18th century quartered in and around Portsmouth. On 25 December 1787 the regiment was reduced and a marching regiment with fresh officers and men raised in its place. The original officers were retained for a time on full pay, before eventually being retired on to the half pay list, while those rank and file still fit for duty were drafted into the Independent Companies of Invalids.

The rather old-fashioned uniform depicted by Morier was common to all the Invalid corps and, indeed, with the rather obvious exception of the firelock and accoutrements, was also worn by the inmates of Chelsea Hospital. Morier shows the soldier wearing rather ill-fitting white gaiters, but as this particular battalion seldom if ever marched anywhere it is likely that they were only worn on formal parades. Oddly enough, out of all the regiments painted by Morier in 1748, this is the only one to be represented by a battalion company soldier – perhaps because it was easier to use a Chelsea In-Pensioner as a model than to fetch a grenadier of the 41st up from Portsmouth. According to the 1751 Warrant grenadiers wore the usual caps, bearing a rose and thistle on a red ground, within a crowned garter.

C2: Invalid c. 1780

Besides the 41st and a number of other Invalid battalions raised during the Seven Years War, Independent Companies of Invalids were widely scattered around the country. In 1793, for example, there were no fewer than 50; ten on Jersey, eight on Guernsey, four on Alderney, one each on Scilly and at Pendennis, six at Plymouth and four at Portsmouth,

three at Berwick, two each at Sheerness, Hull and Chester, one company each at Dover Castle, Tilbury Fort, Landguard Fort, and four in Scotland. In addition, a battalion of Invalids was maintained on the Irish Establishment and there was also an Invalid battalion of artillerymen.

Although the style of the uniform kept pace with the rest of the Army, the Invalid companies were still distinguished by an absence of lace, buff coloured accoutrements, and most noticeably by the wearing of blue waistcoats and breeches. This uniform became even more distinctive when regiments of the line formally adopted white waistcoats and breeches in 1768 but it was not until 1794 that the Invalid companies were permitted to follow suit.

C3: Invalid Officer, Edinburgh Castle 1773

This rather puzzling figure is based on a report of an inspection carried out at Edinburgh Castle on 8 June 1773; 'Officers' uniforms very good, faced with green and laced with gold.' Why this particular company apparently wore green instead of the usual blue facings is not explained, but it may perhaps have

Officers saluting according to the 1794 Manual, from Hall's New Royal Encyclopaedia (2nd edn 1794). Note how the battalion company officers wear boots while the light company officers wear half-gaiters. (Author's collection)

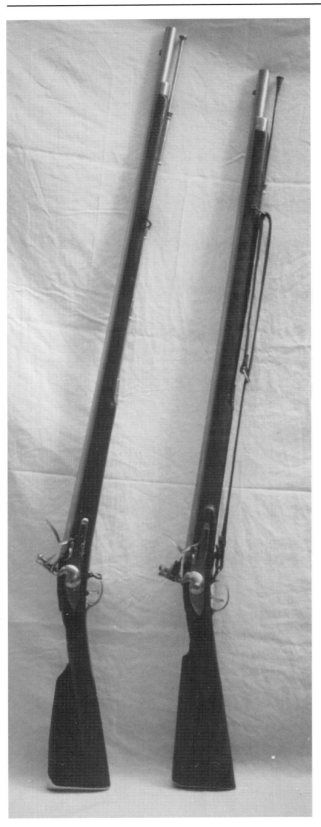

been a distinguishing feature of the four companies stationed in 'North Britain'. Both officers and men presumably wore white waistcoats and breeches.

The Scottish companies were rather widely scattered with one serving at Edinburgh, one at Stirling, a third at Fort George and the fourth at Dumbarton. Smaller detachments, presumably drawn from one or other of these companies, lay even further afield, occupying the various highland forts. In 1745 the permanent staff of Ruthven Barracks comprised three Invalids, and a locally recruited Barrackmaster who actually lived in the nearby village.

D: Marines
D1 & D2: Private 6th Marines and Sergeant 5th Marines 1740s

In November 1739 the King announced the formation of six Marine regiments and these were joined by four more in January 1741. The senior officers were found for the most part from the half pay list, though serving subalterns could usually gain a step in rank by volunteering. The remaining officers, as was usual for newly raised corps were either drawn from the half pay or more commonly were 'new entrants' into the military profession. Had these new and rather hastily raised units proceeded on service as complete battalions the experienced officers and NCOs would no doubt have knocked them into shape without too much difficulty. Unfortunately, they were not given the opportunity to do so.

In the first place, although raised as Marines, they were, for administrative purposes, part of the Army. This quite naturally irked the Lords of the Admiralty but it was not until February 1747 that the battle was won and control of the regiments passed a few doors along Whitehall from the Horse Guards to the Admiralty building. In the meantime confusion reigned.

Marines were required to serve in small detachments aboard just about every ship in the Royal

Short Land Pattern Firelock and India Pattern Firelock. The former, having a 42 inch (107 cm) barrel, was introduced in 1768 and was the standard infantry weapon during the American War and afterwards. The 39 inch (99 cm) barrelled India Pattern was carried by European and native troops of the East India Company from the 1760s, and apparently also by British regulars serving in India for some years before its official adoption in 1794. (Author's collection)

Navy. There was no question therefore of keeping the battalions together, or even as it soon transpired, exerting any meaningful central control over them. Ships of 90 guns or more were supposed to embark a full company of three officers and 100 marines, but the smaller ones could have as few as 15. Keeping track of these men and settling their accounts literally became a nightmare and undoubtedly led to the Army's relinquishing control in 1747. Even so the pay warrants were not finally cleared until 1764, fifteen years after they were disbanded!

Another peculiarity of these regiments was that since no more than a single company was embarked, even on the largest warships, there was no requirement for officers above the rank of captain to go to sea. This made a field officer's post in one of these regiments a rather attractive proposition. It also meant that during the Jacobite emergency in 1745 the Government was able to draw at very short notice upon a pool of otherwise unemployed field officers to lead the provisional battalions formed from 'Additional Companies' (depot companies of regiments serving overseas).

The uniforms depicted in the 1742 Cloathing Book appear rather old fashioned, though it may safely be assumed that, like their comrades in the land forces, all ten regiments wore lapels after 1743. The fact that coat skirts are worn unhooked may be attributed to the fact that they were not expected to undertake much in the way of marching and the provision of a belly-box rather than the larger cartouche box worn on the hip also reflects their rather limited role.

The most distinctive feature of the uniform is the grenadier style cap, presumably worn by all companies. It is not clear from the Cloathing Book illustrations whether it simply lacked the usual tassel on the top, or whether, as is more likely, the cap was an old fashioned style with a separate front and hanging bag. At any rate this type of headgear was probably adopted as being much more practical on shipboard than a wide-brimmed cocked hat.

D3: Grenadier Company, Marines 1775

Marines were once again raised in 1755. This time they were very firmly under the control of the Admiralty, but their officers continued to be carried on the Army List. Their uniform, again following Army styles, was a red coat with white facings, though the extent to which this was actually worn is open to doubt. While on board ship they were expected to keep their uniforms in store and wear a sea kit of slop

Light infantry drill, 1794. The officers demonstrating the drill all wear Tarleton helmets, which appear to have been the most popular style of headgear for light infantry after the American War. None appear to have a sword and all wear half-gaiters. (Author's collection)

clothing similar to that issued to ordinary seamen. Practice doubtless varied from ship to ship and red coats may have been worn over loose trousers and checked shirts during sea actions, but generally speaking the uniform depicted was probably only worn on shore, as in the actions at Lexington and Concord at the start of the American war in 1775.

Officially headgear was the usual cocked hat but officers at Boston in 1775 were ordered to provide themselves with jackets and round hats. With two battalions present it was decided to form grenadier and light infantry companies – an otherwise unknown species of Marine. Grenadier caps with distinctive plates were sent out; the device being the inevitable anchor in the centre of an eight pointed star, surmounted by a crown and surrounded by a laurel wreath. The light infantry caps presumably bore a similar device.

E: English Militia
E1: Private, Norfolk Militia 1759
The existing county militias had proved to be utterly ineffective during the Jacobite emergency in 1745, therefore the 1756 invasion scare saw a new Militia Act. Apart from putting the militia on a more efficient footing, it permitted the Crown to embody it for permanent duty anywhere in England and Wales during wartime. Only arms (a rather basic 'Militia' pattern musket) and coats were provided at Government expense. Other clothing and equipment was the responsibility of the county in which the regiment was raised. Contemporary illustrations indicate that these coats were often quite different in style from those worn by the regular army, perhaps sometimes for reasons of economy.

The appearance of the Norfolk Militia is unusually well documented in a series of sketches illustrating a contemporary drill book, Wyndham's 'Plan of Discipline for the Use of the Militia of the County of Norfolk' (1759). The lack of marching gaiters reflects their largely sedentary role but the general cut of the uniform appears rather French in style. In 1759 it was noted that; 'The Drummers and fifers were all little boys with fur caps and looked very pretty.' Black facings

Scots Guardsman, by Edward Dayes, 1792. This soldier wears the uniform prescribed in 1768 in its final form with a stand-up collar and calf-length gaiters. (NMS)

were still being worn by the two regiments of Norfolk Militia at the time of the American War and during the Napoleonic Wars, and this may explain why the short lived 106th Foot (Norwich Rangers) also adopted black facings when raised in 1794. At any rate, although few of the senior officers and captains of the 106th had any discernible connection with the county, a number of the newly gazetted ensigns and lieutenants are known to have previously served in the Norfolk Militia.

E2: Officer, Norfolk Militia 1759

This figure, again based on sketches in Wyndham's drill book, displays some interesting features, not least the single breasted coat. The sketches depict both junior officers and company commanders wearing boots and carrying fusils and bayonets in place of the regulation spontoon or half-pike. In so doing they were presumably aping regular army practice. Surviving orderly books and standing orders belonging to regular battalions invariably prescribe the wearing of boots on active service and muskets were obviously more practical than spontoons.

Generally speaking militia officers' uniforms appear to have been more elaborate and richly decorated than those worn by regulars. Unlike most regular army officers, whose origins more frequently lay amongst the middle classes, militia officers were almost invariably drawn from the county aristocracy and gentry. Their uniforms naturally reflected their superior wealth and social status, but the fact that they were not liable to be spoiled on active service may also have been a factor.

The band, grenadiers and some very diminutive drummers and fifers of a regiment of Foot Guards at St. James's Palace 1790. Although identified as the 3rd or Scots Guards, the button loops are spaced evenly, which would suggest the 1st Regiment. The curious shako-like headdress worn by the fifers is interesting. (NMS)

E3: Officer, Durham Militia 1760s

This figure, based on a portrait of a grenadier company officer named Crozier Surtees, again displays some interesting variations in style from regular army uniform. Unlike the Norfolk Militia, the Durhams had lapels, but the cuffs and lacings are in light dragoon style. A surviving grenadier cap is black fur with an embroidered front and a green bag. The use of dark, slightly bluish green facings, is intriguing since the same facing colour was adopted in 1758 by Colonel John Lambton's 68th Foot. Although the 68th did not receive their 'Durham' title until after the American War, there is little doubt that it merely regularised an existing county affiliation established by Lambton, who belonged to a prominent Durham family.

F: Scottish Fencibles
F1: Officer, Sutherland Fencibles 1759

At the outbreak of the Seven Years War the Scottish militia was even more moribund than its English counterpart and with no existing structure to remodel, the Government opted instead in 1759 to raise two battalions of 'Fencibles'; one in Argyllshire and the other in Sutherland. Both were areas which had been conspicuously reliable during the Jacobite emergency 14 years previously. A 'fencible' was an old Scots term for a militiaman or more precisely someone capable of carrying arms 'defencible' and, although in a manner of speaking regulars, both units were to be employed in home defence duties and could not be sent overseas. In this respect they were not unlike the ten provincial battalions raised in England during the Jacobite emergency. However, while the officers of those corps had succeeded in obtaining regular commissions and the certainty of half pay to follow, fencible officers did not enjoy equality with their regular counterparts and unless injured in the service were not entitled to half pay when their corps were disbanded.

Both battalions also wore very similar uniforms

with yellow facings and plaids of the ordinary Government sett. The same facings and tartans were consistently adopted by other regular and fencible battalions subsequently raised in these areas. It is not at all clear how the two regiments were distinguished, though the arrangement of the lace loopings probably differed. The wearing of regimental tartans by officers of highland regiments at this early period was by no means universal. While some did so, others like William Gordon of Fyvie, Lieutenant Colonel of the 105th Highlanders, evidently wore whatever took their fancy. [See MAA 261.]

F2: Private, Light Company, South Fencibles 1778

Fencible Regiments were again raised during the American War and although they were still predominantly 'Highland' corps, the South Fencibles were, as their title suggests, raised by the Duke of Buccleuch in southern Scotland in 1778. Their only recorded action took place on 20 April 1779 when a party of recruits for the 42nd and 71st Highlanders mutinied at Leith on being drafted into the 83rd (Glasgow Volunteers). Some 200 men of the South Fencibles suppressed the mutiny in a short, but vicious fight on the quayside. Captain James Mansfield, a sergeant, corporal and two grenadiers were killed and six wounded. Nine mutineers were killed and 22 wounded.

Based upon a contemporary painting, this light infantryman is dressed pretty much according to regulations with the rather unpopular black leather chain cap. Although intended to be a more practical alternative to the ordinary cocked hat, these caps were all too frequently made rather too small for the sake of neatness, predictably resulting in a distressing tendency to fall off. Another frequently expressed criticism was the lack of a peak to shade the eyes when firing and it is little wonder that substitutes were sought.

Sir James Grant of Grant, Colonel of the 1st or Strathspey Fencibles, raised 1793. This well-known print by John Kay illustrates a typical highland officer's uniform of the period – only the short jacket and bonnet are distinctive features. Note how a light spadroon is carried in place of the expected basket-hilted broadsword. (Author's collection)

F3: Subaltern, Hopetoun Fencibles 1793

War with France in 1793 once more saw the raising of a considerable number of fencible regiments in Scotland and eventually in England and Ireland as well. One of the first was the Earl of Hopetoun's regiment, raised in the Edinburgh area. Under their terms of service they could not be marched out of Scotland unless and until there was an actual French invasion. It was quickly realised, of course, that this stipulation was quite unworkable, but subsequent attempts to persuade the fencibles to serve south of the border at first met with some resistance and, in the case of the 1st (Strathspey) Fencibles, outright mutiny. The Hopetoun Fencibles, stationed for some reason at Banff in the north of Scotland, hardly a strategically important location, were slightly less vociferous; which did not prevent some of their more excitable officers dumping the regimental ammunition into the harbour as a precautionary measure. In the end, however, both they and the 6th (Gordon) Fencibles agreed to serve in England.

Drawing on this unhappy lesson, subsequent letters of service stipulated that fencible regiments could be employed anywhere within the British Isles. Eventually this was widened still further to take in service anywhere in Europe, although it was rather pushing things when one Irish unit ended up in Egypt.

The uniform of the Hopetoun Fencibles is usefully illustrated in a number of sketches by the celebrated Edinburgh caricaturist John Kay. The blue-grey facings are unusual but were also adopted by the MacKay or Reay Fencibles. The curved sabre fit for a hero also appears in a sketch of Hopetoun himself and may therefore be a regimental pattern carried in preference to the straight-bladed spadroon.

G: Edinburgh units
G1: Private, Edinburgh Defence Band 1781

Although there was no centrally organised militia system in Scotland during the 18th century, the burghs were generally quick enough to raise forces for their own defence in times of crisis. The Jacobite emergency is an obvious case in point, but the Seven Years War also saw the raising of local volunteers. In August 1759 the Aberdeen Town Council resolved to 'borrow or buy from two to three hundred stand of small arms for the use and defence of the inhabitants, with ammunition conform'. The arms were duly obtained from the government and a body of 500 part-time volunteers was formed. A rather more useful step by the council was to assist in the raising of recruits for a regular light infantry unit; Craufurd's 85th Royal Volunteers. [See MAA 285.] A subsequent offer to raise a battalion of volunteers in 1778 was politely declined by the government and defensive preparations were more or less limited to cleaning and oiling the muskets obtained in 1759.

In Edinburgh it was a very similar story, but in 1781 a part-time volunteer battalion was actually raised. Rather quaintly entitled the 'Edinburgh Defence Band', they adopted blue coats faced with orange. As in 1745 the choice of blue coats seems to have been deliberately intended to distinguish the middle-class volunteers from the regulars – a distinction which would be abandoned in the 1790s. This figure and the light blue coat is based on a contemporary print, but a description in the Scots Magazine for October 1781 refers to a *dark* blue coat with blue cuffs and lapels.

G2 & G3: Edinburgh Town Guard

The Edinburgh Town Guard was a paramilitary police force, originally established in 1607, and very largely made up of old soldiers. Like the notorious Edinburgh caddies or street porters, most of them were also highlanders and by all accounts a pretty tough bunch indeed. By the middle of the 18th century they generally comprised about 120 soldiers divided into three companies and, although regularly clothed and equipped, they lived at home and could work at what trade they pleased when off duty. Not surprisingly they were far from popular and according to Sir Walter Scott, who remembered them only too well, they 'were neither by birth, education, or former habits, trained to endure with much patience the insults of the rabble, or the provoking petulance of truant schoolboys, and idle debauchees of all descriptions, with whom their occupation brought them into contact . . . with their grim and valiant corporal, John Dhu, (the fiercest-looking fellow I ever saw), [they] were, in my boyhood, the alternative terror and derision of the petulant brood of the High-school.'

John Dhu had served with the grenadier company of the 42nd at Ticonderoga, but other veterans, including many of the officers, came from the Scots Brigade in Dutch service.

The uniform is usefully depicted in a number of sketches by John Kay and pretty well conforms to regular army style with the notable exception of the red waistcoat and breeches. Firelocks and bayonets were carried as required, but for ordinary policing duties lochaber axes were apparently preferred. Kay's sketches show the officers armed only with swords but it appears that they too paraded with fusils on occasion - the most celebrated being in 1736 when Captain John Porteous shot a member of a mob trying to free a condemned smuggler.

H: The East India Company

Strictly speaking the military forces maintained by the East India Company were not part of King George's Army at all, though it took a near mutiny in 1796 to preserve their independence. Nevertheless, no study of the 18th century British Army would be complete without some consideration of the Company forces.

The East India Company's army only began to take shape in the middle of the 18th century. The Company's charter had long given it the power to maintain armed forces in the East, but this provision was originally intended to do no more than allow it to recruit small bands of native mercenaries to serve as guards on the Company's premises. However, the rather haphazard expansion of the Company's spheres of influence, and growing conflict with the French, saw a dramatic expansion in the size of the Company's forces in the three Presidencies of Madras, Bombay and Bengal, and the development of a growing professionalism besides.

H1: Capt. R. Bannatyne, Madras Army 1759

Even as late as the 1750s the Company forces were rather loosely organised. The sepoy units were to all intents and purposes free companies, recruited and largely commanded by native officers. Prior to 1759 battalions formed from these companies were often temporary formations placed under the command of quite junior British officers.

Entrants into the Company's service were first appointed as cadets, through the patronage of the directors. Thereafter promotion was regulated

strictly by seniority, rather than by the rather haphazard combination of purchase, interest and merit to be found in the regular service. 'We are not,' said one officer, 'generally speaking, men of interest, else we should not have preferred a service in which seniority gives command.'

In the early days, promotion could be quite swift, offering considerable opportunities for ambitious young men. However, after the Seven Years War, promotion became much more difficult to obtain. Moreover, when the regular 39th Foot were sent out to India in 1754, Parliament passed a Mutiny Act For

and provincial officers in North America, but it caused considerable resentment. As Company officers never failed to point out, it was not simply a matter of seniority. It was bad enough, as one put it that officers grown grey in the Company's service should be 'superseded by young Gentlemen recent from the Academy, many of whom have not been so long in existence as the Dates of our Commissions'. What made matters worse was the very different nature of their duties; a captain in the Company's service was normally expected to command a battalion.

In 1788 this inequality was partially remedied when Company officers were granted brevet regular commissions, backdated to 1783, but there was no improvement in the slow rate of promotion or any other attempt made to put Company officers on an equal footing with their regular colleagues.

An early entrant into the Company's service was a Scot named Robert Bannatyne who was appointed to a cadetship in 1754 and within six months was commissioned an ensign of 'English Infantry', i.e. the Madras Europeans. Subsequently he received command of a sepoy battalion while still only a lieutenant and by 1758 was a captain and town major of Madras during the unsuccessful French siege. During the siege he distinguished himself in leading a sortie which routed the Franco-Irish Regiment de Lally. Unfortunately this promising career was cut short by his death at the storming of Conjeveram on 12 April 1759.

This figure is based in part on a portrait and a surviving coat belonging to a Swiss mercenary officer named Frischmann, and partly on an inventory of Captain Bannatyne's effects auctioned off after his untimely demise. His uniforms and copy of Bland's *Treatise of Military Discipline* were bought by an Ensign Dormand.

There is little or nothing to distinguish him from his regular army counterparts. At this early period all European soldiers in the Company's Madras army, including those serving with sepoy units, wore red coats with buff facings, probably because their first commander, Major Stringer Lawrence, had originally served in the regular 14th Foot.

H2: Private, Madras Europeans 1776

European recruits for the Company's armies were always a rather dubious lot, and the independent company which originally garrisoned Madras was

Above left: Reconstruction: officer 1st Battalion, The Royals, San Domingo, 1794. A round hat and short, unlaced round jacket are worn in preference to the long coat and cocked hat worn in temperate areas. On active service boots were invariably substituted for shoes and gaiters. Above: this reconstruction is based in part on contemporary descriptions and in part on a slightly later sketch of an officer of the 16th by William Loftie. (Author's collection)

India which stipulated, *inter alia*, that regular officers would always outrank Company officers in the same grade, irrespective of their actual seniority. A similar situation existed and was accepted *vis à vis* regular

not known as the 'Gun Room Crew' for nothing. In 1787 an admittedly prejudiced Lord Cornwallis complained that recent drafts had included 'broken gentlemen', former army officers, half pay naval officers and even the odd clergyman, all united only by a pressing need to leave England as quickly as possible. Foreigners, too, were to be found in the ranks and in the early days there were even a couple of companies of Swiss mercenaries.

This reconstruction is largely based on orders issued by Major General James Stuart on 11 December 1776:

'The Acting Commander in Chief has thought proper to diminish the quantity of necessaries formerly to be provided by each soldier, which are now to be four shirts made full and long, three black neckcloths and one white ditto, to clasp, three waistcoats made to button low down, two pair of breeches made full, to come up well upon the belly, and to cover the knees, two pairs of pantaloons, two pair of stockings, regimental uniforms, one pair of black gaiters to button, two pair of shoes.

The Commander in Chief takes this occasion to say that in respect to the dress of the soldier he does not expect all the precision and exactness of a European parade, he knows the climate will not admit of it, but he expects a uniform soldierlike appearance in the whole army, answerable to the means afforded by the Honourable Company which are very ample; for the condition of a private soldier here in their service is to his knowledge better than in any other service in the known world.'

The means referred to was not the miserable pittance which came to a soldier as pay, but to the provision of *Batta*, an additional allowance originally paid only on active service, but soon institutionalised. The very least an officer or soldier could look for was 'Half Batta' – paid in peacetime in Madras – but in Bengal 'Double Batta' was the rule at all times and both officers and men were fiercely protective of this right – as Robert Clive discovered to his cost in the 'Batta Mutiny' of 1766.

H3: Bengal Sepoy 1790s

The best of the Company's officers were appointed

An attractive modern study, by Skeoch Cumming, of a drummer of the 100th (Gordon) Highlanders, 1794. (NMS) to the locally recruited sepoy battalions.

In 1786 Cornwallis made the interesting observation that the sepoys were; 'fine men and would not in size disgrace the Prussian ranks.' He went on to praise their courage but got distinctly sniffy about their drill. Most of the officers in these units were actually themselves Indians and in 1794 it was reckoned that the ratio between (British) officers and other ranks in Bengal was 1:48. Largely in order to speed up their promotion prospects British officers v appointed in ever greater numbers to Sepoy units from the early 1800s onwards, effectively reducing the native officers' status to that of senior NCOs – a source of considerable grievance in years to come.

At first the Sepoys appear to have been un-uniformed, but in September 1759 the Madras units were put into a simple uniform combining short red jackets with native clothing. The other presidencies followed suit and by the 1790s their uniforms were as strictly regulated as their European counterparts.

This figure is based on some watercolour sketches by an unknown artist. Madras and Bombay sepoys wore broadly similar uniforms. The blue facings and yellow lace suggest he could be a member of the 1/20th Bengal Native Infantry, originally raised as a Marine battalion.

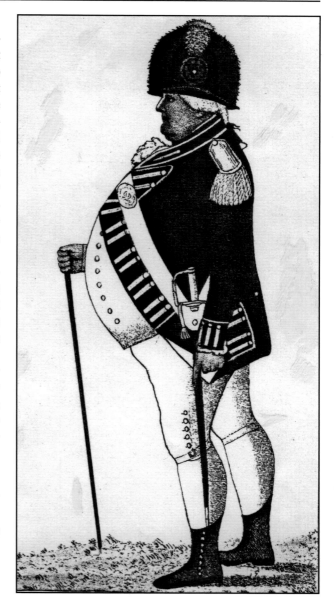

Captain John Rose of Holme; another print by Kay, this time depicting a company officer of the Strathspey Fencibles wearing breeches and a fur-crested round hat. Surviving Orderly books reveal that this uniform was very common in highland regiments in the 1790s. Indeed an order that officers of the Reay Fencibles should parade in highland dress was greeted with consternation since none of them apparently possessed any! (Author's collection)

INTRODUCTION

In 1740, there were some 500 cavalry officers on the regular establishment, compared to about 1,450 infantry officers. The inevitable expansion of the army during the War of the Austrian Succession saw the number of infantry (and marine) officers increase to about 2,500, but the number of cavalry officers remained constant. Indeed, only two new regiments were raised during the war, both of them at the height of the Jacobite emergency in 1745. After 1748, the number of cavalry officers again dropped to around 450 against some 1,650 infantry officers.

The outbreak of the Seven Years War again slightly lifted the cavalry total this time to 600. But, by contrast, nearly 4,000 infantry officers were carried on the Army List at the height of the conflict. Further fluctuations followed the end of the war in 1763 and the American War of Independence 1775-1783, but although the total number of cavalrymen had remained higher than in 1740, their relative importance was less. In 1740 cavalrymen accounted for a quarter of the King's officers (excluding Ordnance officers), but by 1793 that proportion had dropped to only a sixth.

However, the figures can be slightly misleading. The steady expansion of the infantry largely reflected the increased need to man imperial garrisons. In operations closer to home though, the perceived importance of the cavalry was undiminished.

During the War of the Austrian Succession two troops of Horse Guards, one troop of Horse Grenadier Guards, the Blues, two other regiments of Horse and seven Dragoon regiments served in Flanders – a total of ten regiments, besides the Horse Guards, while 14 British cavalry regiments served in Germany during the Seven Years War. At the same time 22 infantry regiments had served

Officer's grenadier cap, 2nd (Royal North British) Dragoons. The Greys were famously distinguished not only by their grey horses, but also by the wearing of grenadier caps in place of hats. The prominent display of the garter star rather than the star of St. Andrew is rather surprising but also appears in the depiction of a trooper of the Greys in the 1742 Cloathing Book. *The replacement of the usual white horse on the little flap is also unusual, but a distinction shared at this time with the 21st Foot. (Author)*

in Flanders and 17 in Germany. By contrast, during the American War of Independence, only two regular cavalry regiments; the 16th and 17th Dragoons saw service, although they were of course supported by a number of locally raised provincial units.

The British Army had three classes of cavalry in 1740: Household units, Horse and Dragoons.

Trooper 13th Dragoons as depicted in the 1742 **Cloathing Book**. *This uniform survived virtually unchanged in the 1751 Warrant, but the elaborately decorated saddle housings and holster caps were replaced by a much simpler style sometime before Morier painted a trooper in 1748. (Trustees of the National Museums of Scotland)*

Highest in order of precedence, the Household cavalry comprised four grossly over-officered troops of red-coated Horse Guards (amalgamated into two troops in 1746) and two troops of Horse Grenadiers. Although unquestionably a social elite, the fact that the Horse Guards rarely ventured outside London did nothing for their military efficiency. Only the Horse Grenadiers, originally raised as specialist Dragoons were reckoned to have any real military value and in 1788 both they and the two remaining troops of Horse Guards were amalgamated to form the Lifeguards.

After the Household cavalry proper came the Royal Regiment of Horse Guards (the 'Blues'),

and seven other regiments of Horse. The greater part of the British Army's cavalry however comprised 14 regiments of Dragoons – increased to 15 in 1746. These had originally been no more than mounted infantry and were still looked down upon as such by the Horse. But although regularly trained as infantrymen in the platoon exercise, in reality there was very little – other than their uniforms and rates of pay – to distinguish them from the Horse.

In 1746, the same economy drive which saw the four troops of Horse Guards reduced to two, also saw a change in status for three of the regiments of Horse. Mindful of the fact that the differences between Horse and Dragoons were very largely cosmetic ones, it was decided to convert the regiments of Horse into Dragoons. However, in order to preserve the all important order of precedence and to sweeten the pill a little, those converted regiments were called Dragoon Guards. The Blues, who had previously ranked as the 1st Horse, were spared. Otherwise, there ought, in theory to have been seven regiments of Dragoon Guards and 15 of Dragoons. But in fact, Dublin Castle for reasons best known to itself decided against converting the four regiments of Horse then maintained on the separate Irish Establishment.

As a result, the 2nd or King's Horse became the 1st or King's Dragoon Guards, the 3rd or Queen's Horse became the 2nd Dragoon Guards and the 4th became the 3rd Dragoon Guards. The 5th to 8th Horse were then redesignated as the 1st to 4th (Irish) Horse, although eventually they too finally became Dragoon Guards in 1789.

This round of alterations did not affect the total number of units, and consequently the disbandment of the short-lived 15th Dragoons in 1748 left the army with the same number of line cavalry regiments as in 1740, except that they now comprised three regiments of Dragoon Guards, four regiments of Horse and 14 regiments of Dragoons. Each category was distinguished one from another only by various peculiarities of dress.

Co-operation with the Imperial army in Flanders during the 1740s had pointed up the usefulness of light cavalry and the 15th Dragoons,

originally raised during the Jacobite emergency as Kingston's 10th Horse, are said to have been trained as hussars. General Henry Hawley (who was nobody's fool despite his quite undeserved reputation as a vicious martinet) had in fact advocated the raising of such a unit as early as 1728. But to Cumberland's dismay the regiment, although a good one, was disbanded in 1748. It was all the more galling of course that the 13th and 14th Dragoons, who had distinguished themselves during the late Jacobite emergency only by the speed with which they ran away every time they met the enemy, were retained on the Irish Establishment.

The outbreak of the Seven Years War in 1756 brought a slight increase in the size of the cavalry. At first, as was the case with the infantry, this simply took the form of an augmentation in the strength of existing units carried on the English Establishment. But because of the desperate need for some kind of light cavalry 11 additional troops authorised on 14 April 1757, were intended to fill that role. After that, there was no looking back and beginning in March 1759 Letters of Service were granted for no less than seven new cavalry regiments, all of them designated as Light Dragoons. Similarly all the new cavalry units raised during the American War of Independence

and those raised after 1793 were also designated as Light Dragoons. The 19th, 20th and 21st Light Dragoons were actually formed by brigading together the newly raised Light Troops of the Heavy cavalry regiments and by 1783 nearly all the old regiments of 'heavy' dragoons had been converted to light cavalry.

Unfortunately, although attended by considerable enthusiasm this preoccupation with the merits of light cavalry in reality extended little further than the intricacies of military millinery. The sad fact of the matter was that, in contrast to the solid professionalism of the British infantry, all too many cavalry officers did indeed subscribe to the not entirely apocryphal view that their chief function was to lend some tone to what might otherwise be a vulgar brawl. And their tactical

Cornet, 8th Horse. Said to have been carried and defended by Cornet Richardson at Dettingen in 1743, this rather fine cornet is of crimson damask with a gold fringe and the arms of General Ligonier. The small union in the canton appears to have been suppressed in 1743. (Author)

repertoire was almost entirely limited to the charge.

In 1758 the intention had been very different. The *Weekly Journal* for 23 May reported approvingly on the Light Troop of the 11th Dragoons, then preparing to take part in one of the raids on the French coast: 'The hussars of the nine regiments are now preparing to go on the expedition. The flower of these Hussars is the Troop commanded by Captain Lindsay quartered at Maidenhead where they have been practising the Prussian exercise and for some days have been digging trenches and leaping over them, also leaping high hedges with broad ditches on the other side. Their Captain on Saturday last swam with his horse over the Thames and back again and the whole Troop were yesterday to swim the river.'

This was all well and good, but the work done by the likes of William Lindsay was undone when the first of the new Light Dragoon regiments went into action. In July 1760, the newly landed

15th Light Dragoons were ordered to take part in a heavy raid on the French garrison of Marburg. En route the raiders unexpectedly ran into five French battalions near Emsdorf. An attempt to surprise this detachment failed, but after the 15th cut the Marburg road the French tried to escape across country. One battalion got clean away but the others were twice charged by the 15th. Finally, as the exhausted dragoons formed for a third charge the French – actually a German regiment, the Royal Baverie – decided that they had had enough and surrendered.

In the euphoria which followed this notable feat of arms, the fact that they had lost 125 men and 168 horses in the action and afterwards had to be sent back to Hanover to reorganise was quietly overlooked. Thereafter, the mundane demands of outpost work and skirmishing were subordinated to training for the charge and in the hope of another such glorious enterprise as Emsdorf. The regiment made so much of this victory that they emblazoned the details on their helmet plates

There was little chance of finding a similar triumph during the American War of Independence. While the infantry learned valuable lessons there, the cavalry learned little. Much of the work done there did indeed centre around the demanding skills of outpost work, reconnaissance and skirmishing. But only two regular dragoon regiments, the 16th and 17th, served there. Even the 16th came home in 1778 and their influence at home was negligible.

Consequently, at the outset of the great war with Revolutionary France in 1793, there was virtually nothing save their uniforms to distinguish Light Dragoons from their heavier brethren. This point was dramatically emphasised by the action at Villers-en-Cauchies on 24 April 1794, which again involved the 15th Light Dragoons. Two squadrons of the regiment, together with two squadrons of the Austrian Leopold Hussars, charged and dispersed six battalions of French infantry. From then on, it was useless to expect British light cavalry to do anything more complicated than to charge straight at the enemy.

ORGANISATION

In 1740, each troop of Horse Guards mustered no fewer than 18 officers, comprising a colonel, first and second lieutenant colonels, first and second majors, four 'exempts', four brigadiers, four sub-brigadiers and an adjutant. When the four troops were being consolidated into two at the end of 1746, they were ordered to be completed to 150 privates apiece.

The line regiments however, including the Blues, were much more conventionally officered, and were normally made up of six or occasionally seven troops, each commanded by a captain, lieutenant and a cornet. The latter was the equivalent of the infantry ensign. As in the infantry three of the troop commanders were also field officers: the colonel, lieutenant colonel and major, and the colonel's own troop was actually led by a captain-lieutenant.

In addition to its officers, each troop of Dragoons or Dragoon Guards comprised three sergeants, three corporals, two drummers, and 59 troopers. The establishment also included a hautbois or oboist in each troop, but this individual existed only on paper, his pay being one of the colonel's traditional perquisites.

In action, cavalry troops were normally paired

Colonel James Gardiner, 13th Dragoons (1688-1745). Born in Linlithgow, the son of another professional soldier, Gardiner was killed at Prestonpans in 1745 while commanding the 13th Dragoons. (NMS)

off to form squadrons and drew up three men deep, either in line or with two squadrons up and the third in reserve. It was possible to vary this practice if the tactical situation demanded it. At Prestonpans in 1745, General Cope formed both his Dragoon regiments in two ranks deep rather than the usual three. In the following year at Culloden, General Hawley deployed the two regular Dragoon regiments in their individual troops rather than pairing them off into squadrons. In both cases this was done because the likelihood of action against hostile cavalry was nonexistent.

Although trained for dismounted action, British cavalrymen almost invariably went into action sitting on their horses' backs. The night battle at Clifton in 1745 appears to be the only occasion

Colonel Gardiner of the 13th Dragoons lived at Bankton House on the fringe of the Prestonpans battlefield. Breaches were made in the park walls in the hours before the battle in order to allow free passage through them by General Cope's troops. The subsequent repairs to the wall linking the main house with one of two flanking pavilions can clearly be seen. (Author)

during the period in which extensive use was made of dismounted dragoons.

UNIFORMS AND EQUIPMENT

As in the infantry the clothing and equipment issued to each soldier was set out in the *Regulations for the Cloathing of His Majesty's Forces in Time of Peace 20 Nov. 1729*. This specified:

For a trooper
  A new cloth coat, well lined with serge.
  A new waistcoat.
  A new laced hat.
  A pair of new large buff gloves, with stiff tops, once in two years.

A pair of new boots, as they shall be found wanting.

As it is difficult to fix a period of time for providing saddles, it is to be left to the judgement of the general officer, who may be appointed to review them.
Housings, (holster) caps, new horse furniture, bitts, and stirrup-irons; cloaks faced with the livery of the regiment, entirely new; and new buff or buff coloured cross-belts, to be provided as they shall be wanting.
The second mounting is to consist of new-laced hats, and horse collars.

For a dragoon
  A new cloth coat, well lined with serge.
  A new waistcoat.
  A pair of new breeches.
  A new laced hat.
  A pair of new large buff-coloured gloves with stiff tops.
  A pair of new boots, as they shall be wanting.
  Saddles to be left to the judgement of the general officer who may be appointed to review them.
  Housings, [holster] caps, new horse furniture, bitts and stirrup-irons; and cloaks faced with the

livery of the regiment, entirely new, as they shall be wanting.

New buff or buff-coloured accoutrements; viz. A shoulder-belt, with a pouch, a waist-belt, sufficient to carry the sword, with a place to receive the bayonet and sling for the arms, such as the general officers, appointed to inspect the cloathing, shall approve of, as they shall be wanting.

The second mounting is to consist of new-laced hats, gloves, and horse-collars.

Perhaps the most striking difference between these lists and the similar ones relating to the provision of clothing for infantrymen is the degree to which the clothing and equipment issued was expected to last longer. Instead of a regular two year replacement cycle the cavalryman could expect to be clothed every year – including a new waistcoat and not a red one cut down from the previous year's coat, but everything else was to be replaced only as and when required.

An inspection report on the 4th 'Irish' Horse in 1771 disapprovingly noted that the boots had been received as long ago as 1767. Consequently, while the commanders of infantry regiments were required to certify annually that they had supplied their men with the clothing to which they were entitled, commanders of cavalry units only had to do so every two years.

Regiments of Horse, Dragoon Guards, Dragoons and Light Dragoons were distinguished in the following ways. Regiments of Horse had fairly narrow lapels which stretched from the collar to the hem of the coat. Dragoon Guards had smaller, broader, 'half lapels' like those worn by infantrymen. Dragoons had no lapels at all, but Light Dragoons wore narrow lapels similar to those worn by infantrymen after 1768. The 16th were, at first, an exception and Morier's painting

Contemporary map of the battle of Falkirk (17 January 1746). General Hawley's three regiments of Dragoons were posted on the left of his front line and opened the battle with an unsuccessful attack against the Jacobite infantry. A miserable performance was then compounded by riding over the loyalist Glasgow Volunteers in their flight – and naturally being shot up by them in the process. (NMS)

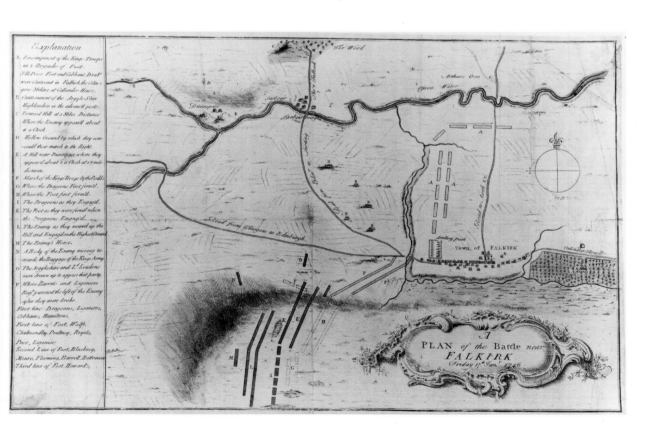

Drummer's cap, 13th Dragoons. Like those worn by infantry drummers this cap has a rather lower front than a grenadier cap and the bag or stocking therefore hangs down at the back. The trophies displayed on the front are simply a conventional design and do not reflect any particular battle honours – indeed the only active service seen by the 13th Dragoons throughout the 18th century consisted of running away from the rebels at Prestonpans and Falkirk. (Author)

shows the original uniform to have been a single breasted coat of 'heavy' dragoon style with black collar and cuffs. They did however subsequently adopt lapels.

Apart from their leather, copper or brass helmets, the Light Troops attached to regiments of Dragoon Guards and Dragoons during the Seven Years War wore the uniform of their parent regiment – that is, with half lapels for Dragoon Guards and no lapels for Dragoons. With the exception of the Blues, all cavalry regiments wore red coats until 1784 when blue jackets were adopted by Light Dragoons. At that point, those regiments which had previously worn blue facings were ordered to adopt red ones instead.

Under King George II, cavalry regiments were also distinguished from their infantry counterparts by generally wearing waistcoats and breeches of the facing colour rather than plain red ones. In 1768, however, they too were ordered to adopt white linings and small-clothes, although inspection reports reveal that a number of units wore buff linings in the early 1770s.

The trumpeters and kettledrummers of the Horse (and Dragoon Guards) and drummers of Dragoon regiments wore the traditional reversed coat colours liberally decorated with lace. Dragoon drummers had the same small mitre style caps worn by infantry drummers prior to 1768, but trumpeters of Horse and Dragoon Guards wore the same cocked hats as the troopers and officers. Light Dragoon drums and trumpets however wore helmets from the outset. This distinctive clothing reflected the fact that drums and trumpets were signallers rather than musicians and had to be readily identified by officers in the midst of battle. Consequently many regiments also went so far as to mount them on greys as a further distinction, although inspection reports reveal that this was far from being a universal practice.

Cavalrymen required more necessaries than their infantry counterparts and these included black woollen gaiters for dismounted drills and guards, half gaiters, forage caps, curry combs etc. and 'frocks'. These were presumably some kind of smocks to be worn for stable duties – although a 1759 order to the Greys laid down that they were to be worn over coats on the march, perhaps because the roads they were travelling on were particularly dusty at the time.

Accoutrements comprised a sword belt, worn over the right shoulder by Horse and around the waist by the Horse Grenadier Guards, Dragoons and Dragoon Guards, and either a carbine belt or a cartridge box and sling, according to arm. Camp Equipage issued by the Board of Ordnance included the usual canteens and haversacks, and picket poles. On the march these were strapped to the trooper's firelock and if time permitted were thrown away at the commencement of an action.

Weapons were somewhat more varied. Generally speaking at the outset of the period all cavalrymen carried broadswords (or occasionally single-edged backswords) with basket hilts. These hilts were often Scottish in origin, differing from those carried by highlanders by an oval ring set into the inside of the basket to allow the trooper to hold sword and reins simultaneously. As the swords were purchased by the colonel there was no fixed pattern and particularly after the introduction of Light Dragoons a number of varieties abounded. Not until 1788 was there any real attempt at standardisation.

Most cavalrymen also carried a pair of pistols, though Light Dragoons were originally supposed to have only one. In theory Dragoons were supposed to thrust their pistols into their belts when dismounted but there is no indication that they did so at Clifton in 1745.

All cavalrymen also carried a carbine of some description. Again there were a number of patterns in use. Until 1770, Dragoons carried a .65 Short Land Pattern firelock with a 42-inch barrel and a wooden ramrod. They were also equipped with a bayonet for it. On march past in review order they were expected to carry their firelocks with bayonets fixed. Doubtless to their dismay, Dragoons Guards were also encumbered with this weapon after their conversion in 1746.

The regiments of Horse were equipped instead with a slightly lighter carbine which, after 1757 at least, had a barrel length of 37 inches and was of .65 or .68 calibre. It was fully stocked to the muzzle and, in place of the usual sling fitted to Dragoon firelocks, it had a ring and bar fitted over the sideplate. This arrangement permitted it, in theory, to be clipped to the carbine belt so that it could be fired from horseback, though it is questionable whether this was ever done. Normally the carbine was strapped to the saddle, butt downwards in Dragoon style.

Light Dragoons on the other hand were in theory expected to skirmish on horseback using their carbines. Kingston's 10th Horse were certainly described as doing so, although it was not until they were taken over by the Duke of Cumberland as the 15th Dragoons that they received a special carbine. This was of .65 calibre with a 42-inch barrel capable of taking a bayonet. Fitted with both an infantry sling and a ring and rather large bar for attaching to a carbine belt, it only really differed from the Short Land Pattern normally carried by Dragoons in its lighter calibre. Having seen comparatively little use these

weapons were appropriated by the Horse Grenadier Guards when the 15th were disbanded in 1748. Subsequently this weapon formed the pattern for the Heavy Dragoon Carbine of 1770.

The Light Dragoon Carbine of 1756 was rather handier with a 36-inch barrel but, in 1760, General Elliot of the 15th Dragoons designed a still shorter one with a 28-inch barrel. Although generally agreed to be an improvement this

Artillery officer 1742, after a contemporary watercolour sketch. The chief points of interest are the comparatively plain appearance of the uniform and his being armed with a fusil. His waistcoat and breeches are scarlet in contrast to the blue small-clothes worn by gunners. (Author)

important, if seldom used, facility to fix a bayonet on to it. In the 1780s experiments were also made with rifled carbines.

Each cavalryman was also provided with harness and saddle housings for his horse. In 1742 the latter, comprising a shabraque or decorative blanket and a pair of holster caps (covers), were quite elaborate with what appears to have been an embroidered edging enlivened by knights' helmets and trophies of arms. By 1748, however, they had been replaced by a much simpler pattern. Probably introduced at the Duke of Cumberland's behest, they displayed the regiment's facing colour and were edged with coloured stripes. The shabraque bore a cartouche with the regiment's number surrounded by a Union wreath, while the holster caps had the Royal cypher in the middle and the number was repeated on the edging – for example, XIII D for 13th Dragoons.

Gunner, Royal Artillery, 1742, after a contemporary watercolour sketch. The coat at this period is substantially unlaced but by 1748 when David Morier painted the train at Roermond in Holland a considerable amount of yellow tape binding had appeared. Although depicted here as carrying only a linstock, large powder-horn and brass-hilted hanger, Morier's painting shows that firelocks were also carried on active service. (Author)

REGIMENTAL DISTINCTIONS

The details here are all taken from the 1742 *Cloathing Book*, Morier's paintings c1748, and the Clothing Warrants of 1751 and 1768. Under the 1768 Warrant, coloured waistcoats and breeches were replaced by white ones and coat linings became either buff or white. Other variations are culled from the inspection reports of various dates and officers' portraits. With the exception of the 1st Horse (Blues), all regiments wore red coats until the 1784 when blue jackets were adopted by light Dragoons.

1st Horse (Royal Regiment of Horseguards)
Blue coats, red facings & waistcoat, blue breeches. No lace on coat. Buff small-clothes worn after 1768.

1st (King's) Dragoon Guards
Blue facings, waistcoat and breeches. Buff small clothes 1768. Yellow lace with buttons arranged in pairs. Red furniture, latterly with "Royal" lace: yellow with a blue stripe. Drummers mounted on greys.

weapon was fully stocked to the muzzle, precluding the use of a bayonet. In 1773 though Elliot produced a second version again with a 28-inch barrel, which this time could be fitted with a bayonet. This version was adopted as the standard Light Dragoon carbine. Another Light Dragoon carbine, issued to the 21st (Royal Forresters) was very similar to the first pattern Elliot except for a better standard of workmanship and the all

Lieutenant Edward Harvey, 10th Dragoons, 1740s. Harvey (1718-1778) entered the army as a Cornet in the 10th Dragoons in 1741 and remained with that regiment until gaining a Captaincy in the 7th Dragoons in 1747. Promoted to Major in 1751 he became Lieutenant Colonel of the 6th (Inniskilling) Dragoons in 1754 and was promoted to full Colonel in 1760. A Major General in 1762 he briefly commanded the 12th Dragoons 1763-4 and then the 3rd (Irish) Horse until 1775 when he resumed command of the 6th Dragoons. He died in 1778 while simultaneously holding that post, serving as Adjutant General, Governor of Portsmouth and sitting as the Member of Parliament for Harwich. Interestingly although his coat lining and gorget patches are yellow (the 10th's facing colour), his rather plain cuffs are red. (Original in Dundee Art Gallery, photo courtesy of NMS)

Captain Lord Robert Kerr. A Scotsman, he was killed at Culloden while commanding the grenadier company of Barrell's 4th Foot. (NMS)

2nd (Queen's) Dragoon Guards

Buff facings, waistcoat and breeches. Black facings ordered 1783 but not noted until 1785. Yellow lace with buttons set three and three. White small-clothes instead of buff ordered 1774. Red furniture, by 1768 this was buff with 'royal' lace. Bay horses 1768. Drummers and farriers mounted on greys 1776.

3rd (Prince of Wales) Dragoon Guards

White facings and waistcoat, red breeches (white by 1748). Yellow lace with buttons set two and two – a report of 1768 comments on buff tape button loops instead of yellow. White furniture, 'Royal' lace. Trumpeters on greys and farriers on blacks 1776

1st (Irish) Horse – 4th Royal Irish Dragoon Guards 1788

Blue facings, waistcoat and breeches (pale blue by 1748). Officers wearing buff waistcoat and breeches 1768. Dragoon style clothing and accoutrements were not altered to the 'Dragoon' pattern until 1790 although NCOs had 'Dragoon' style uniforms in 1788. Yellow lace – white by 1768 with buttons set two and two. Blue furniture, white lace with red stripe. Trumpeters mounted on greys 1769

2nd (Irish) Horse – 5th Dragoon Guards 1788

Green facings, waistcoat and breeches. 'Full Green' facings 1768, but yellow in 1788. White lace, yellow by 1768 and back to white in 1788 with buttons set two and two.

Green furniture, white lace with red stripe 1768. Yellow furniture, white lace with green stripe ordered in 1788 but old (ie. green) furniture still noted as late as 1792. Trumpeters on bays 1768 and 1775.

3rd (Irish) Horse – 6th Dragoon Guards or Carabineers 1788

Pale yellow facings, buff linings, waistcoat and breeches. White facings by 1769. White lace with buttons set two and two. Buff furniture, then white edged with yellow lace bearing black stripe. Trumpeters on long-tailed greys 1769

4th (Irish) Horse – 7th (Princess Royal's) Dragoon Guards 1788

Black facings, buff small clothes – white 1788. Yellow lace with buttons set two and two. Buff furniture – white 1788 – white lace with black stripe. Trumpeters on greys 1772.

1st (Royal) Dragoons

Blue facings and waistcoat, red breeches (blue by 1748). Yellow lace, buttons set two and two. Sergeants had blue sashes in 1753. Blue furniture, red by 1768 with 'Royal' lace. Drummers and Farriers initially mounted on greys, but blacks by 1777. All horses long-tailed.

2nd (Royal North British) Dragoons

Blue facings, waistcoats and breeches. White lace, buttons set two and two.

Cloth grenadier caps worn by all ranks until 1778, then black bearskin ones. Officers' bearskins 'handsomely' embroidered and ornamented. White accoutrements. Blue furniture with 'Royal' lace. Whole regiment mounted on greys.

Allegedly taken by the French at Fontenoy in 1745 this yellow guidon rather intriguingly bears the combined arms of Robert Rich and his wife. The yellow ground might suggest the 8th Dragoons were it not for the fact that Rich transferred from that regiment to the 4th in 1735. Moreover the 8th (St. George's) Dragoons did not serve in Flanders. Unlikely though it may seem therefore Rich's 4th Dragoons may have been carrying this yellow guidon in 1745, losing both it and the green one illustrated elsewhere at Melle on 9 June 1745 where the regiment lost very heavily. The reverse of the guidon bears a rather old-fashioned doubled GR cypher. (Author)

3rd (King's Own) Dragoons

Light blue facings, waistcoat and breeches. Buff small-clothes 1768. Yellow lace with buttons set three and three. Red furniture, blue by 1768 with 'Royal' lace.

4th Dragoons

Pea-green facings (full green 1768), waistcoat and breeches. White lace with buttons set two and two. Green furniture, white lace with red stripe – changed to 'Royal' lace by 1790. Trumpeters all negroes 1776.

5th (Royal Irish) Dragoons

Blue facings, waistcoat and breeches. Yellow lace, but white by 1768 with buttons set three and three.

Two troops wearing grenadier caps as late as 1768. Said to have been a distinction conferred on the regiment in Queen Anne's time, but ordered to be discontinued 1769 in conformity with 1751 Warrant. Blue furniture with 'Royal' lace. Trumpeters on bays 1775.

6th (Inniskilling) Dragoons

'Full Yellow' facings, waistcoat and breeches. Yellow lace – white by 1768 with buttons set two

and two. Yellow furniture, white lace with blue stripe. Trumpeters and farriers on greys 1777.

7th (Queen's) Dragoons

White facings, waistcoat and breeches. White lace with buttons set three and three. Converted to Light Dragoons 1783. Officers' sword belts noted to be worn under the jacket 1789 and 1790 – ordered to be worn outside. White furniture with 'Royal' lace.

8th Dragoons

Orange facings, waistcoat and breeches before 1748 and thereafter yellow. White lace with buttons set three and three. Orange, then yellow furniture, white lace with a yellow stripe. Apparently using goatskin furniture from c1787. Permitted to wear cross belts as a distinction from Queen Anne's war. This distinction was apparently lost when they converted to Light Dragoons in 1775.

9th Dragoons

Buff facings, waistcoat and breeches. White lace with buttons set two and two. Buff furniture, lace white with a blue stripe.

Officer's cap, Light Troop, 2nd Dragoons c1760. In contrast to the rather ambiguously decorated cap worn in 1742 this design, first seen in Morier's painting of 1748 is uncompromisingly Scottish in character. (Author)

10th Dragoons

Yellow facings, waistcoat and breeches. White lace with buttons set three, four and five. Yellow furniture, white lace with green stripe. Officers' swords in form of scimitars without guards to the hilt 1770. Light Dragoons 1783, but 1789 inspection comments on heavy dragoon furniture

11th Dragoons

White cuffs, buff linings, white waistcoat, red breeches – all buff by 1748. White lace, buttons set three and three. White linings reported 1776, but buff in the following year.

Buff furniture, white lace with green stripe. 1775 report noted that housings which had been made up in 1763 but not delivered until 1775 were moth-eaten. Trumpeters on greys 1777.

Light Dragoons 1783 – inspection report for following year comments on clothing being the same as worn when heavy dragoons, only cut shorter and still without lapels.

1789 inspection mentions old heavy dragoon furniture still in use, and buff wings on shells – ordered to be discontinued 1790. Same inspection mentioned swords left on horses when regiment dismounted.

12th Dragoons

White facings and waistcoat, red breeches (white by 1748). On conversion to Light Dragoons (Prince of Wales) received black facings – including half-lapels. White lace with buttons set two and two. Originally white furniture but 1768 Warrant specifies 'black with stripes of white goatskin'. No lace.

13th Dragoons

Green cuffs, buff linings, white waistcoat and breeches – all light green by 1748. Buff small-clothes 1768. Facings also changed to buff on conversion to Light Dragoons in 1783. White lace, although officers had gold lace as early as 1751, but yellow lace specified in 1768. Buttons set three and three. Buff furniture, green by 1768, white lace with yellow stripe.

14th Dragoons

Pale or lemon yellow facings, white waistcoat and breeches – all pale yellow by 1748. Facings briefly changed to green on conversion to Light Dragoons in 1775. Yellow lace, white by 1768 with buttons set three and three.

Pale yellow furniture, white lace with red and green stripes. However, letter of March 1792 gives permission for change from black to yellow furniture. Trumpeters on greys 1775.

15th Dragoons (disb. 1748)

Green facings, buff waistcoat and breeches. Yellow lace. Green furniture.

15th King's Light Dragoons (raised 1759)

Green facings, white linings, waistcoats and breeches. White lace. Granted blue facings in 1766. Buttons set two and two.

Facings changed to red on adopting blue jackets in 1784. 1789 inspection mentions red wings on shells – ordered to be discontinued in the following year.

Black helmets with white fittings, initially green

turban and red mane. Sergeants originally had green sashes.

White furniture, originally edged white with red stripe, but edged with 'Royal' lace after 1766.

Trumpeters on greys 1777. Same inspection mentions swords left on horses when dismounted 'as is practised by the other Dragoon regiments'.

16th Queen's Light Dragoons
Black collar and cuffs, white linings. No lapels on coat, but white lace loops in threes. White waistcoat and breeches. Blue facings – including lapels granted in 1766. Buttons set two and two in 1768. White furniture with 'Royal' lace.

17th Light Dragoons
(No details are known of the uniform worn by the original 17th Dragoons raised but never completed in Scotland by Lord Aberdour. The regiment now known as the 17th was originally raised as the 18th Light Dragoons.)

White facings, waistcoat and breeches. Officers had blue cloaks lined white 1771.

Surviving first pattern helmet has a red front plate, edged with fur and bears a crossed bones badge over the skull. Subsequently skull and crossbones were joined with the skull on top. White turban mentioned in 1768 inspection. White furniture, white lace with black edge.

18th Light Dragoons
White facings, waistcoat and breeches – unauthorised scarlet edging to waistcoat noted in portraits and inspection reports. White lace with buttons set two and two. White furniture, red and white lace.

Hogarth's celebrated March of the Guards to Finchley. This is, no doubt, as exaggerated as most caricatures but nevertheless succeeds very well in conveying the often chaotic nature of military operations. (NMS)

. A REPRESENTATION of the MARCH of the GUARDS towards SCOTLAND, in the YEAR 1745.

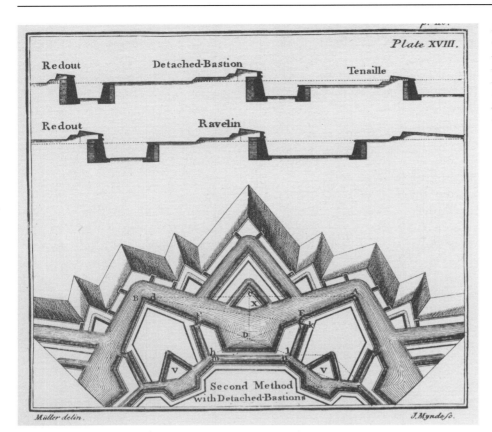

Plate XVIII.

Redout   Detached-Bastion   Tenaille

Redout   Ravelin

Second Method
with Detached-Bastions

Müller delin.   J.Mynde sc.

Eighteenth-century fortifications as depicted in Muller's 'Elements of Fortification'. As far as the British Army was concerned the standard work upon the subject in English. (Author's collection)

19th Light Dragoons (raised 1779 – disbanded 1783)
Green facings, white small-clothes.

19th Light Dragoons (1783-)
See 23rd Light Dragoons.

20th Light Dragoons (raised 1779 – disbanded 1783)
Yellow facings, white small-clothes.

20th (Jamaica) Light Dragoons (raised 1792)
Dark blue jacket with yellow facings. Tin helmet with horsehair mane and alligator badge on front.

21st Light Dragoons (Royal Foresters)
(disbanded 1763)
See text accompanying plate C3.

21st Light Dragoons (raised 1779 – disbanded 1783)
White facings and small-clothes.

22nd Light Dragoons (disbanded 1763)
No details known but possibly black facings.

22nd Light Dragoons (raised 1779 – disbanded 1783)
Green jackets.

23rd Light Dragoons (raised 1779)
Red coats with green facings and white small clothes. Buttons looped two and two. Apparently went out to India wearing green jackets. By virtue of serving there escaped disbandment in 1783 and redesignated 19th Light Dragoons. Facings changed to yellow 1786.

THE BOARD OF ORDNANCE

The Board had a variety of functions in the 18th century, including the supply of guns and ammunition to the Royal Navy as well as to the army. In very general terms it was responsible for supplying the various forces of the crown with all the lethal and non-lethal hardware which they required (including powder, cannon and small arms for the navy), for training and administering the Royal Artillery (including the quite separate Irish Artillery raised in 1755) and Engineers. From there it was a short step to supplying fortifications and, increasingly, purpose-built barracks.

As an organisation it was also, in theory, quite independent and its officers and men were not, strictly speaking, part of the army. Officers received their commissions from the Board, not from the crown. In this respect they were rather like the officers and men of the navy and marines who answered to the Board of Admiralty rather than the King.

This relationship could at times produce some curious anomalies. In the early days, it was common for engineer officers to simultaneously hold military commissions in regiments of the line – and commoner still for regimental officers to fill in as engineers when Woolwich trained personnel were wanting. Indeed, in 1772 Thomas Simes, *The Military Guide for Young Officers* specifically recommended that newly commissioned infantry officers should furnish themselves with a copy of John Muller's 1746 treatise on fortification, but said nothing about other books. Moreover although an Army officer receiving half pay could not serve at the same time in another regiment of the line or even in the militia as these were 'offices of profit under the crown' there was nothing whatever to prevent his working for the Board of Ordnance and drawing his half pay at the same time.

Although the Board's independence could be quite jealously guarded on occasion, it was little exercised in the field. The most obvious distinction was the wearing of blue coats by the King's artillerymen. Curiously enough this sartorial distinction was not extended to the Board's engineer officers until 1782. Until that time they wore red coats, perhaps as a hangover from the days when they also held infantry commissions but more likely to make them less conspicuous. The necessity for close reconnaissance of fortified places made the engineer's job dangerous enough without drawing attention to himself unnecessarily. Having changed to Ordnance blue in 1782,

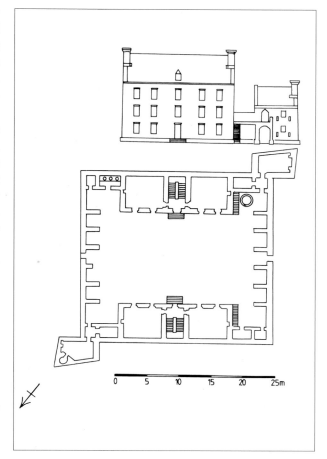

In practice the army's fortifications were often much less elaborate than those described by Muller and other experts. This is a plan of Ruthven barracks, built in 1719-21 and successfully defended by Sergeant Terry Molloy and a dozen men in 1745. It was originally hoped to build four flanking towers (one hesitates to describe them as bastions) 'if the money answers' – very evidently it did not. (Author)

the Engineers reverted to red in 1811 precisely for that very reason, having suffered very high casualties in the Peninsula.

The real distinction between King's officers and Ordnance officers lay in the system of training and promotion. Due to the technical nature of the service, the Board's officers could not purchase their commissions and promotion was entirely a matter of seniority. Moreover while the training, if any, received by the young infantry or cavalry officer was a matter for his regiment, the Board's officers were trained in the intricacies of their craft at Woolwich, and just as importantly

Northern flanking tower, Ruthven Barracks. Terry Molloy and his men shot down a party of Jacobite sappers from these loopholes as they attempted to set fire to the sally-port gate in the foreground.

received 'hands on' experience as Cadet Matrosses (unskilled labourers), Cadet Gunners and Cadet Fireworkers (Corporals) before gaining their commissions.

The four battalions of Royal Artillery, and the quite separate Royal Irish Artillery, were purely administrative units. The basic unit was the company and the one commanded by Captain Lieutenant John Godwin at Culloden was perhaps typical in comprising ten officers, a number of volunteers and 106 NCOs and men. Between them they were responsible for looking after ten 3lb cannon and six Coehorn mortars.

This particular artillery train had been assembled specifically for operations in Scotland and generally speaking the Royal Artillery displayed considerable flexibility in providing the appropriate weight of artillery support for a particular operation. This could vary, according to circumstances, from a single curricle gun and a couple of gunner/instructors, to two or more 'brigades' of artillery. At Minden for example the Royal Artillery mustered a brigade of nine light guns under Captain Foy and nine heavy (12-pounders) under Captain MacBean.

THE PLATES

Plate A: Regular Cavalry 1740s
A1: Trooper, 2nd (Royal North British) Dragoons 1748
The 2nd Dragoons, better known as the Scots Greys, had a solidly impressive combat record during the reign of King George II. In 1742 they were ordered to Flanders and served there until the cessation of hostilities in 1748. In 1745, they were one of only six cavalry regiments left there during the Jacobite emergency. During the Seven Years War, they served in Germany, led by the eccentric Lieutenant Colonel George Preston, who insisted on wearing a 17th-century buffcoat in action.

This figure is based primarily upon Morier's painting of a soldier of the regiment c1748, and a surviving coat in the Scottish United Services Museum. With the obvious exception of the headgear the characteristics of the uniform were common to all dragoon regiments. The coat is double-breasted and unlaced. By 1753, only the 2nd and 3rd Regiments of Dragoons were wearing

buttons and holes on both sides of the coat and in January of that year they were both ordered to fall into line with the other regiments who by then were wearing single-breasted coats.

Thin white lace binding appeared on the buttonholes by 1748, but otherwise the only real decorative feature is the shoulder-knot worn on the right. The elaborate version worn by officers is said to represent the points or ties on a knightly arming doublet, but it is questionable whether those worn by troopers of dragoons did so. Since troopers ranked with infantry corporals, the shoulder knot may simply have been a method of displaying that equality. Another notable distinguishing feature of cavalry uniform (apart from the boots) was the fact that while infantrymen invariably wore red waistcoats, and with the exception of Royal regiments, had red breeches too. Cavalrymen wore small-clothes of the regimental facing colour – in this case blue – or else a neutral white or buff. Similarly while all but a handful of infantry units wore plain white lace on their hats, irrespective of whether their officers

Culloden Moor as depicted by Bowles. The grouping of the Duke of Cumberland and his staff in the central foreground is done purely for dramatic effect, but otherwise the print usefully depicts General Hawley's cavalry breaking through the Culwhiniac enclosures on the left and on the right Barrell's 4th Foot receiving the rebels with bayonets charged breast high. Intriguingly one of the rebels can just be seen with his hand on Barrell's colours – an oblique reference to the temporary loss of one. (NMS)

wore silver or gold lace, in the cavalry white or yellow lace was used as appropriate.

Apart from their caps, this regiment was famously distinguished by its grey horses – hence the 'Scots Greys' nickname – and also by wearing white accoutrements, 20 years before the rest of the army.

The grenadier cap worn by this regiment instead of the usual tricorne hat appears to have changed between 1742 and 1748. *The Cloathing Book* version featured a red front embroidered strangely enough with the red cross of St. George within the garter, superimposed on a white star. The frontlet is blue with a thistle and *NEMO ME*

William Augustus, Duke of Cumberland (1721-1765) at Culloden by David Morier. Cumberland was one of the most able and influential commanders of the British Army in the 18th century. In this important portrait he wears a scarlet coat faced with very dark blue and lavish quantities of gold braid. The saddle housings are also red and gold and interestingly enough do not include separate holster caps. The infantry battalion in the middle distance has yellow facings and appears to represent Pulteney's 13th Foot. Close examination reveals that both officers and men are wearing back gaiters. (NMS)

IMPUNE LACESSIT on a white lapel. The rear of the cap is red over blue and the whole is piped in yellow. By 1748 however the design, as shown, was much more Scottish in character and is not unlike that displayed on the grenadier caps of the 21st Foot. In the 1750s if not before, waterproof oilskin covers were worn over the caps in foul weather. Black bearskin caps were authorised in 1768, bearing the same badge on the front.

Like their infantry counterparts, cavalrymen also had forage caps (called for the sake of distinction watering caps). These were red with a hanging hood, or bag, and a small frontlet of the regimental facing colour, bearing its number on it. Gaiters were also supposed to be worn by Dragoons when dismounted.

A2: Officer, 2nd (Montagu's) Dragoon Guards c1747

Montagu's 2nd Horse, not to be confused with the short-lived 9th Horse raised during the Jacobite emergency, was a good solid regiment. Like both the other regiments of Horse on the English establishment it was converted into Dragoon Guards in 1746. Based on a portrait of

an unknown officer, this figure usefully illustrates some of the differences between the uniforms of dragoons and heavy cavalry.

The principal and most obvious difference is the presence of lapels on the coat. All regiments of Horse had worn rather old-fashioned lapels which were quite narrow and extended the full length of the coat from the neck to the hem – despite the fact that even as early as 1742 troopers wore their coat skirts hooked back. By way of a distinction, those regiments converted into Dragoon Guards adopted infantry-style half-lapels. As Horse, they had worn two cross-belts – a broad carbine belt over the left shoulder and an equally broad baldric or sword-belt over the right shoulder. On becoming Dragoon Guards, however, they adopted Dragoon accoutrements comprising a substantial waistbelt for the sword and a cartouche box and sling over the left shoulder. Oddly enough on the other hand, one Dragoon regiment, the 8th, bore their swords in a baldric instead of a waistbelt. This, according to General Severne who was Colonel of the regiment from 1760 to 1787, was a distinction gained at the battle of Almenara in 1710, when they had

Heavy cavalry officer, c1780. After a caricature published by Bowles and Carter. The regiment is unidentified but the carbine belt suggests one of the troops of Lifeguards.

captured a Spanish regiment of Horse and appropriated their belts. At any rate all accoutrements were invariably yellowish buff coloured at this period, as indeed were the troopers' gauntlets – the only exception being the white accoutrements of the 2nd Dragoons.

A3: Farrier, 11th (Kerr's) Dragoons 1748

Originally raised in Scotland and still by this period largely officered by Scots, Lord Mark Kerr's 11th Dragoons were one of the better cavalry regiments and distinguished themselves at Culloden in 1746 by forcing their way across a heavily defended re-entrant to get into the Jacobite rear. The 1742 *Cloathing Book* shows them wearing the white facings which appear to have been characteristic of Scots regiments before and for some years after the Union in 1707. But by 1748 when they were painted by Morier their facings had changed to buff, an alteration confirmed in the subsequent Royal Warrant of 1751.

Like the pioneers borne on the strength of infantry battalions, farriers were at once tradesmen and perhaps paradoxically were invariably some of the more impressive figures on parade, marching with their axes displayed. The purpose of the axe was a means both for dispatching wounded animals and for recovering the hoof branded with the animal's regimental number. Lacking such proof that a horse had been lost on service it was extremely difficult for the regiment to recover the cost from the government.

His uniform is quite unusual. He wears a fur cap. But while trumpeters and drummers wore the customary reversed clothing and infantry pioneers were distinguished only by their caps and aprons, farriers wore blue coats turned up with the regimental facing colour. This distinction did not however extend to the cloak, which was an ordinary trooper's red one, lined in the regimental facing colour. In 1768, the coats appear to have been modified slightly in that all were to have blue linings and where appropriate blue lapels as well. Only the collar and cuffs were to be of the facing colour, with the exception of Royal regiments which had red ones instead of their customary blue. At the same time all farriers were also put into blue waistcoats and breeches.

Apart from the axe, Morier shows the farrier to be unarmed and the only visible accoutrement is a small case for the axe, carried on a fairly narrow sling. The pistol holsters on the front of the saddle were also replaced by churns or cylindrical leather panniers carrying horse-shoes and nails. This would indicate that the farrier was intended

Regular Cavalry 1740s
1: Trooper, 2nd (Royal North British) Dragoons, 1748
2: Officer, 2nd (Montagu's) Dragoon Guards, c1747
3: Farrier, 11th (Kerr's) Dragoons, 1748

A

The Jacobite Emergency 1745/6
1: Trooper, Duke of Cumberland's Hussar's
2: Private Gentleman, Yorkshire Hunters
3: Private, Georgia Rangers

3

1

2

B

The Seven Years War
1: Sergeant, Light Troop 2nd Dragoons, 1756
2: Officer, 13th (Douglas') Dragoons, 1767
3: Trooper, 21st Light Dragoons (Royal Foresters), 1760

2

3

1

The American War of Independence
1: Private, Light Infantry Troop, 16th Light Dragoons
2: Sergeant, 17th Light Dragoons, 1776
3: Trooper, Castleknock Horse, 1779

2

1

3

D

1: Officer, 7th Dragoons, 1770
2: Trooper, 16th Light Dragoons, 1790
3: Captain Alexander Grant, Madras Governor's Bodyguard

E

Royal Artillery
1: Forbes MacBean, 1748
2: Gunner, Royal Artillery, 1748
3: Conductor, 1748

2

1

3

F

1: Gunner, 4th Battalion Royal Artillery, 1777
2: Officer, Corps of Engineers, 1778
3: Military Artificer, 1786

1: Officer, Royal Artillery, 1794
2: Gunner, 2/Madras Artillery, 1790
3: Gunner, Invalid Battalion, Royal Artillery, 1793

H

Sir John Burgoyne (1723-1792). Entered the army as a sub-brigadier in the Horse Guards 1737, Cornet 1st Royal Dragoons 1744-1751. Re-entered army as Captain 11th Dragoons, Captain Lieutenant 2nd Footguards 1758, Lieutenant Colonel commandant of his own 16th Light Dragoons 1759 and subsequently promoted to full Colonel 1763. Major General 1772, sent to Boston 1775 and to Canada in the following year. Intrigued his way into command of expedition to Albany in the following year but led it to disaster at Saratoga. Although not without ability his various appointments were all achieved through influence, intrigue and purchase. (Author's collection)

to be a non-combatant, no doubt because on campaign a good one was very hard to replace. Nevertheless it is interesting that a farrier of the 1st (Royal) Dragoons is depicted in a later drawing going over a jump with his sword in his hand.

Plate B: *The Jacobite Emergency 1745/6*

As the Jacobites retreated from Derby in December 1745 the British Army made strenuous efforts to intercept them before they managed to reach the Scottish border. Two cavalry brigades eventually made contact at Clifton Moor on the afternoon of the 18th and a lengthy rearguard action commenced. Most of the cavalry units

involved were regulars, but they also included some rather unusual units. One brigade, commanded by Major General Humphrey Bland, was made up of his own 3rd Dragoons, Cobham's 10th and Kerr's 11th Dragoons. The second brigade was considerably less conventional in its composition. It was made up of St. George's 8th Dragoons, Montagu's 3rd Horse, the blue-coated Yorkshire Hunters and the green-jacketed Georgia Rangers.

After an initial skirmish largely involving units of Oglethorpe's Brigade, Cumberland, who was taking personal charge of the operation, ordered Bland's brigade to dismount and attack the Jacobite rearguard under cover of darkness. The rebels promptly counter-attacked. In the fight which followed six men of Bland's 3rd Dragoons were killed, three of Cobham's 10th and one of Kerr's 11th, besides four officers of Bland's were wounded along with an unknown number of men. Jacobite losses were said to have been comparable and the night ended in a draw with the Dragoons left in possession of the field and the rebels getting clean away.

Major John Andre depicted in the uniform of an Aide de Camp. (Author's collection)

afterwards wrote, 'As the Horse was coming off Clifton Moor into the town, our Hussars and Rangers engag'd all the Rebel Hussars, who were headed by one Captain Hamilton..... he was cut down and taken by one of the Duke's Hussars, after a stout resistance.'

At least one other contemporary account refers to the hussar in question as being an Austrian which may mean that they were, in fact, Hungarians. The detachment is also known to have fought at Culloden, on 16 April 1746, where one of them was credited (wrongly) with capturing one of the rebel leaders, Lord Kilmarnock.

This reconstruction is based on some rather small figures painted by David Morier. The green and crimson uniform is the Duke's personal livery and although the basic outline conforms to the traditional 'Hungarian' pattern, there are some interesting peculiarities such as the dragoon style boots, the unbraided jacket worn in place of a dolman, and the rather long pelisse.

B2: Private Gentleman, Yorkshire Hunters

The Hunters were a volunteer unit raised in September 1745: 'Several Gentlemen of considerable Fortunes have resolved to form themselves and their Servants, into a Regiment of Light Horse for the King's Service. Such as compose it are to be mounted on stout Fox Hunters and are to serve at their own expence, under the Command of the Hon. Major General Oglethorpe. They were on this day (30 September) muster'd upon a place called Knavesmire, and made a very fine Appearance. The Gentlemen who composed the first Rank, were all dress'd in Blue, trimm'd with Scarlet, and Gold Buttons, Gold Lac'd Hats, Light Boots and Saddles &c. their Arms were short Bullet Guns slung, Pistols of a moderate size, and strong plain Swords. The second and third Ranks, which were made up of their Servants, were dress'd in Blue, with Brass Buttons, their Accoutrements all light and serviceable, with short Guns and Pistols, and each with a Pole-axe in his hand.'

The reference to 'short Bullet guns slung' is rather puzzling as carbines at this period normally had 42-inch barrels, and it is just possible that they actually had blunderbusses. At any rate a

Light Dragoon officer, c1780. After a caricature published by Bowles and Carter. The regiment is unidentified but the chief point of interest in this figure is his wearing of short gaiters instead of boots while dismounted. This order of dress is often referred to but rarely illustrated. (Author's collection)

B1: Trooper, Duke of Cumberland's Hussars

This small unit primarily existed as the Duke of Cumberland's personal bodyguard but were evidently not averse to getting involved in any fighting. A volunteer surgeon with Bland's brigade

A very atmospheric 19th-century evocation of a siege battery at Yorktown in 1781. Although the gunners can be identified as French by their moustaches, a British gun emplacement would have looked remarkably similar. (Author's collection)

subsequent description of their arrival in Doncaster on 20 October makes no mention of the pole-axes, but does add the curious detail that they all wore green cockades. This distinction may have been a compliment to General Oglethorpe, the nominal commander of the unit, whose own regular regiment had green facings.

B3: Private, Georgia Rangers

Brigadier General James Oglethorpe was Governor of the colony of Georgia and Colonel of the 42nd Foot, a regular battalion raised specifically for the defence of the colony. It was 'broke' in 1748 and reformed as three independent companies. In 1745, Oglethorpe was in England recruiting both for his infantry regiment and a green-jacketed mounted infantry unit attached to it called the Georgia Rangers. (Frustratingly, the Commission Registers fail to distinguish between officers appointed to the two units.) On the point of embarkation when the rebellion broke out the Rangers were diverted to Hull and attached to General Wade's army assembling at Newcastle.

Oglethorpe's 42nd Foot wore the usual red coats with green facings but less is known of his Rangers and contemporary accounts refer only to a green uniform and leather cap. Although this particular individual is wearing infantry-style gaiters, it is probable that most Rangers wore boots as their intended role was to patrol the Georgia coastline, looking out for Spanish raiders.

The most exotic member of this unusual unit was mentioned in a tantalisingly offhand report from Brough in January 1746: 'On Saturday last Gen. Oglethorpe and his Lady, and his Georgia Rangers, with the Indian King and Queen &c. passed over Stainmoor on their road to York.' History, alas, does not record whether the Indian 'King' and his attendants were painted for battle at Clifton.

Light Dragoons (probably Provincials) wearing Tarleton helmets get in amongst an American battery. (Author's collection)

Plate C: The Seven Years War
C1: Sergeant, Light Troop, 2nd Dragoons 1756

In 1756, a Light Troop was added to the establishment of all three regiments of Dragoon Guards and the Dragoon regiments then carried on the English Establishment. In practice they served detached, grouped like the flank companies of infantry regiments into *ad hoc* squadrons. While most of the Greys were serving with some distinction in Germany their Light Troop took part in the coastal raids against St Malo and Cherbourg.

The men recruited for these Troops were to be 'light, active young men' mounted on 'well turned nimble road horses'. Light jockey boots with stiff tops and leather caps were prescribed but otherwise they were to wear the uniform of their parent corps. The caps were to have turned-up fronts bearing the Royal cypher and regimental number, and a brass crest on the skull. Apart from

the number, the only regimental distinction authorised was a horsehair tuft, half and half red and the unit's facing colour.

Rather predictably most units arranged matters to their own satisfaction. A painting by Morier shows a trooper of the 11th Dragoons wearing a cap with a red front, edged with brass, and an all white tuft. Not surprisingly the 2nd Dragoons' cap was more distinctive still. Effectively the regulation leather cap was covered by a smaller version of the grenadier cap peculiar to this regiment. Apart from size this differed from the normal version only in lacking the red 'bag' at the rear – thus exposing the brass-crested skull – and having a red, white and blue horsehair plume at the side.

Saddlery, weapons and accoutrements were suitably lightened and included a new carbine with a 36-inch barrel in place of the normal 42-inch barrel version, a single pistol and a straight-bladed sword. Although Kingston's 10th Horse raised in 1745 and disbanded in 1748 as Cumberland's 15th Dragoons had carried swords with curved blades, straight-bladed weapons seem to have been pretty universal in British service for most of the 18th century. Accoutrements were supposed to be made from tanned rather than buff leather, but there is no doubt that the Greys once again contrived to whiten theirs.

C2: Officer, 13th (Douglas's) Dragoons 1767

The 13th were an all too typical product of the inefficient Irish Establishment. Raised in 1715 their Colonels included good soldiers such as Henry Hawley (1730-1740) and Humphrey Bland (1741-1743). But they failed dismally when committed to action in the Jacobite Rising of 1745. By that time they were commanded by a Scots professional soldier, James Gardiner and promptly abandoned him to his fate at Prestonpans. They also ran away at Falkirk some months later. As soon as the emergency was over they were quietly returned to the obscurity of the Irish Establishment from whence they had come in 1743. This reconstruction is based on a portrait by Pompeo Batoni of Captain James Stewart of Killymoon. The uniform, conforming to both the 1742 *Cloathing Book* and 1751 Warrant, shows how cavalry units wearing the same facing colours were distinguished. In this case the buttons and gold braid loops are arranged in three, and white small-clothes are worn instead of the green waistcoat and breeches worn by Rich's 4th Dragoons. Stewart's portrait appears to depict silk small-clothes, explicable perhaps by his wearing the uniform on a social occasion rather than on duty. This impression is reinforced by his wearing stockings and shoes rather than riding boots. But otherwise his uniform conforms to regulations.

C3: Trooper, 21st Light Dragoons (Royal Foresters) 1760

When the experiment of raising Light Troops for existing Dragoon regiments proved successful, the logical step was to raise complete regiments. The first and most spectacularly successful of these was the 15th, who distinguished themselves at Emsdorf. Others soon followed. Perhaps the most interesting was Granby's 21st Light Dragoons, otherwise known as the Royal Foresters. Although Granby himself could take little more than a proprietorial interest in the regiment since he was otherwise fully engaged in commanding the

Sir William Howe (1729-1814). Entered army as Cornet 15th (Cumberland's) Dragoons 1746, Lieutenant 1747, Captain 20th Foot 1750, Major 60th 1756, Lieutenant Colonel 58th 1757, Colonel 46th 1764. Major General 1772 and commander-in-chief North America 1775-1778, being promoted to Lieutenant General in 1777. Colonel 23rd Foot 1775-1786, then 19th Light Dragoons until his death. Promotions and appointments were managed through his connections (being a half cousin of the King helped) nevertheless he was an able strategist who quite literally ran rings around George Washington. Nevertheless he lacked the killer instinct necessary to press home his victories. (Author's collection)

British contingent in Germany, the regiment was generally agreed to be a first class one reflecting the very latest and best continental practice. Indeed Captain Robert Hinde, author of the influential *Discipline of the Light Horse* (1778), served in the regiment. Unfortunately it was destined never to see action as a unit although a number of men were drafted into units serving in Germany. Strangely enough a solitary officer of the Royal Foresters was included in the prisoners taken by the Americans at Yorktown in 1781 – eighteen years after the regiment was disbanded!

The uniform is depicted by Morier and particularly noteworthy is the German-style helmet with the rather curiously shaped frontlet – a form usually associated with Hessian troops. Officers' helmets were edged with fur. All of the new regiments of Light Dragoons wore lapels on their coats and in this particular case the horse fur-

Guidon, Horse Grenadier Guards c1780. Crimson with lavish gold embroidery and fringing. (Author)

niture was also unusual in comprising a large hussar style shabraque of white goatskin for rank and file, and white bearskin for officers. The latter were edged with wolf-toothed silver braid (with a blue silk line running down the middle) and all ranks had a blue badge over the holsters, bearing the regimental number and royal cypher picked out in white or silver.

Plate D. The American War of Independence

D1: Private, Light Infantry Troop, 16th Light Dragoons

Lieutenant Colonel John Burgoyne (as he then was) received Letters of Service to raise the 16th Light Dragoons on 4 August 1759. Two troops took part in the Belle-Ile expedition in 1761 and the following year the whole regiment sailed for Portugal. In 1766, they became the Queen's Dragoons and adopted blue facings in place of the original black ones. At the same time a badge comprising the Queen's cypher within the garter was placed on their helmets. One of two cavalry regiments sent to America, their six mounted troops were augmented by a seventh, dismounted one in 1776.

'These were provided with a loose cloak or mantle instead of the cloak, which they carry over their knapsack. They are not provided with boots but have brown cloth gaiters. They have no broadswords, have a leather helmet a good deal like that of the Light Infantry. Each man carries a hatchet. They act separately as Light Infantry.'

It might be tempting to view this experiment as a move in the direction of the 'legion' organisation which had already proved popular on the continent and which would soon be widely adopted by both the Loyalist and Colonial provincial units. However the proportion of horse to foot (the dismounted troop had a strength of only 29 men) suggests that the true purpose of this formation was not to act as an integrated combat unit, but in fact to provide local security for the regiment's quarters and foraging parties.

In 1778, the regiment was ordered home and in accordance with the usual practice only the officers and senior NCOs actually embarked, the effective rank and file being turned over to the 17th Light Dragoons. Then the Light Infantry Troop appears to have been disbanded.

D2: Sergeant, 17th Light Dragoons 1776

Raised in 1759 as the 18th Light Dragoons by Colonel John Hale, this regiment became the 17th in 1763. (The original 17th Light Dragoons, a Scottish unit commanded by Lord Aberdour, was never completed.) Traditionally, the 'scalped face and shinbones' badge is said to have been worn in remembrance of General Wolfe. Although this is quite possible it is rather more likely that the actual inspiration was the very similar badge worn by the famous Black Hussars in the Prussian service. It is uncertain just how long this particular style of helmet continued to be worn. A 1784 drawing by Bunbury shows another sergeant of this or another regiment with white facings wearing a Tarleton Helmet.

Like the 16th, this regiment was sent to America in 1775 and served there with some distinction throughout the war, mainly in the north – a small party was even present at Bunker Hill. A better known detachment later served in the south where they provided some badly needed stiffening for Banastre Tarleton's rather undisciplined British Legion. Oddly enough, this provincial corps was originally raised by an officer of the 17th named Cathcart. Despite this connection the detachment resisted all Tarleton's attempts to have them drafted into the Legion after it was taken on to the regular establishment in June 1781.

D3: Trooper, Castleknock Horse 1779

The despatch of considerable numbers of troops from Ireland to America aroused fears of a repeat of Thurot's virtually unopposed descent on Carrickfergus in 1760. A lack of funds prevented the implementation of the 1778 Militia Act, but instead a volunteer movement sprang into existence. Originally, it had no object beyond the immediate defence of the country, but this soon changed and the volunteers threw their weight behind pressure for the repeal of the infamous Poyning's Act, a medieval statute which subjected all Irish legislation to ratification by the English Parliament. The growing politicisation of the volunteers eventually led to their suppression in 1793. Paradoxically however, although some of the members went on to found the United Irishmen, the vast majority of the volunteers went on to

Sir Henry Clinton. Howe's successor as commander-in-chief North America, he had been a more than capable subordinate but lacked the self-confidence necessary for independent command. (Author's collection)

represent the Protestant ascendancy.

This trooper is reconstructed from a painting by Wheatley depicting a parade of volunteers on College Green in Dublin, on 4 November 1779, celebrating the birthday of King William III – which is a pretty good indicator of their real political sympathies. The uniform, and particularly the helmet, is very French in style.

E1: Officer, 7th Dragoons 1770

The Royal Warrant of 1768 did little to alter the uniforms of dragoon regiments. Only the 12th, 15th, 16th, 17th and 18th were designated as Light Dragoons and distinguished from the 'Heavy' Dragoon regiments by the wearing of lapels on their coats and the substitution of

Officer of Light Dragoons (probably 16th) after Bunbury.
Note the very long fur trimmed shell or 'kitt'. (Author)

helmets for cocked hats. The 7th were not converted to Light Dragoons until 1783.

This officer, based on a portrait, still wears the, by now, rather old-fashioned single breasted coat. The 7th were supposed to have white facings but the portrait shows a distinct buff tinge to both facings and small-clothes. It is also notable that the riding boots are now much lighter and less clumsy than those worn before.

E2: Trooper, 16th Light Dragoons 1790

In the aftermath of the American War there was a wide-ranging review of the army's uniforms and equipment. A number of changes were recommended, but the most dramatic alteration was seen in the clothing of Light Dragoons. The old long-tailed red coat was abandoned and replaced by a short single breasted round jacket in hussar style. There appears to have been an initial move in favour of a plain green jacket as previously worn by some Provincial cavalry units, and the 23rd Light Dragoons appear to have gone to India wearing them even though their uniform was actually supposed to be a red coat turned up with green.

The eventual choice, however, ordered in 1784, was for a dark blue hussar style dolman, braided with white cords. A second, sleeveless jacket or shell was worn on top, presumably for the sake of warmth. At the same time, the boots were lightened still further and the Tarleton helmet was officially authorised. The popularity of this new uniform may be gauged by the fact that, with the exception of the shell, it survived virtually unaltered until 1812.

This reconstruction is based on surviving items of clothing and a painting by Wheatley. The 16th had worn blue facings on the old red uniform, but when ordered into the new blue uniform the facings were changed to red. A sketch by Bunbury shows that the officers of the regiment wore rather long, Hungarian-style shells (which were apparently referred to as 'kitts') and that between 1785 and 1788 they had them rather dashingly lined with leopardskin. On 14 June 1788, all regiments of Light Dragoons were ordered to be dressed in the same uniforms and to be distinguished only by the facing colour on the collar and cuffs.

This order provoked an immediate protest from the 16th Dragoons and on 22 June the Adjutant General wrote rather apologetically to the regimental colonel, Major General Harcourt: 'The only object of this new order is to introduce a greater uniformity in the dress of the Light Cavalry Corps, than there was before. His Majesty therefore hoped you would not regret the exchanging the leopard skin lining of your Officers' uniforms, for that which is now ordered to be worn by all the officers of all the other Light Dragoon Regiments.'

E3: Captain Alexander Grant, Madras Governor's Bodyguard

Despite maintaining a solid core of European infantry and artillery units, the East India Company came to rely almost entirely upon native cavalry units with a few British officers. There were however occasional attempts to raise European cavalry units. Perhaps the most notable was a 'foreign legion' raised by a Swiss officer named Abraham Bonjour in 1768. This comprised a company of light infantry and a troop of hussars – the latter being, for the most part, French veterans who had originally come out to India with the Hussards de Conflans. The light infantry were to wear: 'a light jacket of green, faced with red, and a cap…They should have breeches and stockings all in one with black gaiters'.

No mention was made of the Hussars' dress but as Conflans' regiment also wore green faced with red (and red breeches) it would seem quite possible that Bonjour's troopers were still wearing their old French Army uniforms. The Hussars were dismounted in 1769 and the rest of the legion disbanded in 1769. The Company also had a troop of Dragoons in the early days of the Madras Army. But although favourably reviewed this was broken up in 1777, briefly reinstated and eventually disbanded in 1779.

The native cavalry regiments which replaced this rather raffish crew wore uniforms very closely patterned after European styles. This figure is based upon a representation of Captain Alexander Grant (1763–1801) in a well known painting by Home depicting the capture of Bangalore in 1791. Grant's background was typical of many EIC officers. He was the son of Ludovick Grant, minister of Ardchattan in Invernessshire. Commissioned a cornet in the Company's service on 19 June 1783 and a lieutenant in January 1786. The date of his captaincy is uncertain but he was promoted to Major in September 1799.

Apart from the fact that his jacket is scarlet rather than blue Captain Grant is distinguished as an EIC officer rather than a British regular only by his leopardskin sabretache, worn high up on the hip. A native trooper or Sowar standing beside Captain Grant in the Bangalore painting wears a very similar uniform to that shown here

Charles, Earl Cornwallis (1738-1805). A Guardsman like a great many other general officers he is best known for his southern campaign during the American War which culminated in the disastrous defeat at Yorktown in 1781. Despite this he went on to rebuild his career by serving as Governor General and commander-in-chief in India 1786-1793, Lord Lieutenant and commander-in-chief Ireland 1798-1801 and again Governor General of India in 1805. His appointments appear to reflect his well-attested popularity rather than any great ability. (Author's collection)

although the jacket is worn open from the throat to the belly and instead of a Tarleton helmet he wears a fairly tall pinkish red turban.

Plate F: Royal Artillery
F1: Forbes MacBean 1748

It was far from uncommon to find officers of relatively humble origins serving in the British Army during the 18th century. However, lacking money and influence few of them advanced far beyond the rank of captain, except in the Royal Artillery where seniority, and to a lesser extent merit, counted for everything. A notable example was Forbes MacBean, the son of an Inverness minister and step-brother of Lieutenant William Bannatyne

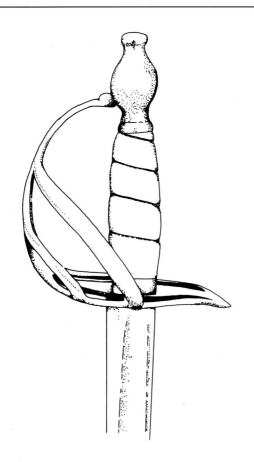

1788 pattern heavy cavalry sword. Prior to 1788 there was no regulation pattern and regimental colonels were free to equip their men as they pleased. Neither this weapon nor the 1788 pattern light cavalry sabre proved to be satisfactory and both were replaced in 1796. (Author)

(see MAA 285) and Captain Robert Bannatyne (see MAA 289). Entering the Royal Artillery as a Cadet Matross on 3 August 1743, he commanded two guns at Fontenoy in 1745, and later that year again served under Cumberland at the siege of Carlisle. For some reason he did not serve in Scotland, but at Lauffeldt and Rocoux he commanded the battalion guns attached to the 19th Foot. Promoted to Captain in January 1759 MacBean commanded a heavy artillery brigade using ten 12-pounders at Minden with some effect. In 1762 he went with the British expedition to Portugal and subsequently served as a colonel in the Portuguese Army between 1765 and 1768. Posted to Canada between 1769 and 1773 he returned there as CRA (Commander Royal

Artillery) in succession to Major General Phillips in 1778. This brought him a well merited promotion to lieutenant colonel in 1782 and then the appointment of Colonel Commandant of the Invalid Battalion in 1793. Promotion to Major General followed almost at once and active to the end he died a Lieutenant General at Woolwich in 1800. One of the Royal Artillery's more intellectual officers, MacBean was elected a Fellow of the Royal Society in 1786.

This reconstruction is largely based on a painting by David Morier, depicting the train of artillery encamped at Roermond in Holland in 1748. MacBean wears the traditional gunner's uniform of a dark blue coat faced with red, but is distinguished from the rank and file by his red waistcoat and breeches. The wearing of white gaiters in the field is extremely unusual and presumably reflects the fact that the artillery train was then at rest.

F2: Gunner, Royal Artillery 1748
The 1742 *Cloathing Book* depicted a very plain uniform without any lace and rather short 'half-lapels'. C.C.P. Lawson quotes a 1750 order that sergeants' coats were to be laced with gold and the other NCOs with yellow worsted. This might suggest that the gunners's coats were still unlaced at this date. But Morier's painting which can be positively dated to the spring of 1748 clearly shows lace worn by all ranks. This gunner, taken from the painting, displays a number of other interesting features. His gaiters are black as would be expected on campaign and in contrast to the red small-clothes worn by his officers this man wears blue. A rather curiously shaped belly-box and black bayonet-frog is carried on a thin belt around his waist. In 1742, gunners and matrosses were supposed to be armed with linstocks – combination spears and slow-match holders. A 1749 order directed these to be laid aside in favour of carbines and bayonets, but once again Morier's painting shows this order to have been widely anticipated. Those carbines carried during the 1740s were presumably the same 42-inch barrel weapons issued to dragoons, but in 1757 a cheaper version specifically intended for issue to artillerymen was set up. The buff sling supports a

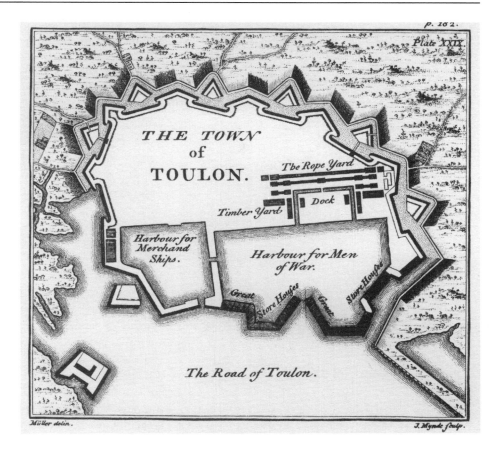

p. 162.

Map of the defences of Toulon from Muller's **Elements of Fortification** *This particular illustration was no doubt studied with great interest during the Allied occupation of the port in 1794.*

large powder-horn on his right hip. At the Court of Inquiry held into the débâcle at Prestonpans in September 1745, General Cope's CRA, Major Eaglefield Griffith, testified that while he had provided the usual 40 rounds for each of the six - pound curricle guns attached to the army, he had only been able to get off one round apiece from each of them since his men fled the field at the outset of the engagement, taking the priming horns with them!

F3: Conductor 1748

The Royal Artillery prided itself on its professionalism, but as in many other armies of the time, was forced by Treasury constraints to rely upon civilians to actually transport the guns. Although these drivers were not subject to military discipline their recruitment was far from being a haphazard process. Arrangements would be made at the outset of a campaign, or even on a fairly long term basis with conductors (haulage

contractors) who provided both the horses and the personnel required and saw to it that they moved the guns in roughly the right direction. Contemporary paintings show that these drivers did not wear military uniform as such, but were easily recognised by their drab coloured waggoners' smocks and occasionally by some form of uniform headgear provided by the haulage firm for which they worked. The conductors also pleased themselves as to how they were dressed, but often opted for a semi-military style and this reconstruction is once again based on a figure in Morier's painting of the encampment at Roermond.

G1: Gunner, 4th Bn Royal Artillery 1777

Being administered by the Board of Ordnance rather than the Horse Guards, the uniforms of the Royal Artillery were not covered by the Royal Warrant of 19 December 1768. But somebody must have mentioned this to the Board because,

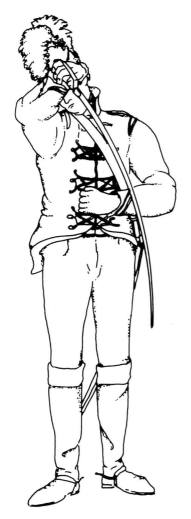

Trooper 16th Light Dragoons demonstrating the Horse near side Protect. After sketch in **Rules and Regulations for the Sword Exercise in the Cavalry 1796.** *Note the curious arrangement of the lace on the jacket, and the high boots. (Author)*

on 21 February 1769, they rather belatedly noted: 'His Majesty has given certain regulations for the cloathing of the several marching Regiments which may occasion some small alterations in the cloathing of the Royal Regiment of Artillery...'. Some dithering then followed until it was realised that by then it was too late to alter the clothing already ordered for that year and so new patterns were not sealed until January 1770. When they eventually appeared the new uniforms substantially followed the infantry in style and white small-clothes replaced the blue ones, except in the

invalid companies who clung to the old pattern. Still, white accoutrements were not ordered until 1772 and the coat linings were not ordered to be changed from red to white until 1782. Even then it still took over a year to get everybody into the new uniforms and even longer to replace the old embroidered drummers' caps with bearskin ones.

Cocked hats bound with yellow tape were still prescribed for gunners but one of the von Germann sketches shows a gunner serving under General Burgoyne wearing a light infantry cap. In March 1777, the Board ordered a pattern jacket, waistcoat and breeches to be made up for the gunners about to be sent to America. The waistcoat and breeches were to be the same pattern and price as those already ordered for the Artificer Company at Gibraltar, but the jacket was evidently a new pattern priced at 17s 1d apiece. As this is very close to the 17s 6d paid at the time for an ordinary soldier's coat, it may be inferred that these jackets had lapels and were not the single-breasted round jackets which became increasingly popular during this period. The gunner depicted by von Germann is presumably wearing one of these new jackets rather than a cropped coat.

The Royal Irish Artillery wore a uniform similar to their counterparts on the English establishment, but a watercolour sketch of c.1773 shows a white lining to the coat and buttons arranged in pairs, with a light dragoon-style cuff and chevrons of lace on the lower arm. Predictably a harp badge is worn on the cartouche box, but perhaps the most unusual feature shown in the watercolour is a very long Prussian-style queue reaching down into the small of the gunner's back.

G2: Officer, Corps of Engineers 1778
Engineers were also the responsibility of the Board of Ordnance, but their military status was at first somewhat ambiguous and some officers obtained their commissions by serving in infantry regiments. This was obviously a far from satisfactory state of affairs and on 14 May 1757 officers were for the first time commissioned as Engineers. Until that time, there was no prescribed uniform for engineers and many

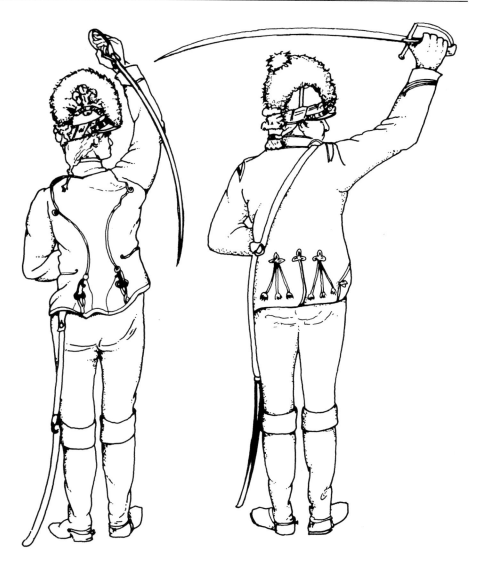

Rear view of troopers of the 10th and 16th Light Dragoons from the same source. Note the loose, comfortable fit of the jackets, especially that worn by the trooper of the 10th on the left. (Author)

apparently wore the uniform of whichever infantry regiment they then happened to belong to. This also had to change and just two weeks later the *Ipswich Journal* of all things noted that the uniform of the newly formed Corps of Engineers was 'red lapelled with black velvet, buff waistcoats and breeches'. Perhaps because there were so few of them the Board of Ordnance took rather a long time to get round to considering the modernisation of their uniforms in the wake of the 1768 Warrant and it was not until 20 August 1772 that the pattern shown in this reconstruction was authorised. As it happened, this particular uniform did not last very long. In December 1782 it was ordered to be changed to a blue coat again

faced with black velvet and lined with white.

G3: Military Artificer 1786

All Engineers were officers and prior to 1772 all the army's labouring work was carried out either by infantrymen or by civilian contractors working under engineer's direction. Every summer for many years parties of soldiers laboured on General Wade's network of roads in the Scottish Highlands. Roadwork was apparently popular as it attracted extra pay and was generally characterised by much looser discipline than usual. But it was only practical to employ soldiers as workmen during peacetime and at the same time difficult to find skilled craftsmen during wartime, especially in remote areas. Consequently in 1772, a Soldier Artificer Company was formed for service in Gibraltar. The experiment was a considerable success and led to the formation of a Corps of Royal Military Artificers and Labourers in 1787.

The Gibraltar company's uniform comprised a plain red coat faced with orange-yellow, white waistcoat and breeches. This figure is wearing the company's working dress, a fairly long red wool jacket with large side pockets – a white linen version similar to those used by the 25th on Minorca was worn in summer.

When the Corps of Royal Military Artificers and Labourers was formed an entirely new uniform was adopted, closely conforming in colour at least to that worn by Engineer officers. The full dress uniform was a dark blue coat faced black and lined white, but their working dress was similar in style to the Gibraltar company. Originally white Russia duck jackets were worn but in 1792 dark blue cloth ones were authorised for use in winter. In 1789 the Gibraltar Artificers also adopted blue coats faced black, but the two units were not combined until 1797.

H1: Officer, Royal Artillery 1794

Loutherberg's sketches of the siege of Valenciennes provide a useful illustration of how regulation and practice could often part company. Round hats actually appear to have been worn by all ranks of the Royal Artillery at this time, until the order came to replace them with the more usual cocked hats in April 1796. The order was evidently an unpopular one, because subsequently on 23 May a sternly worded reminder came instructing officers to provide themselves with the required cocked hats by the 4th of the following month.

In 1794 officers were also supposed to be wearing cloth (wool) or kerseymere breeches and top boots bound with white leather. However this unknown officer actually appears to be wearing a pair of gaiter trousers rolled up over his boots. The prescribed sword was the so-called 1786 pattern or spadroon – a straight bladed weapon. But Mercer, who had joined the Royal Artillery at this time, refers to the occasional use of a dirk instead.

H2: Gunner, 2/Madras Artillery 1790

The dress of the East India Company's artillerymen, who were invariably Europeans, broadly conformed to regular army styles. But as this reconstruction based on a watercolour by a Company artist shows, there were some significant differences. The most obvious, of course, is the hat. Instead of the ubiquitous round hat worn in the Indies by regular units of infantry and artillery from the 1770s onwards, this appears to be an early forerunner of the 19th-century solar topee. It was made of cloth stretched over a split cane frame. The blue coat turned up with red also differs from the regular army pattern in having cavalry-style chevrons of thin yellow lace on the cuff and forearm. Double-breasted waistcoats were quite popular among regular officers, but rarely worn by the rank and file. It is not clear whether they were worn by all ranks of the Madras Artillery at this time or whether this soldier has merely chosen to cut a dash by wearing one of his own while 'walking out'.

H3: Gunner, Invalid Battalion, Royal Artillery 1793

Each of the four battalions of the Royal Artillery included two invalid companies until about 1784 when they were consolidated into a single battalion under a Major Whitmore. Comprised of officers and soldiers no longer fit enough for active service in the field, their task was to man the guns in fortresses and other fixed positions. In practice, this was not always as easy as it might at first appear, since fortress guns were invariably of a large and heavy calibre. Consequently, it seems to have been the practice to employ invalid gunners to instruct and direct detachments of volunteers drawn from any infantry units which may have been handy.

On 8 March 1771, the Board of Ordnance, then still trying hard to catch up with the changes ordered to infantry uniforms in the 1768 Warrant, paused to consider the clothing of the invalid companies and had 'thoughts of making some alterations therein'. The precise nature of these alterations is not clear. But four days later the usual contractor, Mrs Elizabeth Benford, was ordered to make the coats for the invalid companies plain, 'but in all other respects the same as the present pattern'. Since Mrs Benford was also asked to report 'what abatement she will make for the lace and sewing on' it is likely that the reference to the coats being made plain means that they were unlaced.

Another thing likely to have been considered by the Board at this time was whether or not to alter the small-clothes from blue to white. In 1784 however, Major Whitmore obtained permission from the Board to have his men's breeches made with a fall-down flap as in the marching companies, which suggests that until that time they had still been wearing the old style blue breeches with a fly front. Although he succeeded in having the cut brought up to date, no alteration was made in the colour, and in a list of prices approved for the clothing of the Royal Artillery in 1792 specific mention is made of blue cloth waistcoats and breeches for invalids.

INDEX

Figures in **bold** refer to illustrations, plates are shown with caption locators in brackets.

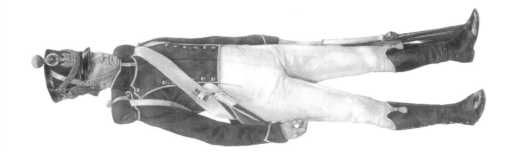

FIND OUT MORE ABOUT OSPREY

❏ Please send me the latest listing of Osprey's publications

❏ I would like to subscribe to Osprey's e-mail newsletter

Title/rank

Name

Address

Postcode/zip   state/country

e-mail

I am interested in:

❏ Ancient world
❏ Medieval world
❏ 16th century
❏ 17th century
❏ 18th century
❏ Napoleonic
❏ 19th century

❏ American Civil War
❏ World War I
❏ World War II
❏ Modern warfare
❏ Military aviation
❏ Naval warfare

Please send to:

USA & Canada:
Osprey Direct USA, c/o MBI Publishing, P.O. Box 1, 729 Prospect Avenue, Osceola, WI 54020

UK, Europe and rest of world:
Osprey Direct UK, P.O. Box 140, Wellingborough, Northants, NN8 2FA, United Kingdom

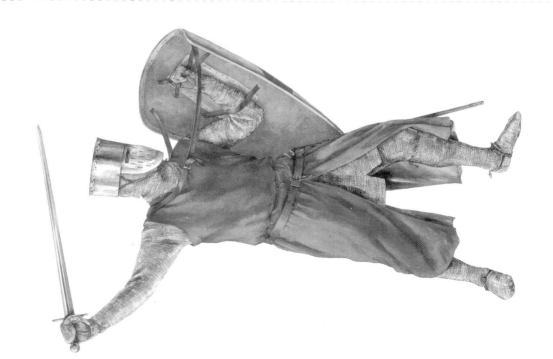

OSPREY
PUBLISHING

www.ospreypublishing.com

call our telephone hotline
for a free information pack

USA & Canada: 1-800-826-6600
UK, Europe and rest of world call:
+44 (0) 1933 443 863

Young Guardsman
Figure taken from *Warrior 22:
Imperial Guardsman 1799–1815*
Published by Osprey
Illustrated by Richard Hook

Knight, c.1190
Figure taken from *Warrior 1: Norman Knight 950 – 1204 AD*
Published by Osprey
Illustrated by Christa Hook

POSTCARD